Americanism in the Twenty-First Century

Public Opinion in the Age of Immigration

This book explores public opinion about being and becoming American, and its implications for contemporary immigration debates. It focuses on the causes and consequences of two aspects of American identity: how people define being American and whether people think of themselves primarily as American rather than as members of a panethnic or national origin group. Importantly, the book evaluates the claim – made by scholars and pundits alike – that all Americans should prioritize their American identity instead of an ethnic or national origin identity. It finds that national identity within American democracy can be a blessing or a curse. It can enhance participation, trust, and obligation. But it can be a curse when perceptions of deviation lead to threat and resentment. It can also be a curse for minorities who are attached to their American identity but also perceive discrimination. The notion of American identity is a predisposition that the government has good reason to cultivate but also good reason to approach with caution.

Deborah J. Schildkraut is an Associate Professor of Political Science at Tufts University. She is also the author of *Press "One" for English: Language Policy, Public Opinion, and American Identity*.

Civic Center

Americanism in the Twenty-First Century

Public Opinion in the Age of Immigration

DEBORAH J. SCHILDKRAUT

Tufts University

CAMBRIDGE
UNIVERSITY PRESS

CAMBRIDGE UNIVERSITY PRESS
Cambridge, New York, Melbourne, Madrid, Cape Town, Singapore,
São Paulo, Delhi, Dubai, Tokyo, Mexico City

Cambridge University Press
32 Avenue of the Americas, New York, NY 10013-2473, USA

www.cambridge.org
Information on this title: www.cambridge.org/9780521145244

First published 2011

Printed in the United States of America

A catalog record for this publication is available from the British Library.

Library of Congress Cataloging in Publication data

Schildkraut, Deborah Jill, 1973–
Americanism in the twenty-first century : public opinion in the age of immigration /
Deborah Schildkraut.
    p. cm.
Includes bibliographical references and index.
ISBN 978-0-521-19175-3 (hardback) – ISBN 978-0-521-14524-4 (pbk.)
1. National characteristics, American.   2. Americanization.   3. United States – Emigration and
immigration – Social aspects.   4. Immigrants – United States – Social conditions.   5. Social
integration – United States.   6. Assimilation (Sociology) – United States.   I. Title.
E169.12.S
973–dc22   2010025203

ISBN 978-0-521-19175-3 Hardback
ISBN 978-0-521-14524-4 Paperback

Contents

Figures and Tables

TABLES

Acknowledgments

As with any book, this one would not have been possible without the support, advice, encouragement, and diversions provided by many people and institutions. As is true of all authors, I cherish the opportunity to offer my thanks.

First, the analyses in this book rely on a data source that was only made possible by a grant from the Russell Sage Foundation (RSF). The advisory board and staff at RSF were generous, helpful, and flexible throughout. Special thanks go to Pam Snyder and Radhika Atit at Oberlin College for helping me put together a successful grant application in the first place.

Once funding was secured, I unexpectedly found myself without an institute to conduct the survey. I was fortunate to be put in contact with the Social and Economic Sciences Research Center at Washington State University, at the recommendation of Jake Bowers. There, the data collection was directed by Ashley Grosse. Ashley is, in a word, amazing. Her professionalism made everything go more smoothly than I could have expected, her challenging questions led to important changes in the survey design, and her hospitality during my visit to Pullman went above and beyond the call of duty.

At many points along the way, I had the opportunity to present the ideas in this book and get important feedback. In addition to participants and discussants at several political science conferences, I am grateful to the people who provided feedback at the Political Psychology and Political Behavior Workshop at Harvard, the Center for Political Studies National Election Studies Workshop at the University of Michigan, the Political Science Department at Michigan State, the Workshop on Political Psychology at Columbia, the Civic Engagement Workshop at Tufts, the Program on Survey Research at Harvard, the Canada Program at the Weatherhead Center for International Affairs at Harvard, and the Research Circle on Democracy and Cultural Pluralism at Brandeis. At these and other venues, there have been people whose generosity with advice and encouragement have been especially helpful, including David Art, Lisa Garcia Bedolla, Robert Devigne, Ioannis Evrigenis, Michael Fortner, Yoshiko Herrera, Dan Hopkins, Greg Huber, Don Kinder, Steve Macedo, Scott

McClurg, Phillip Muñoz, Kent Portney, Elizabeth Remick, Sam Sommers, and Elizabeth Theiss-Morse. Special thanks go to Jeff Berry and Natalie Masuoka, who read the full manuscript. I started this project while at Oberlin College and finished it at Tufts University. The ethos at both departments is to do whatever can be done to help each other succeed. I appreciate my good fortune at ending up in such collegial settings.

Thanks also go to anonymous reviewers at various journals and presses, who sent me pages upon pages of suggestions over the years. The book is uniformly stronger for it. A version of Chapter 3 appeared in the *Journal of Politics* (August 2007, Cambridge University Press) and portions of Chapter 4 appeared in *American Behavioral Scientist* (September 2009, Sage Publications). They are reprinted here with permission and gratitude. I am also grateful for the support and dedication from the people at Cambridge University Press, including Lew Bateman, Emily Spangler, and Anne Lovering Rounds. Thanks also to Blythe Woolston and Christine Dunn.

My acknowledgments would be incomplete if I didn't call attention to my parents. Their encouragement and enthusiasm never wane. They have, on several occasions, lifted me up when I really needed it. They also regularly send me news articles and Web links related to my research. I would not have discovered the compelling news stories on bilingualism in South Florida that I describe in Chapters 2 and 5 had my mother not sent them my way.

Finally, I dedicate this book to my boys. First, to my sons Evan and Nate, who make me work more efficiently, challenge me in ways I never imagined, and are endless sources of wonder and entertainment. Second, to my dog Sparky, who slept at my feet as I wrote much of this book and made me go on countless long walks during which some of my best brainstorming took place. And finally, to RJ, whose unyielding support has literally and figuratively gotten me to the tops of mountains. This book is but one of many accomplishments that I owe to him.

Introduction

American Identity in the Twenty-First Century

ENGLISH-ONLY CHEESESTEAKS

In 2006, a landmark cheesesteak shop in Philadelphia garnered national attention not for its menu but for a sign posted by its owner telling customers,
"This is America. When ordering, please speak English." Owner Joey Vento
argued that the sign was aimed not at tourists but at illegal immigrants from
Mexico. He gave many media interviews during the controversy, stating in
one of them that it is "wrong, wrong, wrong that a Mexican girl comes here
to pop a baby," and that he is only saying "what everybody's thinking but
is afraid to say." Though some potential customers chose to avoid the shop
during this time, others eagerly voiced their support for Vento as they waited
in long lines for their cheesesteaks (Zucchino 2006). In 2007 then–presidential
candidate Rudolph Giuliani campaigned at the shop (Dale 2007). A panel of
the Philadelphia Commission on Human Rights ruled in 2008 that the sign was
not discriminatory. In response to the flood of support Vento received from
across the country, he said, "I woke up America" (Maykuth 2008).

SCARED TO REPORT CRIMES TO THE POLICE

As the federal government failed to enact immigration reform amid cries for
change in the early years of the twenty-first century, states, counties, and cities
began devising their own policies to address issues that arise from legal and
illegal immigration. One increasingly common approach is to enlist local law
enforcement agencies in efforts to determine whether a person is in the country
legally and to detain them if they are not. In 2007, for example, the supervisors
of Prince William County, Virginia, passed a resolution that directed "officers
to check the status of anyone in police custody who they suspect is an illegal
immigrant" (Miroff 2007). Because the directive does not require all people
in custody to be asked their status, Latino residents have voiced fears that the
resolution would render them targets of racial profiling. For their part, police

officers affected by similar measures in other locales have expressed worries that residents will be less willing to report crimes for fear of increased scrutiny (Ford and Montes 2007). An Arizona statute passed in 2010 sent shock waves across the country for calling on officers to check the status of anyone they suspect of being in the country illegally, regardless of whether the person was already in custody for some other offense. Not only did this law spark fears of reporting crimes to police, but it also generated comparisons to South Africa's apartheid and to Nazism.

ATTITUDE ADJUSTMENT NEEDED

During the 2008 presidential primaries, with growing attention devoted to the preferences of Latino voters, journalist and talk-radio host Bob Lonsberry wrote a column questioning why Latinos are considered a minority group while Italian and German Americans are not. The main difference between Latinos and these other groups, he argues, is one of "attitude," writing that Latinos "typically make choices that perpetuate their minority status," such as not learning English and maintaining a strong identification with their country of origin. He goes on to say that once Latinos Americanize, they can not only achieve the American Dream but can also strengthen America with their achievements.[1]

What all of the preceding situations highlight is that all levels of American society across the nation are finding themselves dealing with a tangled web of ethnic change, language diversity, national security, effective law enforcement, and civil liberties. They all stem from the changing demographic makeup of the United States and how various levels of government address the policy needs that arise from such change. More importantly, these policy debates and local controversies can have long-lasting consequences for the relationships people have with American political institutions. For whites and nonwhites, legal immigrants and illegal immigrants, first-generation and fourth-generation Americans, one's very sense of self vis-à-vis his or her national identity is brought to the fore when such controversies arise. All of these debates touch in one way or another on the concept of American national identity, what it means, and who can be a part of it. When people are confronted with such issues, they look to their views of the norms and values that constitute American national identity in order to help them determine what they think are appropriate policy responses (Citrin, Reingold, and Green 1990; Schildkraut 2005a). Moreover, they can begin to question the extent to which they think their membership in the national community is an important part of who they are, especially if they feel that political institutions or their fellow Americans do not treat them as full and equal members.

---

[1] Column available at http://www.boblonsberry.com/writings.cfm?story=2301&go=4 (accessed January 21, 2008).

The question of what consequences ethnic change has on American society is a recurring one in our history. From Ben Franklin worrying about the impact of Germans on the Anglo way of life in the colonies, to the Know-Nothing Party campaigning against Irish Catholics in the 1840s, to Chinese exclusion in the 1880s, to national origin quotas in the 1920s, and to Japanese internment in the 1940s, fears of the cultural and demographic changes brought by immigrants have always sparked outrage and division.[2] This story is as American as the story of the shots fired at Lexington and Concord. We continue to add chapters to it in the current era as the percentage of foreign-born residents in the country has been rising steadily, from a low of roughly 4 percent in 1970 to approximately 13 percent today.[3] Although in the past our immigration politics concerned immigrants from various European and Asian countries, today the focus is largely on immigrants from Latin America, and especially from Mexico. Not only do Latin Americans constitute the vast majority of immigrants today, but they also comprise a majority of illegal immigrants. The Department of Homeland Security reports that illegal immigrants from North America constitute 76 percent of all illegal immigrants to the United States, 78 percent of which is attributable to Mexico alone. An additional 12 percent of illegal immigrants come from Asian countries (Hoefer, Rytina, and Baker 2008).

When viewing current immigration politics in its historical context, it is also important to note that the concept of an "illegal immigrant" did not exist for much of American history. The Johnson-Reed Act of 1924 (aka the National Origins Act) created the restrictionist framework that established the notion of illegality. Though the quotas from that act were abolished in 1965, numerical limits on immigration remained, and thus, so did illegality. It took on new political significance as the 1965 immigration reforms have been credited with exacerbating the rate of illegal immigration (Ngai 2004). Further immigration reforms in the 1980s increased the rate even more. Estimates suggest that the number of illegal immigrants in the country grew from 2.5 million in 1980 to 3.5 million in 1990 to close to 12 million today (Edwards 2006; Hoefer, Rytina, and Baker 2008). Due to these trends and the subsequent immigration-related policy debates that accompany them, we find ourselves once again challenged to address public policy issues that arise from ethnic change and the debates about the meaning of American identity that such change brings. This book is not an analysis of such policies. Rather, it is about the American people – how they feel about the changes around them, how they feel about the policies in question, and about how much – or little – commonality there is among Americans of different backgrounds regarding these matters.

There is a significant amount of heated rhetoric on immigration, ethnicity, and identity, and the rhetoric can be consequential for the very phenomena under investigation here. When Vento says his Mexican customers are there

---

[2] See Chapter 7 for a more detailed history of attitudes toward immigrants in the United States.

[3] Data on demographics were found at the Migration Policy Institute, http://www.migration information.org/datahub/charts/final.fb.shtml (accessed June 19, 2008).

just to "pop a baby," how are those customers ever going to feel like they belong or are proud to be members of that community? When police officers are told to use their own judgment when deciding whether to inquire about immigrant status, how are Latino residents going to feel that they can trust those officers or the county government that issued the directive? When there is a constant barrage of political discourse that chastises immigrants for not wanting to become American and rejecting American values, how can that not affect the very likelihood that those immigrants (or their children) will come to think of themselves as American?

I do not mean to give the impression that a majority of Americans is hostile to immigration or to immigrants. Many points exist throughout this book in which I demonstrate otherwise. Although it is true that when asked if immigration to the United States should be increased, decreased, or kept the same, since 1965 a plurality of Americans has consistently said it should be decreased with only three exceptions (1965, 1999, and 2001 – pre-9/11), it is also true that Americans have consistently been more likely to say that immigration is, on the whole, a good thing for the country rather than a bad thing.[4] Moreover, majorities throughout the past several years consistently voice support for providing an opportunity for undocumented immigrants to earn legal status, even if the words *amnesty* and *illegal* are used in the survey question (Schildkraut 2009). Americans are often sympathetic to immigrants who do not know English (see Chapter 4), and they routinely credit immigrants for being hardworking (see Chapter 7). In short, proimmigrant and ambivalent attitudes about immigrants appear to be as widespread – if not more so – than hostile ones. Ambivalence is a key analytical concept that I employ at points in this book. Nonetheless, hostility is also present. By its nature, it has been more noticeable and newsworthy than the proimmigrant and ambivalent voices, and it needs to be addressed. It shapes the political debate and thus has consequences for how policy makers approach immigration-related issues and how the hostility's targets relate to American society.

The concerns raised in immigration discourse – about citizenship, law enforcement, and a sense of common purpose – are valid ones for citizens in a multiethnic society to have. Given the pace of demographic change in recent years, it would be foolish if we did not think about these issues. But the rhetoric is often devoid of careful empirical analysis, and a major goal of this book is to fill some of that void, to provide the kind of data and assessment that allow us to examine, for instance, whether the alleged traditional consensus on what it means to be an American is breaking down or whether people are increasingly rejecting an American identity and instead prioritizing panethnic or national origin identities. In doing so, it also examines where such patterns of identity prioritization come from and what their consequences are.

---

[4] Trends on these questions were found at Gallup Brain's "Topics and Trends," http://institution .gallup.com.ezproxy.library.tufts.edu/content/?ci=1660 (accessed September 10, 2009).

One constant theme among elite commentators and ordinary Americans alike is that the very idea of being American is in jeopardy, and that we have of late failed to recognize just how much work it takes to keep this diverse country together. Such concerns have come from those on the right and on the left. The "work" discussed as essential for national stability often involves wrestling with the competing identities that individuals have and highlights the need to ensure that one's identity as an American achieves and maintains prominence. Public opinion about the contours and dynamics of American identity is where the central focus of this book lies.

Identity Content and Attachment

The starting point for this project is the assumption that national identities are key players in shaping how people respond to diversity and public policy debates. Identities have multiple dimensions, and this research falls within the increasing body of political science scholarship concerned with understanding the political consequences of these dimensions (Citrin et al. 1994; Citrin, Wong, and Duff 2001; Lien, Conway, and Wong 2004; Theiss-Morse 2004; Abdelal et al. 2006; Huddy and Khatib 2007; Theiss-Morse 2009). The aspects of American identity addressed in this empirical political science literature include beliefs about what it means to be a member of this particular national community, examinations of the boundaries people draw that delineate who can be a member of the national group, and more recently, the degree of connection or belonging that individuals have with the group and its members, especially when they might also claim a connection to an alternate group, such as a racial or ethnic group.

There is an increasing recognition that American identity, along with all national identities, is not necessarily unique in its attitudinal dynamics but rather akin to other social identities. The term *social identity* refers to the part of a person's sense of self that derives from his or her membership in a particular group and the value or meaning that he or she attaches to such membership (Tajfel 1982a). Accordingly, one's degree of attachment to the group and particular understanding of what it takes to be a member of "group X" are key factors shaping the role that social identities – including national identities – play in determining subsequent political attitudes and behaviors (e.g., Citrin, Wong, and Duff 2001; Huddy and Khatib 2007; Theiss-Morse 2009). The research presented in this book is not an attempt to confirm or challenge this view of national identity as a social identity but rather to use its insights for guidance when assessing contemporary debates about a wide range of attitudes and behaviors that stem from the politics of immigration. As such, the book focuses on two particular individual-level dimensions of American identity that derive from an understanding of national identities as social identities and are implicated in today's heated rhetoric about immigration. These two dimensions are *content* and *attachment*.

IDENTITY CONTENT

The first part of the analysis is centered on identity content, understood here to be the set of "constitutive norms" that provide "formal and informal rules that define group membership" (Abdelal et al. 2006, 696). Content applies to institutions (formal content) and citizens (informal content). For institutions, content refers to the rules of the game. Is ours a society that protects speech rights, or is speech limited? What, if any, restrictions are placed on eligibility for citizenship? Is political participation – such as voting – a requirement, or are people free to abstain? These kinds of regulated norms define the legal boundaries of membership. They also set expectations for how group members behave and allow government officials to impose sanctions when citizens violate those expectations.

For citizens, content also refers to expectations about what our compatriots are like but in an informal manner and without the force of law when norms are violated. When citizens contemplate the constitutive norms of American identity, they are thinking about what makes us American – and what they think *should* make us American. It is this informal boundary making that leads us to use terms such as *true American*, *all-American*, and even *un-American*. Constitutive norms encompass behaviors (such as political participation), beliefs (such as tolerance and patriotism), and personal characteristics (such as where a person was born or the language she or he speaks).

In this study, the focus is on identity content from the perspective of citizens rather than institutions. It examines the expectations people have of each other as living and breathing embodiments of American identity. Recent scholarship has underscored the importance that setting these kinds of boundaries plays in social identities like national identities, in which people yearn for both a sense of belonging and distinctiveness. The boundaries emerge from the group's history and from ideas about what "typical" group members are like (Theiss-Morse 2009). Previous work has called the collection of informal boundaries associated with American identity "Americanism" (Citrin, Reingold, and Green 1990). A wide range of boundaries that fall under this label is examined as is the extent to which they should be thought of as a single construct or whether it is more appropriate to analyze multiple "Americanisms." Then the impact of peoples' understanding of Americanism on immigration-related policy debates is explored.

In his 2004 book *Who Are We?*, Samuel Huntington warned of the loss of a common set of norms and values uniting Americans. He wrote, for example, that "the battles over racial, bilingual, and multiculturalist challenges to the [American] Creed, and America's core culture had become key elements of the American political landscape by the early years of the twenty-first century. The outcomes of these battles in the deconstructionist war will undoubtedly be substantially affected by the extent to which Americans suffer repeated terrorist attacks on their homeland and their country engages in overseas wars against their enemies. If external threats subside, deconstructionist movements could achieve renewed momentum" (2004, 177). In other words, the very meaning of American identity is under siege from within, and without an external enemy to unite us, we may do ourselves in. He argued that a multicultural America will become a multicreedal America, and that a multicreedal America cannot survive because a common creed has historically been essential in holding this country together.

Huntington's book garnered national attention not only because it provocatively targeted Latinos as a key source of the problem, but also because it tapped into an increasingly widespread sentiment that there is a loss of a common core in terms of beliefs and behaviors. Huntington was far from alone in voicing such concerns (Pickus 2005; Farmer 2006; Wilson 2006; Geohegan 2007). One particularly successful issue entrepreneur in the area of immigration has been Lou Dobbs of CNN. During George W. Bush's second term as president, Dobbs expressed consistent outrage about proimmigrant and proimmigration arguments and policy proposals. He regularly chastised immigrant-friendly political leaders as betraying the country, its values, and its people. His outrage found a receptive audience in the American public. During the height of congressional debates about so-called comprehensive immigration reform in 2006, Dobbs was getting more than eight hundred thousand viewers per night, an impressive 46 percent increase in his viewership from the previous year.[5] As a reporter from the *Los Angeles Times* noted, Dobbs seemed to "add viewers in direct proportion to [his] fiercely expressed views against illegal immigration" (Collins 2008).

This outrage is consequential. Recent research shows that people who cite CNN as their main source of television news exhibit higher levels of antiimmigration sentiment than viewers of network news (as do people who cite Fox News and their main source of news). Using data collected during the 2006 midterm elections, Facchini and colleagues find that people who watched CNN were 8 percentage points more likely than people who watched news on CBS to oppose the Senate's rather immigrant-friendly reform bill even after controlling for ideology and partisan identification (Facchini, Mayda, and Puglisi 2009). Even though a majority of Americans were supportive of the key elements of comprehensive immigration reform (Schildkraut 2009), the vocal minority drowned them out and won the day. The reform bill that Bush worked so hard to advance, which would have created a guest-worker program and provided an opportunity for illegal immigrants to become legal residents, died in Congress.

Antiimmigration rhetoric is thus fueled, in part, by the notion that the country's growing ethnic diversity is fracturing popular consensus about the meaning of American identity. One goal of this book is to assess that claim. If this claim turns out to be a misperception and is not supported by the evidence, findings from social psychology indicate that it is imperative to set the

---

[5] Newsmax, "Lou Dobbs' Ratings Up at CNN," http://archive.newsmax.com/archives/ic/2006/5/10/104603.shtml (accessed March 3, 2009).

record straight. Decades of research show that "people respond systematically more favorably to others whom they perceive to belong to their group than to different groups" (Gaertner and Dovidio 2000, 15). It does not take much for "we/they thinking" to emerge, and when it does, a wide range of group conflict processes are set into motion (Tajfel 1982b).[6] (Mis)perceiving that immigrants and their descendants reject "traditional American values," such as the work ethic or the value of political participation, would be sufficiently threatening such that native-born Americans close ranks and devalue the perceived out-group. Thus, whether native-born Americans and their immigrant compatriots actually share common perceptions about – and commitments to – the American political community needs to be investigated, and commonalities need to be highlighted. Prosocial behavior and cooperation increase when people of different backgrounds are led to focus on a common identity (Gaertner and Dovidio 2000).

Investigating the degree of consensus about what Americanism means is not only important from the perspective of group conflict theory, but it is also important from the perspective of democratic theory. Although democratic theorists disagree over the extent to which shared norms and values are essential for democratic stability, an impressive roster of scholars advance some version of this claim (e.g., Walzer 1983; Kymlicka 1995; Dahl 1998; Gutmann 2003; Müller 2007; Miller 2008). Robert Dahl, for instance, writes that a shared democratic political culture among the participants of self-governance is an essential condition for a stable democracy. Kymlicka goes further, writing that "the health and stability of a modern democracy depends, not only on the justice of its basic institutions, but also on the qualities and attitudes of its citizens: e.g. their sense of identity" (Kymlicka 1995, 175). Jan-Werner Müller writes that constitutional patriotism, a perspective developed by Jürgen Habermas that maintains that "political attachment ought to center on the norms, the values, and more indirectly, the procedures of a liberal democratic constitution" is especially important in "established democracies with increasingly diverse populations" (2007, 1–4).[7] According to this reasoning, the lack (or loss) of a shared identity and shared commitment to democratic procedures threatens the viability of the self-governing process.[8]

Theorists who debate the extent of commonality and common identity necessary for democratic stability often fall into – and pit themselves against – different camps, such as liberal nationalism, communitarianism, constitutional patriotism, and liberal multiculturalism (Song 2009). The nuances that distinguish these perspectives are interesting and important but are not the main concern here. Rather my point is that although proponents of these different

---

[6] See Ellemers et al. (1999) for discussion of the conditions under which group conflict might be more or less likely to occur.

[7] See Mason (1999) for another version of this argument.

[8] See Abizadeh (2002) for a rebuttal.

perspectives may disagree on the degree of commonality that is necessary for democratic stability, they all accept (some reluctantly) the premise that some commonality and sense of shared commitment is necessary. Charles Taylor, for example, a critic of the notion that a common culture is necessary in liberal societies, admits that "democratic states need something like a common identity" (1998, 143), but he laments rather than promotes this observation. He continues, "In practice, a nation can only ensure the stability of its legitimacy if its members are strongly committed to one another by means of a common allegiance to the political community" (144).

Of late, scholars who argue for the importance of shared values and a common sense of purpose in democratic societies point to empirical work that shows that cultural heterogeneity and/or rapid cultural change is often associated with both lower levels of generalized trust and expenditures on public goods, including education and infrastructure (Alesina, Baqir, and Easterly 1999; Alesina and La Ferrara 2002; Putnam 2007; Hopkins 2009). These negative correlations are likely due to the social psychological consequences of perceiving that the majority group's value is threatened through its encounters with the ever-growing outgroup.

But before the claim that immigration is leading to national disintegration can be assessed, the set of norms that Americans rely on to define their national identity must first be established. One argument of this book is that political commentators and public opinion scholars need to employ more accurate and wide-ranging measures of what Americanism is than they have used previously if they hope to shed light on debates about how changing demographics affect the meaning of American identity and to examine how ideas about identity content shape the contours of such debates. People engaged in these debates either neglect relevant opinion data altogether or rely on a narrow set of norms that typically pit inclusive norms (such as the belief that true Americans respect American political institutions and laws) against exclusive norms (such as the belief that true Americans are Christian). Yet in reality, the American public relies on a broader and deeper set of norms when they think about what uniquely distinguishes Americans from non-Americans. In particular, the norms of civic republicanism (based on participatory democracy) and incorporationism (based on being a "nation of immigrants") need to be examined in order to conduct a more complete assessment of the state of identity content in the United States today.

We know from existing scholarship that beliefs about constitutive norms have strong influences on policy attitudes (Frendreis and Tatalovich 1997; Citrin et al. 2001; Citrin, Wong, and Duff 2001; Schildkraut 2005a; Theiss-Morse 2009), but I argue that we need more accurate assessments of what those beliefs are if we strive for a deeper understanding of their power. Only when such assessments are in place can we appropriately gauge whether dissensus exists and if it falls along racial and ethnic lines. In this book, I develop such measures and use them to investigate claims that increasing diversity in the

United States threatens consensus over what it means to be American. I also use them to explore how ideas about identity content affect attitudes on policy debates related to ethnicity and immigration, such as whether government documents should be provided in multiple languages and whether racial profiling is an acceptable counterterrorism tactic.

I also argue that public opinion about the content of a national identity is not just about the expectations we have regarding our compatriots, but that it also involves judgment. We judge others based on whether we think they live up to or violate the ideals embodied in our constitutive national norms. Studies of norm violation have a long and storied history in public opinion scholarship. The concept of symbolic racism, or racial resentment, was developed to capture the notion that race-based policy views in the United States are now shaped not by beliefs about biological differences between blacks and whites but rather by the belief that African Americans *choose* to abandon the traditional American norms of individualism and the work ethic (Kinder and Sanders 1996; Sears, Henry, and Kosterman 2000; Mendelberg 2001; Henry and Sears 2002). It is this norm violation that sustains modern aversion to government efforts aimed at reducing inequality, racial resentment scholars argue. Though other scholars have vigorously challenged whether racial resentment exists and if it is free of "old-fashioned" beliefs about biological inferiority (Sniderman and Piazza 1993; Sniderman and Carmines 1997), many compelling studies have shown that perceptions of norm violation are persistent and powerful (see Mendelberg 2001).

Judgments about whether other groups in American society violate American norms exist as well, though they have not received nearly the same degree of scholarly scrutiny as judgments involving African Americans (see Paxton and Mughan 2006 for an exception). In analyzing public opinion about the content and boundaries of American national identity, I therefore address the issue of norm violation once belief in the norms has been established. My earlier qualitative research uncovered a great deal of resentment toward immigrants and their descendants, and such resentment was often based on the perception that traditional American norms were being consciously abandoned (Schildkraut 2005a). Unlike the norms invoked in racial resentment, which stem from America's legacy of classical liberalism, the immigration-related resentment on display by participants in my qualitative research had more to do with notions of identity (whether immigrants wanted to become American or think of themselves as American), active citizenship (whether immigrants were willing to "do their part"), and incorporation (whether immigrants aspired to "blend in"). In this book, I take these qualitative observations and test their generalizability. To what extent do such perceptions of norm violation exist in American society today? What is the best way to measure them? What are their consequences? As with the analysis that develops measures of constitutive norms, the analysis of perceptions of norm violation speaks to contemporary concerns in American politics as well as to scholarly debates in public opinion research about the more abstract phenomenon of how identities shape public opinion.

IDENTITY ATTACHMENT

The second dimension of national identity under investigation in this book is identity attachment. Identity attachment is defined here as the extent to which people consider their group membership to be an important part of how they see themselves. This union of the group identity with one's own self-perception is central to the perspective that national identities are social identities. It recognizes that understanding one's own identity in the context of a national group sets a variety of group processes into motion, including the desire to promote the well-being of the group (Theiss-Morse 2009).

Existing studies that characterize American identity as a social identity conceive of attachment as the extent to which people consider themselves typical Americans, how strongly they feel American, and whether they feel strong ties to the American people (Huddy and Khatib 2007; Theiss-Morse 2009). Such measures have been shown to affect a range of political outcomes, such as one's degree of political involvement, the extent to which people exclude others from group membership, and whether people are willing to make sacrifices for the collective. Although I use such a measure of attachment at some point in the book, my main investigations into identity attachment expand the literature to focus not on perceived typicality but rather on the extent to which seeing oneself as American takes precedence over other, potentially competing, identities, such as racial, ethnic, or national origin identities. Doing so builds on the social identity approach to studying national identities by applying it to the context of today's debates about immigrants in American society. The question of whether people are attached to ethnic or national origin identities at the expense of an attachment to an American identity – and the alleged consequences – is what fuels these debates. As such, the relevant measure of attachment here is one that asks people to prioritize these potentially competing commitments (see Chapter 5). In short, identity attachment is increasingly recognized as an essential element to explore when examining the dynamics of national identities. In this project, the particular form of attachment employed is one that addresses the issue of identity prioritization, or the extent to which people think of themselves primarily as American instead of primarily as a member of an ethnic or national origin group.

Today's immigrants and their descendants are often criticized as violating the long-standing American norm of assimilation, of lacking the desire to become American and instead choosing to pursue narrow group interests. Their attachment to American national identity is explicitly called into question in these critiques. Examining such claims empirically is thus a central focus of this book. I investigate the route by which people come to see themselves as American (and the ways in which this process is hindered) and assess how the presence or lack of an American attachment shapes one's experiences as a political actor. Again, simply providing accurate data is the first necessary step. Once such information is in place, I am then able to assess whether the claims of immigration critics and the worries of political theorists noted earlier are valid and whether patterns of identity attachment have political consequences. The types of political consequences under investigation include attitudes toward political institutions, including trust in government and law enforcement, as well as one's sense of obligation to the common good. As with my investigations of identity content, my investigations of identity attachment are motivated by psychological and normative research on the central role that the perception of a shared identity can play in stemming group conflict and shoring up democratic stability.

Moreover, common sense says that we should be concerned about identity attachments and their political consequences, but I find that common sense is often too simplistic or inaccurate. A key argument that emerges from the research in this book is that the normative claim that all Americans should prioritize an American identity instead of an ethnic or national origin identity is more complicated than it is typically cast. It has been argued that a psychological attachment to the national community is essential for developing devotion to the public good and fostering trust and commitment. Immigration critics sound alarms over whether immigrants and their descendants come to think of themselves primarily as American. Democratic theorists argue that a shared identity is important for political stability, especially in multiethnic societies. I investigate such concerns and show that non-American identities are often innocuous, and that they can even help improve attitudes toward government. These findings raise important questions about when – and whether – a psychological attachment to being American is desirable.

In this investigation of identity attachment, I go beyond asking whether it matters if someone thinks of him- or herself primarily as American and examine the conditions under which it matters. I pay particular attention to the perceptions people have of whether they are personally mistreated due to their race or ethnicity and whether they think their ethnic and national origin groups are also mistreated. In this portion of the analysis, I draw heavily on social identity theory and group consciousness theory, which both highlight the role of context, motivation, and perceptions of treatment in shaping identities and their consequences (Miller et al. 1981; Conover 1988; Conover and Sapiro 1993; Flippen et al. 1996; Branscombe et al. 1999; Schmitt, Spears, and Branscombe 2003; Theiss-Morse 2003; Chong and Rogers 2005). I illustrate that the political importance of identity attachments can only be properly understood when examined in conjunction with perceptions of mistreatment.

Existing scholarship has shown that perceptions of mistreatment can be powerful influences over how people see themselves in relation to American society in general (e.g., Portes and Rumbaut 2001), but this research does not investigate how these perceptions can alter the role of identity prioritization nor do they distinguish analytically the different levels at which mistreatment can be perceived. In my analysis, the power of perceptions about one's own treatment, the treatment of one's panethnic group (such as Latino or Asian), and the treatment of one's national origin group (such as Mexican or Korean) are explicitly compared.

The Importance of Public Opinion about National Identity and Immigration

This book is about more than just showing that many of Huntington's claims as well as the claims of other immigration critics are unfounded, though debunking such claims is important given the level of resentment toward immigrants that I uncover and the power of such resentment to shape political outcomes. It is about understanding the roots of that resentment and, more broadly, the impact of national identity on both the majority and minority. This book takes up beliefs on both sides of the immigration coin, through parallel explorations of the content, causes, and consequences of beliefs about American identity and citizenship among the white majority as well as among immigrants. Among the majority, the book documents norms that Americans hold about citizenship; investigates the role those norms play in evaluating immigrants and policies related to immigration; and explores the meaning and measurement of "immigrant resentment," a pattern of beliefs underlying much contemporary hostility toward immigrants. Among immigrants and their descendants, the book measures the ways in which and the degrees to which immigrants adopt American identities and explores the effect of those identities on engagement with American political institutions.

The phenomena I investigate are critical for understanding the political and social dynamics of the evolving ethnic composition of the American populace. Focusing on the causes and consequences of identity content and attachment in the United States broadens and deepens our insights about public opinion on these issues. We know that public opinion can be a strong influence on policy outcomes, especially with the increased prominence of direct democracy at the state and local level. We also know that public opinion is a powerful influence over people's behavior. It is for these reasons that I devote my attention to understanding how opinions form about policies that relate to diversity and immigration and on the role of American national identity in this process.

Additionally, the public policies under investigation here can have profound effects on the nation's newest citizens and residents. For example, policy decisions about bilingual education can affect the quality of education limited-English proficient (LEP) students receive, which can then affect their chances for economic success and social mobility. A recent report, for example, found that the high school dropout rate for LEP students in Boston has doubled since 2002, the year in which Massachusetts voters passed an initiative requiring schools to shift from transitional bilingual education to English immersion. The dropout rate for middle school students has tripled (Uriarte and Tung 2009). Official language policies can also affect whether LEP individuals of all ages have access to the government and public services. Antiterrorism and anticrime policies can affect the extent to which nonwhites trust the government and law enforcement authorities, which can then affect whether they become involved in the political process, which can ultimately affect whether the political system responds to their needs.

All of these policies can affect how ethnic minorities view themselves in relation to American society. They can affect whether people feel alienated from "mainstream" American life, consider themselves to be Americans, or view their national and ethnic identities as compatible or as mutually exclusive. One of the pillars of American national identity is active citizenship. In addition to participating in electoral politics, volunteering in one's community with and donating to charities are widely seen as important civic acts in which "good" Americans should engage. Yet fears of increased governmental powers of surveillance have led many Arab Americans to disengage from their communities and fear that any donations they make will place them under governmental scrutiny (Henderson et al. 2006). The policies of the government might promote the very disengagement and norm violation that critics like Huntington fear.

A 2006 report by the Vera Institute of Justice (funded in part by the Justice Department) found that although racial profiling is not official policy, some police officers in high-density Arab communities have admitted to being suspicious of the Arab citizens in their jurisdictions. In one of the study's focus groups of police officers, one officer said he would not accept free coffee from an Arab American store owner because he "would be wondering if there were strings attached" (Henderson et al. 2006). A recent article in the *Washington Post* was tellingly titled "Distrust Hinders FBI Outreach to Muslims" (De-Young 2007). Figuring out how to bolster trust in American political institutions among all Americans is an important aim, but it is arguably more important when it comes to the newest residents and citizens who are just establishing their sense of self in relation to the national community.

Finally, the analyses in this book yield insights into what people hope policies will achieve, which can ultimately guide policy making in ways that promote national unity and respect for difference while mitigating conflict and meeting the needs of different communities. For example, if many people support restrictive language policies because they want everyone in the society to speak a common language – a desire instilled by the American norm of active citizenship – then designing policies that actually achieve this end would be a more appropriate response than declaring English the official language, a policy option that has not proven to be effective in promoting the learning of English. If, however, support for policies like official-English is driven by more hostile motives, then determining the roots of that hostility can provide prescriptions for minimizing it.

THE POWER – AND LIMITS – OF NATIONAL IDENTITY

To this point, I have largely argued that we need to study and recognize the powerful role that dimensions of American identity play in opinion formation, political behavior, and group conflict. But a critical insight that emerges in several chapters of the book is that this power is constrained in important ways.

How people define *American identity*, for instance, has the power to shape how people interpret new policy debates. But this power is typically only realized if the policy is explicitly connected to the norms in question. For example, people who define *American identity* ascriptively (what I call "ethnoculturally") do not automatically support antiimmigrant policy proposals. Additionally, people who adhere to certain liberal or republican notions of American identity often reject such policies, but again, these national norms are only evoked in targeted ways. Likewise, I find that identity attachment can affect political engagement but in a limited and complicated fashion. In particular, the presence or absence of perceptions of mistreatment crucially conditions the power of such attachments.

My goal, therefore, is not to argue that identity content and attachment are the silver bullets that help us finally and truly understand public opinion. Rather in some cases it is true that our insights are deepened by attending to measures of national identity more thoroughly than we have in the past. But in other cases, concentrating our attention on national identity turns out to be a distraction from the more central phenomena that should concern us, such as enduring divisions among partisans and harmful perceptions of discrimination.

National identity within American democracy can be a blessing, a curse, or none of the above. Under some conditions, it can enhance participation, trust in government, and one's sense of obligation to the American community. This rosy scenario of common understandings and attachments along with civically engaged citizens is what scholars have in mind when they write of the importance of identity for the stability of democratic systems and the provision of public goods. I also find that there is a real yearning among the American people for a sense of unity amid our diversity – rather than a yearning for replacing diversity with uniformity. But national identity within American democracy can be a curse for society as a whole when our attachments are so strong that perceptions of deviation lead to threat and resentment. It can be a curse to members of minority groups who are attached to their American identity, but who also perceive that they suffer from discrimination. It is those people, I find, who are most likely to withdraw from politics and community. Still there are other cases in which conventional wisdom would lead us to expect to find significant impacts of identity attachments, and yet I find none. The notion of American identity is thus a predisposition that the government has good reason to cultivate, but also good reason to approach with caution.

The Twenty-First-Century Americanism Survey

This analysis is made possible by its reliance on a unique survey that collects parallel public opinion data from white natives, African Americans, and Latino and Asian immigrants and their immediate descendants. The survey is called the Twenty-First-Century Americanism Survey (21-CAS), which I designed and implemented in 2004 with a research grant from the Russell Sage Foundation

(RSF) and with the technical expertise of the Social and Economic Sciences Research Center (SESRC) at Washington State University. This nationally representative random-digit-dial survey has unique questions designed specifically for the topics at hand. It has 2,800 respondents and includes oversamples of blacks, Latinos, and Asians. Where appropriate, other data sources are also employed.

Existing data and research have been useful for demonstrating the relevance of identity content and attachment to contemporary policy debates and establishing patterns that justify conceiving of American national identity as a social identity, but this data and research are limited by their question-wording, regional emphasis, and tendency to focus on the views of white Americans *or* minorities, but not both at the same time. The 21-CAS allows the present study to overcome these limitations. It yields insights into the relationship between national and ethnic identity formation, the ways in which conceptions of identity influence policy views, and how other factors, such as individual-level characteristics (i.e., ideology or income) or the ethnic makeup of one's community (measured by census data) shape opinions about policies related to immigration and ethnicity. The survey includes new questions designed to capture the concepts and relationships under investigation and will provide a valuable data set for the growing number of scholars studying these issues. Importantly, the survey also provides a baseline for tracking opinions about these issues over time.

The relationship among conceptions of national identity, racial animosity, and policy preferences has been of central concern to social scientists for some time. To date, few, if any, surveys that investigate these issues are national in scope and have large enough subsamples to permit examinations of the same questions asked at the same point in time across different ethnic groups. The main contributions of the 21-CAS, therefore, derive from including large numbers of minority respondents across the nation, combining important questions that have been asked in disparate studies into one survey, and adding new questions designed specifically to overcome the limitations of existing data. It is a theory-driven survey informed by existing surveys and qualitative studies – including my own focus group research. Several findings in this book confirm insights I derived from focus group analysis. The 21-CAS also helps validate the utility of systematic analysis of focus group discussions in public opinion research.

My goal in this book is also to take the concerns raised in contemporary immigration debates seriously. The data were collected such that I would be able to find dissensus if it exists and identify the political consequences of identity attachments. I aim to treat the concerns of Huntington, Dobbs, and the many Americans who agree with them on their own terms. Moreover, I do not assume that any particular policy preference, such as a desire to make English the official language, is driven simply by racist or nativist concerns. My goal has been to collect and analyze the kind of data that allow the charges being made to be evaluated empirically.

Plan of the Book

The second chapter describes the 21-CAS. It explains how the 21-CAS builds upon the strengths of existing data sources that have been used in related studies, such as the General Social Survey, the National Election Studies, and surveys by the Kaiser Family Foundation and Pew Hispanic Center, while also addressing their limitations. The 21-CAS uses these valuable surveys as guides for asking about the content of American identity, identity prioritization, and policy preferences. It also expands the range of options that are investigated in each of these areas and refines question wording. This chapter also includes a discussion of the benefits, challenges, and limitations of relying on survey data in order to examine the issues under investigation in this project.

In Chapter 3 I take on the empirical task of accounting for how Americans define the content of American identity. I outline the theoretical underpinnings and qualitative findings used to derive the identity content questions in the 21-CAS. The measures are developed to capture America's widely accepted liberal tradition (America as a land of freedom and opportunity), understudied civic republican tradition (America as a participatory democracy with vibrant communities and dutiful citizens), highly contested ethnocultural tradition (America as a nation of white Protestants), and equally contested incorporationist tradition (America as a diverse nation of immigrants) (Conover, Crewe, and Searing 1991; Higham 1993; Hollinger 1995; Glazer 1997; Hackney 1997; Smith 1997; Schildkraut 2005a). I test the adequacy of these measures and use the results of that test to examine factors that influence how people define what being American means. I pay particular attention to claims of immigration critics who fear that our increasing diversity threatens national unity (Huntington 2004; Bauer 2006; Farmer 2006; Wilson 2006). Such fears are hardly outdated or concentrated among a handful of commentators. They found new outlets and energized audiences during debates about immigration reform in the spring of 2006 and tap into enduring concerns that have been raised by scholars of national identity and group conflict for years. I show that a broader range of constitutive norms define being American than has typically been studied in public opinion research. A complex and contradictory set of norms exists, and it is difficult to reduce them to compact scales. Importantly, I show that concerns about national disintegration have little merit. Most Americans, regardless of their ethnic or immigrant background, share this complex view of what being American means, though there are signs of divergence worth monitoring.

Chapter 4 continues the analysis of public opinion about the content of American identity by examining how the norms analyzed in Chapter 3 influence attitudes on salient immigration-related debates. The first portion of the chapter analyzes attitudes regarding policies related to language use, such as whether English should be the official language and signs on businesses should be in English. The second portion of the chapter analyzes attitudes about the use of race and ethnicity in domestic counterterrorism policies, such as whether law enforcement authorities should be allowed to question or detain people who look Arab or Muslim in order to prevent terrorist attacks. Debates about language and profiling policies such as these have inflamed passions in recent years and can have very real consequences for the people affected by them. Moreover, they are intricately tied to broader debates about the boundaries of American national identity and about who is entitled to the full range of rights and opportunities that come with membership in the political community. The goal in this chapter is twofold: first, to provide greater understanding of how America's constitutive norms work as independent variables; second, to provide more depth to our existing understanding of the dynamics of opinion formation on the policies.

I find that using constitutive norms to place boundaries on American national identity does not automatically lead to preferences for policies that restrict the full range of citizenship rights of Americans who do not fit the dominant cultural type. Rather, constitutive norms that have been traditionally overlooked can promote more inclusive preferences. I find, for example, that constitutive American norms are consistently strong predictors of language policy preferences, yet their influence is quite nuanced. Certain civic republican norms, for instance, promote support for bilingual ballots while norms about free speech lead people to reject policies dictating that English must be used in signs on private businesses. Other civic republican norms, however, consistently promote support for a variety of restrictive policies. Overall, I find that some support for restrictive language policies is driven by a narrow cultural understanding of what being American means, but that in the aggregate, concerns about how to find unity in the face of diversity are often more powerful. Controversial statements like those by Joey Vento get the media attention, but many Americans are more concerned about how to preserve a sense of common cause in the face of rapid ethnic change. On profiling, however, having a narrow cultural view of American identity is the main driving force behind opinion formation.

After this policy analysis, the attention shifts from identity content to identity attachment. Chapter 5 starts by discussing debates about self-identification and identity prioritization. Today's immigrants are often criticized for deviating from a notion of the ideal immigrant from earlier eras that welcomed his or her new identity as American without looking back. Critics, like Bob Lonsberry, claim that today's immigrants do not want to become American and fail to internalize their membership in their new national community. Democratic theorists and social psychologists write of the importance of individuals in diverse societies adhering to a common identity. This chapter begins my empirical examination of such concerns by, first, investigating patterns of identity prioritization and, second, analyzing the factors that influence whether a person identifies primarily as American, a member of a panethnic group, such as Latino or Asian, or a member of one's national origin group, such as Dominican or Korean. I find that concerns about the rejection of an American self-identification are exaggerated. Moreover, I find that acculturation plays a significant role and does so in ways contrary to those who claim that experiences in the United States encourage the rejection of an American identity. Rather, the longer one's family has had an opportunity to integrate into mainstream American society and institutions, the greater the likelihood that she or he will identify primarily as American. Yet the results also show that perceptions of discrimination promote the rejection of an American identity. Importantly, such perceptions do not appear to be a by-product of acculturation. In short, experiencing life in the United States both helps and hurts the process of "becoming American." Acculturation promotes an American identity, yet being at the receiving end of discrimination can offset the gains made through acculturation.

Despite finding little evidence to support the claim that people are increasingly reluctant to think of themselves, first and foremost, as American and despite finding that the adoption of an American identity is affected primarily by acculturation, I do not end Chapter 5 ready to dismiss the concerns that immigration critics, democratic theorists, and social psychologists raise. Their concerns regarding self-identification are instrumental in nature. Identity attachment matters, it is argued, because it affects one's relationship with American political institutions and other Americans. Whether this argument is true is assessed in Chapter 6. The analysis uses group consciousness theory and social identity theory to provide frameworks for understanding the conditions under which identity choices do and do not have political consequences and whether those consequences produce engagement with – or withdrawal from – the broader national community. These theories suggest that panethnic identities are often benign and can sometimes even neutralize the negative political consequences of discrimination. Absent that group attachment, mistreatment can lead to a withdrawal from collective action. At the same time, studies of social identity also find that the interaction between identity and discrimination might exacerbate alienation rather than mitigate it, especially with regard to prosocial behavior such as volunteering in one's community or donating to charity.

I show that one's primary self-identification largely fails to influence attitudes. Instead, perceptions of group-level and individual-level discrimination are more damaging and promote various forms of alienation from the American political community. In line with social identity and group consciousness theories, adopting a non-American identity can mitigate the effects of discrimination with respect to trust in government, but it can also activate the alienating power of discrimination with respect to one's sense of obligation to the American people. I also find that perceptions of how one is personally treated are consistently more potent than perceptions of how one's ethnic or national origin group is treated. But more importantly, I find that absent perceptions of mistreatment of any kind, the identity attachments under investigation here are often innocuous. In the end, however, I side neither with the immigration critics who charge that the fabric of American society is at risk when many citizens identify with their ethnic group nor with the optimists who claim that how people identify has little bearing on the political process.

   Chapter 7 brings us full circle by exploring the resentment some white Americans have toward immigrants. This resentment is evident in the claims animating many of today's immigration-related and ethnicity-related debates. Even though many nonwhite Americans, immigrant and native-born alike, define the normative content of American identity the same as whites do (Chapter 3), think of themselves as American (Chapter 5), and differ minimally from whites in their sense of obligation, patriotism, and trust (Chapter 6), many white native-born Americans think otherwise. They believe that today's immigrants and their descendants reject American norms, and this belief generates "immigrant resentment." Immigrant resentment is similar to the modern resentment many whites have toward blacks in U.S. society – aka symbolic racism (Kinder and Sanders 1996; Henry and Sears 2002) – but differs in important respects that involve the nature of the norms being violated. Rather than being seen as lazy (though some Americans do see immigrants that way), immigrants today are often seen as working quite hard. Yet rather than being praised for embodying the Protestant work ethic so central to American identity, they are often criticized, for it is said that their devotion to work detracts from other important facets of American identity, including active citizenship. The irony, as I show in earlier chapters, is that this resentment can *cause* the rejection of American society, which then gives the resentment even more fuel. Though it is prevalent, immigrant resentment has yet to receive much attention from public opinion scholars. In this chapter, I develop measures of immigrant resentment and compare immigrant resentment to racial resentment and more old-fashioned beliefs about the preferred racial and religious background of immigrants. Then I show how immigrant resentment is a powerful influence over public opinion about immigration policy, even after controlling for economic factors, racial resentment, and old-fashioned beliefs. This chapter also contains an extensive discussion of the history of attitudes toward immigrants in the United States. It notes how such attitudes have evolved over time and how the stage was set for immigrant resentment to emerge.

   I conclude the book with Chapter 8, in which I review my arguments, summarize my main findings and discuss their implications, and suggest avenues for future research. When all is said and done, I show that to date there is not much validity to concerns that American national identity is disintegrating or that the newest Americans are more likely than anyone else to reject their own American identity or American institutions. Most differences are at the margins, and majorities of most relevant subgroups arrive at the same broad conclusions regarding the content of American identity and one's own psychological attachment to the nation and its institutions. I underscore the conditional nature of the political impact of panethnic, national origin, and American identities and the extent to which they can become politicized under conditions of threat. Sometimes this politicization generates civic connections although other times it promotes political alienation.

   Studying the causes and consequences of political identities has taken on a prominent role in political science throughout the past decade and with good reason. Much research has shown that political behavior is driven by more than just material concerns, and that commitments to groups motivate a significant amount of human action. The variety of groups, commitments, and actions entangled in this relationship is staggering. Scholars devoted to studying the power of political identities often focus on particular aspects of identities, resulting in frustration in the lack of overarching terminologies and models (Brubaker and Cooper 2000; Smith 2003; Smith 2004). The range of important questions to ask about national identity and immigration is in many ways overwhelming. I tackle several here that at times seem too disparate to include in a single study and at other times too intertwined to untangle at all. What unites the questions explored here is a concern with how people from a variety of backgrounds and experiences view themselves in relation to American society and with how they form opinions on important ethnicity-related public policies.

This research is guided by my concern for how the United States can continue to welcome immigrants while minimizing intergroup conflict and developing appropriate – and popularly supported – policies that ease the transition for immigrants and the native born. My findings offer guidance in this regard, showing potential paths toward consensus. I also argue that we need to continue to monitor the patterns discussed throughout the book. The 21-CAS provides a valuable snapshot and offers guidelines for how to proceed with subsequent analyses. As the United States continues to debate changes to its immigration policies, immigrant policies, language and education policies, and national security policies, it is important to keep assessing the empirical claims made by visible and vocal critics. Moreover, it is important for those critics to recognize that the way in which they voice their concerns could bring about the very alienation and lack of commitment that they fear.

2

The Twenty-First-Century Americanism Survey

Uncovering the causes of attitudes, particularly those related to identities, is always challenging, and a public opinion survey is in some ways an imperfect tool for doing so. Scholars are often confronted with the trade-offs between generalizability and depth of insight. Surveys rely in large part on the "top of the head" responses people offer when asked about how they view themselves vis-à-vis their ethnic and nationality groups rather than on extended reflection. Yet those first responses reveal much about the relative salience of different identity choices; the fact that they regularly emerge as significant predictors of policy opinions and as the product of stable social and demographic factors suggests they are more than superficial. Surveys also remain the best method for interviewing large numbers of people from a variety of backgrounds, testing whether the patterns of their responses are statistically significant, and generalizing from those patterns to the broader population.

Some of the causal relationships under investigation throughout this study are straightforward, such as which demographic factors affect what someone thinks it means to be an American, or to what extent perceiving discrimination affects trust in government. Others are less tractable, such as the relationship between immigrant resentment and different conceptions of American national identity, whether the ethnic makeup of one's community causes certain attitudes, or whether the attitudes determine where a person chooses to live. But even in cases in which determining causality is difficult or in which a more exploratory approach is used, meaningful associations can still be investigated. For instance, knowing the association between certain community contexts and particular patterns of beliefs is valuable, even if we have trouble determining which one is the chicken and which one is the egg. Such exploratory insights can suggest avenues for future research by using alternative methods and can provide guidance for designing public policies that meet the challenge of simultaneously being accepted by the public, effective at achieving their aims, and respectful of the needs of different groups in society.

The depth of insight provided by my previous focus group analysis directly informs the survey design, which prevents some of the pitfalls that surveys can encounter. The most important pitfall the focus groups prevent is the use of questions that do not appropriately measure the phenomena the investigator seeks to study. What makes the Twenty-First-Century Americanism Survey (21-CAS) valuable, therefore, is that it is a nationally representative survey with questions designed specifically to measure the concepts under investigation. The goal of this chapter is to describe the general approach of the 21-CAS and its specific methodological details, and then to provide a profile of the respondents. With this overview of the survey in place, I will then be ready to explore the questions and concerns raised in the introduction.

GENERAL APPROACH

Although the United States is well on its way to becoming a majority-minority population, public opinion data sources remain poorly equipped for systematically studying the views of nonwhite Americans regarding many important issues (Dawson 2000; Bobo 2001). Surveys that do focus on black or Latino public opinion often survey *only* blacks or Latinos, making comparisons across ethnic groups difficult. The types of questions relevant to this project are rarely, if ever, asked in a single survey and asked of large numbers of people from a variety of ethnic backgrounds across the nation. Consequently, most survey-based studies of identity, ethnicity, and relevant policy preferences in the United States have generally taken one of two forms. In the first, they rely on national data collected by omnibus surveys such as the National Election Study (NES) or the General Social Survey (GSS), which has often required trying to make the most of incomplete or vague measures designed without the specific research questions being investigated in mind. It has also meant focusing on the views of white Americans because many national surveys fail to garner sufficient numbers of nonwhite participants. In the second, they employ unique surveys with innovative measures but have restricted their samples in terms of geography or ethnicity. Examples of such data sources include past iterations of the Los Angeles County Social Survey (LACSS, 1994–2000), the Latino National Political Survey (1991), the Kaiser Family Foundation/Pew Hispanic Center National Survey of Latinos (KFF/PHC, 2002), the *Washington Post*/Kaiser/Harvard Survey on Latinos (2000), the Public Agenda "Now that I'm Here" survey of immigrants (2003), the Pilot National Asian American Political Survey (PNAAPS, 2000–1), and the Latino National Survey (LNS, 2006).

The LACSS includes large numbers of people from a variety of backgrounds, but only people from Los Angeles County. The other surveys are national in scope but concentrate on particular subsets of the population. Doing so presents invaluable opportunities for studying particular groups in remarkable depth, but is obviously limited when it comes to assessing whether findings regarding one group help us understand another.[1] Not only does the 21-CAS have measures designed specifically for the questions under investigation here, but also it draws from a national sample, has oversamples of nonwhite groups, and incorporates important survey item innovations from these more restricted data sets. This last feature helps the 21-CAS to provide additional time-series data points for crucial questions that merit routine measurement, such as how people prioritize their country of origin, racial or panethnic background, and American citizenship. In all these ways, the current survey used in this book thus builds on the strengths of existing data sources while addressing some of their shortcomings.

I offer here a more detailed example of how the survey builds upon the insights of previous data sets. I chose to ask the same questions of all respondents, even if doing so led some respondents to be a little perplexed.[2] For instance, when scholars seek to study how people prioritize their ethnic and national identities, they seem to assume that white Americans do not face the same complex choices as Latinos or immigrants and thus only pose questions about identity choice or perceived discrimination to their nonwhite respondents. The 2002 KFF/PHC National Survey of Latinos provides an example of this tendency. It asked valuable questions about perceptions of discrimination against oneself personally and against one's group, which can be used to investigate how perceived treatment affects identity choices and political engagement (Schildkraut 2005b). Even though the sample included non-Latino respondents, such questions were not presented to them. Yet conventional wisdom maintains that in increasingly diverse areas, many whites feel that they face discrimination because of their race or ethnicity, and that this perceived treatment generates hostility toward immigrants and promotes support for restrictive policies.

The following anecdote provides an illustration of this conventional wisdom. The *Sun-Sentinel*, a daily paper in south Florida, ran a series of articles from May 8 to May 13, 2003, about linguistic diversity in the region. The Web-based version of the paper included a discussion board where readers could share their views. Many of the postings from non-Latinos were very hostile toward linguistic diversity, often with people relating stories of how they had been denied a job because they were not Latino or did not know Spanish. Some of the postings were so vitriolic that the paper's editor wrote an editorial commenting on how unsettling the animosity was. He wrote, "We knew when we published our series on language this past week, we'd get an ear full from readers. But,

---

[1] Several studies, especially those by Jack Citrin and various colleagues, employ both kinds of data sets so that the benefits of one can offset the drawbacks of the other (Citrin et al. 1994; Citrin et al. 2001; Citrin, Wong, and Duff 2001). For examples of work using omnibus surveys, see Frendreis and Tatalovich 1997; Hood, Morris, and Shirkey 1997; Hood and Morris 1997.

[2] The only exceptions here are in obvious cases in which, e.g., asking certain questions of noncitizens would not have made sense.

even our most seasoned editors were surprised at the anger, frustration and hate expressed in the dozens of e-mails we received" (Maucker 2003).[3] Yet we have not been able to assess the generalizability of such anecdotes and conventional wisdom or the larger questions they raise about the intersection of race, ethnicity, and national identity because the relevant questions are skipped over when respondents identify themselves as white. Here, the same questions are asked of everyone.

For whites who never feel that their racial or ethnic identity presents challenges, such questions might seem odd. For instance, at one point in the survey, respondents are asked if they feel that their national origin group faces discrimination in the United States. For a fourth-generation white respondent who says her ancestors are from the Netherlands, this means that she is asked if she feels that Dutch people are discriminated against here. Chances are quite good that this respondent has never perceived anti-Dutch sentiment in the United States and might therefore think the question is strange. But for those whites that feel threatened and tie the threat to their racial or ethnic background, such threat can be investigated. Examining whether perceptions such as those that were expressed on the *Sun-Sentinel* discussion board are actually grounded in objective conditions, such as the ethnic makeup of one's community, or whether they arise from more psychological sources will provide useful insights into the understudied role that diversity plays in shaping how whites self-identify and feel about political institutions and contentious ethnicity-related public policies. Census data about the racial and ethnic makeup of respondents' communities is employed in order to aid in this line of inquiry.

In sum, this survey builds upon existing data sources in the following ways: it is nationally representative with a large sample size; has oversamples of nonwhite groups, which will allow for phenomena to be investigated across racial and ethnic groups; adopts useful and innovative questions that have been used in regional or ethnicity-specific surveys and fields them in a more generalizable context; and asks the same questions of everyone, which will allow for investigations of the different ways in which the challenges brought about by ethnic diversity affect people of different ethnic and racial backgrounds. More substantively, it is a valuable tool for probing how people define the content of American identity at the start of the new century, investigating the unique kinds of resentment that immigration fosters, exploring the factors that guide the reconciliation of competing identities, and examining how all of these factors shape policy beliefs and the relationships people of all stripes have with political institutions. But before moving on to these thorny and complicated questions, a description of the survey and the general patterns it reveals are in order. The following description focuses on the overall methodology and on a demographic profile of the participants. I discuss in

[3] See Chapter 5 for excerpts from the angry e-mails.

detail how the wording of specific questions builds on existing survey items where appropriate in later chapters. The text of all questions can be found in Appendix A.

METHODOLOGY

The 21-CAS is a national random-digit-dial (RDD) telephone survey of adults, supplemented with oversamples of blacks, Latinos, and Asians. Data collection was funded by a grant from the Russell Sage Foundation (RSF) and was conducted from July 12 to October 8, 2004, by the Social and Economic Sciences Research Center (SESRC) at Washington State University. The oversamples were generated through a combination of procedures. The primary procedure involved using the 2000 Census to draw samples stratified by region, urbanization, and minority density. Areas were categorized as "high density" if blacks, Latinos, or Asians made up 31 percent to 50 percent of the population in a telephone exchange area and as "medium density" if these groups made up 20 percent to 30 percent of the population. A high- and medium-density sample was drawn for each group. After six weeks in the field, the Asian American samples were supplemented with a sample of Asian surnames due to higher than expected noncontacts. Both procedures are common ways of including larger numbers of people from groups that are traditionally underrepresented when RDD is used alone (e.g., Lien, Conway, and Wong 2004). The SESRC constructed one weighting variable for the sample. This variable weighs each respondent according to his or her self-identified race so that results from the entire sample can be generalized to the U.S. population as a whole. Data from the 2000 Census were used to construct this weight. Unless noted otherwise, all percentages discussed in the book refer to weighted results while raw numbers refer to unweighted results.

For all contacts, interviewers asked to speak with a person in the household who is eighteen years of age or older and had the most recent birthday. The final sample has 2,800 respondents, yielding a margin of error of ±1.89 percentage points at a 95 percent confidence level. The cooperation rate, or the ratio of interviews to interviews plus refusals, was 31.2 percent. Refusal conversion calls were attempted three weeks after a potential respondent's initial refusal. Although a higher cooperation rate would be preferable to a lower rate, recent studies suggest that the cost of extensive refusal conversions are not worth the effort (Curtin, Presser, and Singer 2000; Keeter et al. 2000; Groves, Presser, and Dipko 2004).

The average interview length was twenty-six minutes. A Spanish version of the survey was available and was used by 137 respondents. No Asian-language versions were available. The SESRC did have interviewers conversant in some Asian languages. When non-English-speaking Asians answered the phone, these interviewers were sometimes able to introduce the survey in their language and ask if the appropriate person in the household could complete the interview in English.

PROFILE OF RESPONDENTS

Citizenship

Ninety-three percent of respondents are U.S. citizens, and 85 percent were born in the United States. Of those born elsewhere, the mean number of years spent living in the United States is twenty, with a standard deviation of 14.7. With regard to race, 98 percent of whites are citizens, 96 percent of blacks, 73 percent of Asians, and 68 percent of Latinos.

Generation

I categorized as "first generation" those respondents who were not born in the United States, "second generation" those respondents who were born in the United States but whose parents were not, "third generation" those respondents who were born in the United States along with at least one parent but without any grandparents born in the United States, and "fourth plus generation" those respondents who were born in the United States and have at least one parent and one grandparent that was also born in the United States. According to this categorization, 15 percent of the respondents are first generation, 5 percent second generation, 7 percent third generation, and 73 percent fourth generation or more. Thus, at least 27 percent of the respondents either immigrated themselves or have likely known a family member that did. For many, immigration is not just a romantic element of our national history or a scourge to be debated by politicians but is instead a part of their personal reality.

Language

For 89.5 percent of the respondents, English is the primary language spoken at home. For 5 percent it is Spanish, and for 1 percent it is Chinese. The remaining 4 percent said they speak another language at home; of those, most were Asian languages, including Hindi, Urdu, Vietnamese, Thai, and Korean.

Country of Origin

To measure country of origin, all respondents were asked "What countries did your ancestors come from?" and were allowed to offer three places. If they offered more than one place, respondents were then asked to specify which one they identify with most. Their response to this question was used in all remaining questions that involve inserting the respondent's country of origin (such as whether people feel that "Mexicans" suffer from discrimination). If respondents said they could not decide which one they identify with most, did not identify with any of the places they mentioned, or only named one place, then their first mention was inserted instead. Fifty-five percent of respondents named more than one place. Of those, 31 percent said "neither/none/can't choose" when asked which place they identify with most. The five most common "first mentions" were Germany (17.02%), England (12.85%), Ireland (10.15%), Mexico (5.39%), and Italy (4.65%). Admittedly, one drawback of this sample is that specific national origin comparisons are difficult because of the small sample sizes within most national origin categories. For example, it is difficult to compare Vietnamese respondents with Koreans. The ethnic-specific surveys, such as the PNAAPS and the Latino National Survey (LNS), are clearly better suited for such inquiry. I undertake national origin comparisons where appropriate and feasible, though I primarily concentrate on comparing the causes and consequences of national origin and panethnic identities among people from a wide variety of particular backgrounds. I compare people who prioritize their national origin identity – regardless of what that particular identity might be – with people who prioritize their panethnic identity.

Race and Panethnicity

Two questions were used to establish the racial and panethnic categories used for the analyses in this study. First, respondents were asked if they are of Hispanic or Latin origin or descent (yes/no). Second, they were asked "What race do you consider yourself to be?" The race question was left open-ended. Interviewers coded anything other than white/Caucasian, black/African American, Asian, Hispanic/Latino, Native American, or mixed race as "other" and entered the respondent's answer verbatim. The "other" responses were later recoded if possible. For example, if a person said her race was Mexican, she was later recoded as Latino on the race measure. The race question and the Latino origin question were used in conjunction in order to construct a single panethnicity variable that places each respondent in only one racial or panethnic category. The breakdown of this final variable is the following: 1,633 white, non-Hispanic respondents; 300 black; 441 Latino; 299 Asian; 25 Native American; and 38 "mixed." I use these categories to analyze race and panethnicity throughout the book and focus on whites, blacks, Latinos, and Asians. A detailed discussion of the construction of this variable appears in the following section. It is divided into two parts: the first reviews the logistical details, and the second discusses the conceptual issues with which one must contend when creating a variable such as this one.

Logistical Issues of the Panethnicity Variable. For the panethnicity variable, people were categorized as white if they said their race was white and that they were not Latino. A few respondents were also categorized as white if they said their race was "other" but then named a European country when asked to clarify (e.g., Czech). People were categorized as black if they said their race was black and that they were not Latino. A few respondents were also categorized as black if they said their race was "other" but then said "African American" when asked to clarify. People were categorized as Asian if they said their race was Asian and that they were not Latino. A few respondents were categorized as Asian if they said their race was "other" but then named Asian countries when asked to clarify (e.g., Chinese). People were categorized as Latino if they said their race was Latino and/or that they are of Latin origin, as Native American if they said their race was Native American but that they were not Latino, and as "mixed" if they said their race was mixed but that they were not Latino.

It is worth noting that 62 percent of respondents who said that they were of Latin origin or descent also said that their race was Latino or Hispanic, 17 percent said white, and 10 percent said "other." Of those who said "other," nearly all mentioned a Latin American country when asked to clarify (e.g., Mexican or Dominican). Close to 72 percent of respondents who are of Latin origin or descent identify racially as Latino as well.

In total, 201 out of the 2,800 respondents were recoded as either white, black, Asian, or Latino based on their open-ended responses to the race question and/or their answers to the Latin descent question. A majority of those cases (n = 123) consists of people who said they were of Latin descent.

Conceptual Issues of the Panethnicity Variable. As anyone who uses survey data to study issues related to race and ethnicity can testify, classification decisions such as the ones described here are always challenging methodologically, conceptually, and even morally. Many of us are torn between our recognition of the social construction of racial categories and the reality of mixed heritage, on the one hand, and the methodological need in large-N studies to place respondents in one and only one category on the other hand. We feel the paradox of employing, and even perpetuating, the rigid distinctions that we know to be problematic. It is not unlike the debates that surrounded the 2000 Census and the opportunity to select more than one racial category. At the time, many leaders of ethnic organizations commented that they appreciated the development in conceptual terms while in practical terms advocated that nonwhites select only one race (El Nasser 2000; Schevitz 2000; Davis 2001; Holmes 2001).[4] As these leaders know well, socially constructed racial categories can still have powerful consequences. Studying those consequences requires employing those categories in some shape or form. The conscientious way of dealing with the challenges of constructing a panethnicity variable, I argue, is to be transparent about coding decisions, collect the data in such a way that alternative specifications can be explored, and explain the logic of one's choices. Having accomplished the first and second of these demands, my task now is to address the third.

In particular, the decision here to have one's Latino heritage trump all other heritages might strike some readers as a controversial one. My starting point here is the U.S. Census, which for decades has classified people from any racial

---

[4] In the end, less than 3% of the population selected more than one racial category on the 2000 Census (Grieco and Cassidy 2001).

background as Hispanic if their country of origin sustains that classification.[5] With that precedent in mind, I also noted that many people of Hispanic descent in the United States consider themselves Hispanic racially. In the 2000 Census, for example, 42 percent of Hispanics identified as "some other race."[6] Ninety-seven percent of people who selected "some other race" on the census were Hispanic (Grieco and Cassidy 2001). More importantly, roughly 72 percent of Hispanic respondents to the 21-CAS racially identify as Hispanic or with their Latin American country of origin (62% the former and 10% the latter). Finally, as a scholar of racial and ethnic politics in the United States, it is my suspicion that for those respondents who fall in multiple categories, the increasing public attention over the years to Latino immigration, potential Latino political power (aka "the sleeping giant"), and Latino purchasing power collectively serve to increase the salience of this portion of a person's heritage. Together, these factors drove my choice to prioritize a person's Latino heritage when creating the "race" variable.[7]

Finally, I use the terms *race* and *panethnicity* interchangeably throughout the analysis, and when I use the term *ethnicity*, it is to refer only to one's country of origin. This terminology is the same as that used by Lien, Conway, and Wong in their analysis of the PNAAPS (2004). It also aligns me with scholars like David Hollinger, who critique the rigid distinctions between race and ethnicity and opt for alternative terms such as *ethnoracial bloc* (1995). Both *race* and *panethnicity* are terms commonly used to denote physical appearance and culture and unite peoples according to how the dominant U.S. society has treated them throughout history. Hollinger advocates using *ethnoracial* because "this phrasing better reflects our understanding of the contingent and instrumental character of the categories, acknowledges that the groups traditionally called racial exist on a blurred continuum with those traditionally called ethnic, and more easily admits renunciation, once and for all, of the unequal treatment in America of human beings on the basis of the marks of descent once called racial" (39). Although I do not adopt the term *ethnoracial*, I do share his sense that a single measure of racial and panethnic categories can serve multiple purposes well, and that the practical distinctions between race and ethnicity are quite blurred. Moreover, a person can be Italian and white, or Korean and Asian, and both identities can become politically salient. Though I reserve the term *ethnicity* for indicating national origin ancestry, I share the acknowledgment that the broad racial labels we employ are additionally overarching categories that subsume many smaller ethnic groupings, and that many people identify with both the smaller grouping and the larger one. As such, we should

---

[5] I use the terms *Latino* and *Hispanic* interchangeably throughout this book.

[6] Forty-eight percent classified themselves as white.

[7] Overall, 123 respondents who claimed Latino heritage (28%) chose a racial category other than Latino (or Latin American country of origin). Of those, 78 (63%) chose "white," 11 (9%) chose "black," 21 (17%) chose "mixed," 3 (2%) chose Asian, 2 (2%) chose Native American, and 8 (7%) did not answer the question. All 123 are classified as Latino in the race/panethnicity variable used in this study.

do what we can to capture these different identities when we collect our data, which is what I have tried to do with the methodological choices discussed here.

To summarize, the variable I refer to as "race" has respondents in one, and only one, category. When I discuss respondents' panethnic groups, I am referring to this variable. I view its categories as umbrellas that cover a wide range of national origin ethnicities but that potentially take on their own independent power and meaning.

Additional Demographic Measures

The median age of the respondents is forty-seven. Fifty-eight percent of the respondents are female. The mean education level is "some college." The mean household income is between $45,000 and $49,000.

The sample was more conservative than liberal, but more Democratic than Republican. Thirty-seven percent of respondents identified as conservative, 34 percent as moderate, and 23 percent as liberal, whereas 41 percent identified as Democratic ("strongly" and "somewhat" combined) and 33 percent identified as Republican.

COMPARING THE 21-CAS TO OTHER DATA SOURCES

Table 2.1 compares characteristics of the 21-CAS population with characteristics of the U.S. population based on census data and, where appropriate, with characteristics of respondents from the 2004 NES. It shows that the similarities among the data sources are more substantial than the differences, especially with regard to age, nativity, race, and income. The survey population is more female, more educated, and has more households earning more than $100,000 than the U.S. population, but the median household income compares favorably. Such differences are typical (Lien, Conway, and Wong 2004). Compared to the NES, which overlapped in the field with the 21-CAS, the 21-CAS sample is more Democratic but generally the same ideologically.[8] Readers should keep these differences in mind, but should be assured by Table 2.1 that the 21-CAS sample provides a reasonable approximation of the population of the United States.

Because the majority of respondents reflected in Table 2.1 are white and because the analyses throughout the book focus considerable attention on the attitudes and behaviors of nonwhites, I also compare Latinos, Asians, and blacks in the 21-CAS with data about those groups from the 2000 U.S. Census with regard to three characteristics from Table 2.1: nativity, educational attainment, and income. The results are in Table 2.2. All three groups compare

---

[8] The 2004 NES preelection survey was in the field from September 7 to November 1, 2004, whereas the 21-CAS was in the field from July to October, 2004. See "NES Announcement: Update on the 2004 American National Election Studies," http://www.umich.edu/~nes/announce/newsltr/20050120.htm (accessed July 14, 2005).

TABLE 2.1. *Comparing the Twenty-First-Century Americanism Survey and the American Population*

Characteristic	Twenty-First-Century Americanism	2000 Census	2004 NES
Female	58%	51%	
Median age, 18 and over	47 yrs	35–44 yrs	
White, non-Hispanic	69%	75%	
Black, non-Hispanic	12%	13%	
Asian, non-Hispanic	6%	4%	
Latino/Hispanic	11%	13%	
Born in United States	85%	88%	
Education (age 25 and over for census)			
No high school diploma	7%	20%	
Completed high school	19%	29%	
Bachelor's degree	19%	16%	
Household Income			
Less than $25,000	20%	21%	
$25,000–$49,999	18%	29%	
$50,000–$99,000	32%	35%	
More than $100,000	21%	15%	
Median	$50,000–$59,999	$50,046	
Political Orientation			
Democratic (strong and somewhat/weak)	41%		32%
Republican (strong and somewhat/weak)	33%		39%
Liberal	23%		20%
Conservative	37%		32%

Notes: Racial categories from the U.S. Census are for those people who selected one race only. Data from 21-CAS are weighted; data from NES are unweighted. Variables from 21-CAS (except income) and the NES still include "don't know" and "no answer."
Sources: U.S. Census, American FactFinder, http://factfinder.census.gov (accessed July 12, 2005). American NES, 2004. Data downloaded from NES data center.

favorably on nativity and income. Yet, as with the sample as a whole, these subgroups in the 21-CAS have higher education levels than their counterparts in the general population, with the discrepancies higher for Latinos and Asians than for blacks.

ADDITIONAL QUESTIONS

Respondents were asked many additional questions including how they feel about various public policies and political institutions and about their own political activity. Further, respondents were asked sets of questions designed specifically to measure the major concepts under investigation here, including how they define the content of American national identity, whether they harbor resentment toward immigrants, how they prioritize their identities, and

TABLE 2.2. *Comparing Respondents in the Twenty-First-Century Americanism Survey and the Census, by Race*

Characteristic	Twenty-First-Century Americanism	2000 Census
Latinos		
Born in United States	50.34%	60%
High school diploma or more	79.55%	52.4%
Bachelor's degree or more	23.41%	10.4%
Median income	$35,000–$39,999	$34,379
Asians		
Born in United States	25.75%	31.10%
High school diploma or more	97.99%	80.4%
Bachelor's degree or more	70.57%	44.10%
Median income	$60,000–$74,999	$59,324
Black		
Born in United States	92.7%	93.9%
High school diploma or more	87.63%	72.3%
Bachelor's degree or more	25.75%	14.3%
Median income	$30,000–$34,999	$33,255

Notes: Entries from 21-CAS are unweighted. Education figures from 2000 Census are for people age 25 and older. Census data for Latinos are from people categorized as "Hispanic or Latino (of any race)."

Sources: For Latinos: http://www.census.gov/prod/2004pubs/censr-18.pdf (accessed September 16, 2009). For Asians: http://www.census.gov/prod/2004pubs/censr-17.pdf (accessed September 16, 2009). For blacks: http://www.census.gov/prod/2005pubs/censr-25.pdf (accessed September 16, 2009).

how they feel their racial and national origin groups are treated in the United States. It is these questions that are most unique to the present survey and that are directly informed by my earlier qualitative research. The design of these items and respondents' answers to them are addressed in great detail in later chapters.

3

Defining American Identity in the Twenty-First Century

As streets in cities across America filled with activists rallying to support immigrants in the spring of 2006, renewed attention was drawn to the question of whether the rapidly changing ethnic demography of the United States is changing what being American means. A central concern is one raised by the late Samuel Huntington – that a multicultural America will become a multicreedal America (2004). Conservative icon Phyllis Schlafly, for example, warns that many immigrants today threaten our cultural norms, including our economic norms and the rule of law (2006; also see Bauer 2006; Farmer 2006; Wilson 2006). Even commentators who explicitly link their concerns to national ancestry justify their position by arguing that immigrants reject the norms and values that define being American (Buchanan 2006). It is not just those on the right who voice such concerns. An avowed "lifelong Democrat" and "early and avid supporter of Obama" recently wrote in the *Christian Science Monitor* that "heavy immigration from Latin America threatens our cohesiveness as a nation," and that "Latinos are not melting into our cultural mainstream" (Harrison 2009). He goes on to warn that the instability of democracy in Latin America is being imported to the United States and argues that no equivalent in Spanish exists for the words *compromise* or *accountability*. The message from such warnings is clear: today's immigrants and their children do not adopt American civic norms and therefore threaten our democratic stability.

The fear that the presence of groups of people with varying sets of cultural and civic norms undermines stability is not confined to the pundits. Scholars of social psychology and democratic theory have long examined the dynamics of group relations and the conditions under which conflict is more or less likely to emerge. Research in both of these fields suggests that the perception of a common group identity and a shared understanding of a group's value and meaning can be important ingredients for stability and cooperation.

From the psychological side, John Transue found, for example, that when whites were primed to think about being American they were more likely to support having their own taxes raised to help minorities than whites who were primed to think of their ethnicity (2007). Similarly, Samuel Gaertner and colleagues found that white college students were more likely to agree to a black student's request for help if the black student was wearing a hat with the school's logo (2000, 63). Gaertner and Dovidio call this phenomenon the Common Ingroup Identity Model; their book on the subject details countless more studies to support the general theme that people from different ethnic subgroups can achieve harmony – and even make sacrifices for one another – when they realize their common bonds (2000). Antiimmigration rhetoric such as that noted here (see also Chavez 2008) undercuts the recognition of a common ingroup identity. It serves to perpetuate the salience of subgroup identities and to mask true areas of agreement. The result is greater conflict, less cooperation, a retrenchment from redistribution, and greater preferences for antiimmigrant and antiimmigration policies.[1]

From the democratic theory side, Robert Dahl writes that becoming a "we" is an important condition that enables democratic procedures to thrive (1991). Similarly, David Miller writes that national identities come to exist when a group of people share a public culture, and that this shared identity creates a sense of obligation to one another and fosters the "mutual understanding and trust that makes democratic citizenship possible" (1995, 185). He also defends the idea that it is fair to expect immigrants to demonstrate a familiarity with a nation's culture as a condition of naturalization (Miller 2008; also see Pickus 2005). Michael Walzer likewise writes of the importance of shared meanings in self-governing societies (1983, 1996). Similar ideas about identity, belonging, and democracy can be found as far back as John Stuart Mill's *Considerations on Representative Government*. One should note, however, that not all democratic theorists agree that a shared identity or even a shared sense of "what it means to be X" is necessary for democratic stability (Mason 1999; Abizadeh 2002). Yet as noted in the introduction, even many critics of the strong sense of commonality that people like Miller advance admit that some degree of shared understanding is essential in diverse democracies (Taylor 1998, 1999).

Thus, though it may be tempting to dismiss comments by Buchanan, Schlafly, and others as musings of right-wing extremists that do not merit careful scrutiny, there are reasons to address their concerns. The stability of diverse democracies allegedly rests, in part, on whether people from different backgrounds see themselves as engaged in a common political enterprise and agree on what it is that makes them a "we." For democracies, this agreement often centers on certain principles, such as liberty and tolerance (Dahl 1991, 1998; Gutmann 2003; Müller 2007), but might also include other factors, such as an appreciation of the country's history and even of its diversity (Kymlicka 1995; Miller 1995; Glazer 1997).

The argument that immigrants and their descendants are a threat to American culture and stability through their rejection of traditional national norms

---

[1] Also see the work of Branscombe et al. (1999) for a discussion of the psychological dynamics of perceived threats to the value of one's group.

is nothing new. One only has to look to World War II for evidence. Estimates suggest that around two-thirds of the people interned were American citizens who could not escape the perception that their Japanese ancestry rendered them a perpetual threat (Murray 2000). John Higham's classic examination of nativism throughout American history shows that Asian Americans were hardly the only group to be portrayed as too foreign and unable to assimilate (1963).

Leo Chavez calls the contemporary manifestations of such claims the "Latino Threat Narrative" (2008). Although Latinos certainly draw a significant amount of ire, Asian Americans still suffer from the perception that they are "forever foreign" (Tuan 1998); Muslim Americans continually face charges that their religion is incompatible with the American way of life; and even African Americans, the vast majority of whom are not immigrants, are still sometimes portrayed as undermining American stability. One need only recall characterizations of Barack and Michelle Obama as militant and unpatriotic during the 2008 presidential campaign (e.g., Nelson 2008; Rutenberg 2008; Weisman and Shear 2008).

It is important to acknowledge that antiimmigrant sentiments do not necessarily represent views of the majority of Americans nor do they necessarily constitute a majority of media commentary about immigration. Substantial portions of the American public were in favor of immigrant-friendly reforms promoted by President Bush in 2006 (Schildkraut 2009). The editorial boards of national newspapers regularly criticize antiimmigration messages. The editorial page of the *New York Times*, for example, has been a consistent champion of comprehensive – and compassionate – immigration reform. Several examples throughout American history exist in which immigrant-friendly reforms were advanced successfully, such as in 1965 and 1986. But traditionally – as well as in our current era – the voices that are more hostile to immigrants appear to be louder and better organized (see Chapter 7 for a more detailed account of immigration history in the United States). Political leaders respond to such organization and noise, as evidenced by the recent decisions of Republican officeholders that some experts say will win them support from their base but will threaten the long-term viability of the party through its alienation of Latinos (Wides-Munoz 2009). Recent examples include opposing comprehensive immigration reform, voting against the confirmation of Latina Supreme Court Justice Sonia Sotomayor, and raising the specter of illegal immigrants getting free healthcare under Democratic proposals for healthcare reform (e.g., Stanton 2009).

This chapter provides an empirical assessment of the concerns that recent immigrants and their descendants are rejecting traditional American norms, collectively known as "Americanism." It relies on a wide-ranging set of norms to generate survey data allowing a thorough and generalizable test of the claim that we lack consensus on the norms and values that constitute American identity, and that this lack is due to cultural diversity. In doing so, it also provides an empirical assessment of the "multiple traditions" theory

(Smith 1997) and develops more accurate measures of how Americans view the content of American identity than has typically been included in public opinion research. Previous examinations of opinions about American identity (Citrin, Reingold, and Green 1990; Frendreis and Tatalovich 1997; Citrin, Wong, and Duff 2001; Theiss-Morse 2009) have been hindered by measures that focus on only two components of American identity: liberalism (America as a land of freedom and opportunity) and ethnoculturalism (America as a nation of white Protestants). Although analyses of additional dimensions of American identity have animated political science literature in recent years, empirical investigations into the dynamics of a multidimensional Americanism have been missing. Two often-overlooked elements of American identity are civic republicanism (America as a vibrant participatory democracy with dutiful citizens) and incorporationism (America as a diverse nation of immigrants). Moreover, previous studies generally focus on whites, leaving the study of how nonwhites define American identity underdeveloped.

This chapter uses the Twenty-First-Century Americanism Survey (21-CAS) in order to overcome these limitations. The analysis confirms the multiple traditions perspective, showing that a broad range of constitutive norms define being American. A complex and contradictory set of norms exist, and it is difficult to reduce them into a single measure of Americanism. The findings also suggest, however, that Americans might not "package" constitutive norms into the same broad ideological traditions that historians and political theorists do. Importantly, the results also show that concerns about national disintegration have little merit at this juncture. Most Americans, regardless of their ethnic or immigrant background, share this complex view of what being American means, though there are signs of divergence to monitor, with some social groups in American society less likely than others to see the norms of cultural assimilation and cultural maintenance as mutually exclusive. Whether a person strongly identifies with the American people and one's partisanship and ideology are often more potent determinants of how the content of American identity is defined than ethnicity or nativity.

WHY CONTENT?

The analytical focus of this chapter is on the content of identities, or "the meaning of a collective identity" (Abdelal et al. 2006). One key aspect of identity content is the set of "constitutive norms" that provide "formal and informal rules that define group membership" (Abdelal et al. 2006, 696). These rules dictate normative guidelines about behaviors and processes that are valued and ideally followed by group members, leaders, and institutions (Citrin, Reingold, and Green 1990; Schildkraut 2005a). They help people decide who is and is not a fellow member of this important social grouping and thus determine the targets of outgroup biases, even if those targets are legally and formally members of the ingroup (Theiss-Morse 2009). To understand the power of political identities and assess the claims discussed earlier, we need to study what people think these constitutive norms are. (The extent to which people "think of themselves" as American and its consequences are examined in later chapters.)

Constitutive norms of identity content emerge from an amalgam of elite-driven forces, counterelite contestation, and eventually acceptance among citizens (Smith 2003). They provide rules regarding acceptable behaviors and practices, demarcate the boundaries of membership, and dictate what people expect from other group members and their political institutions. Constitutive norms generate ideal types that serve as information shortcuts; they set expectations for group members for how we should look, sound, think, act, and worship. As with any information shortcut, these ideal types lead to accurate as well as inaccurate expectations. For example, many people assume that someone with an accent is not American. Many people also assume that Americans are active participants in their political system. In both cases, violations of the ideal abound, yet the ideal continues to shape how Americans approach their surroundings. Constitutive norms play a key role in helping people recognize others as fellow group members (Abdelal et al. 2006). As such, the perception that certain people or groups in a society fail to adhere to the norms can lead them to be categorized as outside the group, which has the potential to spur ingroup favoritism and outgroup derogation (Turner 1982; Theiss-Morse 2009).

As previously noted, commentators center their arguments on the norms and values that delineate American identity. Public opinion scholars have confirmed that beliefs about identity content are powerful forces that shape policy attitudes. Yet scholars and pundits alike have too often confined their attention to only a subset of the potent norms that constitute American identity. Centering this analysis on identity content and expanding the scope of norms under investigation is important for at least three reasons. First, given that today's heated rhetoric of disintegrating creedal consensus can exacerbate ethnic tensions, providing a thorough test of whether such rhetoric describes reality accurately is imperative. If it turns out to be inaccurate, misperceptions should be corrected, difficult as this may be (Kuklinski et al. 2000; Sides and Citrin 2007). The concerns at the heart of this rhetoric are valid ones to have, as research from social psychology and democratic theory makes clear. Any nation experiencing rapid ethnic change should examine them. But the data needed to test their validity adequately are rarely invoked.

Second, beliefs about identity content shape how people feel about contentious policy issues, such as language policy, immigration policy, and government spending on race-related programs (Citrin, Wong, and Duff 2001; Schildkraut 2005a; Theiss-Morse 2006). The academic study of public opinion on such policies would therefore benefit from measures that go beyond liberal norms regarding political tolerance and ethnocultural norms regarding race or religion. Only with properly tailored measures can we study *which* components of American identity matter *when* and for *whom*. Note that this inquiry is different from studies of people's core values and how those core values shape policy attitudes (Feldman 1988). Rather, the concern here is the values and norms that people think uniquely and rightly constitute the meaning of American identity. It is the power of the associations people make between the values and the identity – and not just the values – that interests scholars of identity politics. We know that such associations are strong influences over policy attitudes, but we need more accurate assessments of what those associations are in order to more fully understand their power.

Third, such an investigation will provide a snapshot of the dimensions of conflict or consensus at a given point in time. This baseline will be valuable for uncovering the dynamics of identity contestation and change, processes that are difficult to isolate but that are of increasing concern (Gerstle 2001; Abdelal et al. 2006). Given the slow pace at which such change takes place, tracking this cross-sectional data over time is a valuable endeavor.

THE CONTENT OF AMERICAN IDENTITY: MORE THAN LIBERALISM AND ETHNOCULTURALISM

Recent scholarship has identified complex and often competing components of American identity that are rooted in the widely accepted liberal tradition, the understudied civic republican tradition, the contested ethnocultural tradition, and the equally contested incorporationist tradition (Higham 1993; Hollinger 1995; Glazer 1997; Hackney 1997; Smith 1997; Schildkraut 2005a). This perspective has been termed the "multiple traditions" (Smith 1993), or multiple conceptions model of the content of American identity.[2] As noted in the introduction, my focus in this inquiry is on the ways in which these traditions inform the public's perceptions of informal constitutive norms (expectations about what our compatriots are like but without the force of law when norms are violated) as opposed to formal constitutive norms (norms that shape institutional practices and legal rules of the game).

Liberalism and ethnoculturalism merit the least amount of explanation here; both have been examined in detail and at many levels of analysis. Liberalism, in short, is the image of America that comes most easily to mind when people think about what it means to be American and is widely seen as *the* defining essence of American political culture (Hartz 1955). It stresses minimal government intervention in private life and promotes economic and political freedoms along with equality of opportunity. Countless studies have documented its enduring influence over elites, masses, and institutions (Lipset 1963; McClosky and Zaller 1984; Feldman 1988; Citrin et al. 1994). The normative boundaries liberalism places on membership in the American community are that group members endorse liberal principles, try not to infringe upon the political and economic rights and freedoms of others, and try to achieve the

---

[2] Smith's "multiple traditions" model includes liberalism, ethnoculturalism, and civic republicanism only. For more on why and on the rise of incorporationism, see Schildkraut 2005, ch. 3.

American Dream through hard work. Liberalism is the normative tradition Huntington invoked when he wrote of the creedal component of American identity. It is also the normative tradition that democratic theorists highlight most often when describing the ways in which consensus over norms matters for democratic stability (e.g., Dahl 1991; Gutmann 2003).

Ethnoculturalism, though less celebrated than liberalism, has also been a defining element of American identity. It is an ascriptivist tradition that sets rigid boundaries on group membership. In its extreme, ethnoculturalism maintains that Americans are white, English-speaking Protestants of northern European ancestry (Smith 1997). Over time this tradition has been increasingly discredited, but it is far from breathing its last breath. Since 9/11, elites and masses have endorsed restricting the full range of citizenship rights to people of certain ethnic and religious backgrounds (Schildkraut 2002; Lichtblau 2003; Davis and Silver 2004; Malkin 2004). Others decry racial and ethnic exclusions while promoting linguistic and religious ones. Huntington, for instance, wrote that non-Christians are outsiders in America, a status they should accept given the country's history of religious tolerance. For many people who genuinely reject such exclusions, ethnoculturalism still operates beyond their awareness. We have all heard stories, for example, of Asian Americans being asked about where they are from even after insisting they are American. American-born historian Ronald Takaki wrote of one such encounter, when he is told his English is "excellent" and asked how long he has been in America (1999). He noted that people of all backgrounds, even fellow academics, ask him when he came to the United States, showing that they do not see him as American. As with liberalism, many studies have documented ethnoculturalism's past and present (Mills 1997; Smith 1997; Citrin, Wong, and Duff 2001; Gerstle 2001; Devos and Banaji 2005; Schildkraut 2005a).

That, however, is generally as far as quantitative examinations of how people conceive of American identity have gone. Other conceptions of American identity in the multiple traditions perspective have garnered less analytic attention from public opinion scholars. Civic republicanism emphasizes the responsibilities, rather than the rights of citizenship. It advances the notion that the well-being of the community is more than just the sum of individualistic pursuits of private gain. Rather, a vibrant self-governing community needs individual members to act on its behalf (Banning 1986; Held 1996; Walzer 1996). In this view, we should all be involved in social and political life and pursue ends that serve the public good (Sandel 1996). As Tocqueville noted, pursuing the public good engenders pride and patriotism, which further motivate people to "labor for the good of the state" (1835/1990). Seeing oneself and the political community as inseparable is a key part of the civic republican ideal (Dagger 1997; Petit 1997). Civic republicanism thus sets boundaries on American identity by making demands on group members to be an informed and involved presence in public life, prioritize the collective entity, and see the community as a central component of their own identity. Huntington and other immigration critics are particularly concerned about this aspect of civic republicanism.

Studies of the role of civic republican principles in American political culture have proliferated with the ever-expanding attention to social capital (e.g., Putnam 2000). This scholarship often focuses on the extent to which Americans fail to be good civic republicans through their own lack of political involvement or civic engagement. Recent scholarship also examines whether people of diverse backgrounds see themselves primarily as American (Pearson and Citrin 2006). Much less attention has been given to whether people value civic republican ideals and see them as constitutive of American identity. Yet valuing the ideal and living up to it are different because one's normative attachments can shape one's interpretation of political issues even if one's own behavior violates those norms through, for example, political apathy.

Incorporationism is a more recent addition to the set of norms that constitute the content of American identity. The seeds of this tradition were planted nearly a century ago with cultural pluralism (Kallen 1924), and only in the past few decades have elites and citizens come to endorse this notion that America's unique identity is grounded in its immigrant legacy and its ability to convert the challenges immigration brings into thriving strengths (Higham 1993; Glazer 1997; Tichenor 2002). Ethnoculturalism continues to exist, but it does so alongside an incorporationist challenge that has grown stronger during the years due to many factors, including the rights-based movements of the 1960s and 1970s and the political incorporation of immigrants and their descendants. As David Hollinger notes, the end of the twentieth century saw the "sheer triumph" of "the doctrine that the United States ought to sustain rather than diminish a great variety of distinctive cultures carried by ethnoracial groups" (1995, 101). Yet the extent to which triumphal consensus exists regarding incorporationism has yet to be examined adequately with a national sample; such an examination will be provided here.

The simplicity of incorporationism – the idea that the United States is a nation of immigrants – belies complex beliefs about the balance between unity and diversity. Although there are people who advocate one extreme of complete assimilation and others who reject the premise of assimilation altogether, most Americans do not fall at these extremes. Incorporationism celebrates our ability both to assimilate and maintain difference. As Citrin (2001) has posited, many Americans do not view these alternatives as mutually exclusive (also see Schlesinger 1998). The boundaries that incorporationist norms place on group membership involve individual responsibilities to assimilate to American culture to some hard-to-define degree while also maintaining pride in one's ethnic heritage and continuing to observe its traditions. It also places demands on people to value or even celebrate that living in the United States means that one will continually encounter, get along with, and learn from people from a multitude of backgrounds. Day-to-day politics often pits assimilation and diversity against one another, yet many Americans believe that in the ideal, a balance between the two can be reached, and it is this ability that forms the core of this view of what uniquely distinguishes the United States from other countries (Walzer 1996; Tyack 1999; Zolberg and Woon 1999; Schildkraut

2005a). In this sense, incorporationism reflects the bidimensional model of acculturation psychology, in which one dimension represents the acquisition of the new culture in the host country, and a second dimension represents the maintenance of the original culture. According to this model, people can move along each dimension separately. As David Sam (2006, 17) wrote, this bidimensional model illustrates that "it is possible to identify with or acquire the new culture independently, without necessarily losing the original culture." Some theorists suggest that something like incorporationism is a dimension on which diverse democracies should seek consensus, for doing so can guard against the seemingly inevitable tendency for diversity to generate conflict and instability (Kymlicka 1995; Dahl 1998).

The constitutive norms under investigation here, derived from theoretical and historical analyses, suggest guidelines regarding appropriate state action in response to political conflicts and provide expectations about the political, civic, and cultural beliefs and practices of one's compatriots. They are implicated in contemporary debates about immigration and in scholarship on democratic theory and group conflict, and research has shown the power of liberalism and ethnoculturalism to shape policy views. It is for these reasons that this set of multiple traditions drives the present analysis, as opposed to other, generally apolitical, elements of American identity, such as a love of baseball or apple pie. Yet despite the move away from the long-standing view that American identity is primarily liberal in nature, empirical investigations of a multidimensional Americanism are still rare (exceptions include Citrin et al. 2001; Schildkraut 2005a). Civic republicanism and incorporationism are often overlooked, or respondents must choose between assimilation and the maintenance of diversity rather than being allowed to accept both. Qualitative studies, though limited in their geographic scope and generalizability, have thus far provided the primary means for analyzing a broader range of identity content (Waters 1990; Conover, Crewe, and Searing 1991; Schildkraut 2005a).

Additionally, previous studies are often restricted to examining whites, leaving the study of how nonwhites define American identity underdeveloped. A few exceptions have suggested that in regard to some measures, evidence of national disintegration is lacking (e.g., Citrin, Reingold, and Green 1990; Citrin et al. 1994; de la Garza, Falcon, and Garcia 1996; Citrin, Wong, and Duff 2001), though more thorough investigations are warranted given either the age or geographic concentration of prior data sources, narrow range of items gauging the content of American identity, or low numbers of nonwhite respondents.

MEASURING THE CONTENT OF AMERICAN IDENTITY

I use the 21-CAS to address the limitations of existing scholarship. Recall that the 21-CAS has 2,800 respondents: 1,633 white, non-Hispanic; 300 black;

441 Latino; and 299 Asian.[3] The general approach in this chapter is to use closed-ended survey questions to ask people the extent to which they think certain norms should be considered important aspects of American identity. The norms used in the survey were designed to capture the four broad classes of norms previously discussed. Yet three possible drawbacks of this approach need to be addressed. First, closed-ended questions require that people respond to a predetermined list of norms and thus may miss popular norms that are not included. Second, research has shown that people have a tendency to endorse democratic norms in the abstract but not in concrete situations (Prothro and Grigg 1960; McClosky 1964; Mueller 1988; Jelen 1999; Hurwitz and Mondak 2002), which could call into question whether the survey captures ideals that are meaningful to the respondents. Third, some might say that what matters with respect to the charges of immigration critics is how people behave, not how they think. American cohesion is threatened if subgroups actually fail to tolerate free speech or fail to participate in politics, not if they fail to *say* that Americans should tolerate free speech or participate.

The first drawback can be addressed by noting that the wording of the questions in the 21-CAS was designed by relying heavily on open-ended discussions of focus groups (Schildkraut 2005a) in addition to relying on the theoretical and historical references previously noted. Using open-ended questions on identity in a large-N survey would make systematic and generalizable analyses unduly challenging. By using small-N discussions – that were content analyzed – as a first step, the closed-ended questions aim to be broad in scope while still enabling representative statistical analysis. This reliance on focus groups also underlies my decision to focus on the four broad traditions outlined earlier while ignoring other political traditions that might have played a role at times in shaping what Americans think being American means, such as civil disobedience or antistatism.[4]

The second and third drawbacks were tangentially addressed earlier when I noted that even if people fail to live up to the ideals in question, the ideals exist in their minds and are prominent in the public sphere. A major goal of this investigation is to examine if there are differences based on race, ethnicity, or immigrant background in the extent to which people acknowledge the role that these ideals play in popularly defining what it means to be American. A second goal is to examine how the ideals might "matter," and Chapter 4 shows that connecting particular ideals to American identity is politically consequential with respect to policy views related to immigration. That said, in

---

[3] The remaining respondents either identified as mixed race, Native American, or answered the race question in a way that could not be incorporated into this breakdown (e.g., "human").

[4] Antistatism in particular might have played more of a role in my inquiry had I concentrated on formal constitutive norms rather than on informal norms. The antistatist concern with government power played a key role in the design of American political institutions (Kroenig and Stowsky 2006), and focus group participants regularly voiced support for a government that respects citizens' privacy (Schildkraut 2005a).

terms of assessing popular (mis)perceptions that immigrants and their descendants fail to adopt American norms, it would undoubtedly be additionally helpful to examine behaviors as well as attitudes, though such an examination is beyond the scope of this book (for examples along these lines, see DeSipio 2006; Pearson and Citrin 2006; Ramakrishnan 2006; Wong 2006; Chavez 2008).

Two features of the 21-CAS improve upon existing measures of how people define the content of American identity, which can primarily be found in the 1996 and 2004 General Social Survey (GSS) and the 1992 National Election Study (NES) and have been the focus of analyses of the content of American identity to date (Citrin, Wong, and Duff 2001; Schildkraut 2005a; McDaniel and Nooruddin 2008; Theiss-Morse 2009). First, measures in the GSS, ask: "Some people say the following things are important for being truly American. Others say they are not important. How important do you think each of the following is?"[5] Then they ask about a handful of ideas that tap into America's liberal and ethnocultural traditions. This wording makes it impossible to know if respondents are saying what they normatively believe to be important characteristics for Americans to have or if they are simply acknowledging that particular characteristics have been influential in making someone American. For example, I might say that being a Christian is very important in making someone a true American because I recognize that non-Christians have often felt excluded from the American mainstream. I may deplore this reality, but I may still agree that Christianity has played a central role in defining American identity. The 21-CAS addresses this conflation of acknowledgment and normative approval by asking respondents: "I'm going to read a list of things that some people say are important in making someone a true American. The first one is _____. Would you say that it *should* be very important, somewhat important, somewhat unimportant, or very unimportant in making someone a true American?"[6] This wording allows for a greater likelihood that respondents' answers reflect their own American ideal. This change yields lower levels of approval across comparable items (see nn. 8, 9, 11, and 12). Second, the list that follows this introduction includes items that need to be added to develop a more accurate assessment of the content of American identity. Table 3.1 lists each item, the tradition it was intended to measure, and the percentage of respondents that says the item is either very or somewhat important.[7]

The first two ethnocultural items (being born in America, being a Christian) are from the GSS while the last two (having European ancestors, being white)

---

[5] The NES question is similar, asking how important certain items are in making someone "a true American," instead of "truly American."

[6] *Should* is italicized here for emphasis. It was not emphasized during the interview.

[7] Percentages are weighted with the population weights provided by the SESRC. To minimize respondent fatigue, the American identity series was randomly divided into two halves. The first half was asked early in the survey; the second half was asked later. The items within each half were rotated randomly.

TABLE 3.1. *American Identity Items*

Intended Tradition	Question	% Very Important	% Somewhat Important	N
Ethnoculturalism	Being born in America	24.2	27.1	2768
	Being a Christian	19.3	15.6	2745
	Having European ancestors	7.0	10.4	2707
	Being white	3.8	6.1	2747
Liberalism	Respecting America's political institutions and laws	80.9	15.9	2764
	Pursuing economic success through hard work	69.0	21.7	2760
	Letting other people say what they want, no matter how much you disagree with them	65.9	21.9	2698
Civic republicanism	Doing volunteer work in one's community	44.3	41.9	2773
	Thinking of oneself as American	68.9	24.3	2763
	Feeling American	62.1	28.0	2678
	Being informed about local and national politics	65.3	29.7	2770
	Being involved in local and national politics	37.1	43.8	2761
Incorporationism	Carrying on the cultural traditions of one's ancestors, such as the language and food	35.7	37	2751
	Respecting other people's cultural differences	80.1	16.8	2773
	Blending into the larger society	36.9	36.5	2683
	Seeing people of all backgrounds as American	73.1	19.6	2717
Contested/multiple	Being able to speak English	71.0	23.1	2787
	Having American citizenship	76.0	17.7	2773

Note: Weighted results. "Don't know" and "no answer" excluded.
Source: Twenty-First-Century Americanism Survey, 2004.

more directly capture ethnoculturalism's exclusivity. As Table 3.1 shows, endorsement of ethnoculturalism is still at a notable level. Combining "very" and "somewhat important," more than half of the respondents say being born in America should define being American, 35 percent say the same about

Christianity, 17 percent say the same about having European ancestors, and 10 percent say the same about whiteness.[8]

The first liberal item (respecting America's political institutions and laws) is from the GSS and is included here primarily for continuity. The problem with this item is that it fails to describe explicitly the essence of liberalism: political and economic freedom and opportunity. Qualitative studies confirm that Americans strongly associate such freedom and opportunity with the United States and strongly value such association (Conover, Crewe, and Searing 1991; Schildkraut 2005a). I therefore introduced questions aimed at each of these ideals (pursuing economic success through hard work, letting other people say what they want no matter how much you disagree with them). As noted earlier, the exact wording was informed by focus group discussions and theories of classical liberalism. Table 3.1 shows that strong majorities see all of these items as important constitutive norms, though there is more variation on the newer measures.[9]

Four of the five civic republican items are new, with content and wording derived from theorists noted previously and from qualitative studies (Conover, Crewe, and Searing 1991; Schildkraut 2005a). The one older item is from the GSS and asks whether true Americans should "feel American," yet it is not clear what exactly people are being asked to assess here. I suspected it was aimed at gauging whether people endorse the civic republican call for seeing oneself as part of the political community. To provide more specificity, the 21-CAS asks if it should be important for Americans to think of themselves as American, which more clearly taps the "we"-ness of which Dahl and others write and that has been characterized as an important element of the civic republican ideal. The bivariate correlation between "feeling American" and "thinking of oneself as American" is 0.51.[10] For both items, more than 90 percent of respondents think such self-perception should be very or somewhat important, confirming that Americans see this civic republican norm as constitutive of American identity.[11]

The remaining civic republican items ask about doing volunteer work in one's community, being informed about local and national politics, and being

[8] The 2004 GSS, which uses the word *is* rather than *should*, shows that 56% of respondents say that being born in America is a very important element of American identity, and 49% say the same about being a Christian (using the 2004 weight provided by the GSS). These results are higher than the 21-CAS by 32 and 29 percentage points, respectively. These differences are considerably larger than differences on other comparable items (see following notes), which is not surprising given that these are the items most likely to suffer from the conflation of acknowledgment and approval. Comparison with the 1996 GSS yields similar differences.

[9] The 2004 GSS shows that 75% of respondents say that respecting American institutions and laws is a very important element of American identity, 6 percentage points less than respondents in the 21-CAS. This is the only comparable item that garners more support on the 21-CAS than on the GSS.

[10] Bivariate correlations for all American identity items appear in Appendix B.

[11] The 2004 GSS shows that 69% of respondents say that feeling American is a very important element of American identity, 7 percentage points more than respondents in the 21-CAS.

involved in local and national politics. As Walzer notes, "[Americans] expect citizens to participate actively in public life" (1996, 92). He goes on to elaborate that the mere act of participating encourages people to think about the public good and reinforces their common commitments to the nation and its people. My initial inclination was to ask about the importance of being "informed and involved" in a single question, but focus group discussions led me to realize that citizens might see these aspects of political engagement as distinct elements of the civic republican ideal (Schildkraut 2005a). Table 3.1 shows that support for volunteering and being involved is weaker than support for being informed, yet when combined with "somewhat" important, majorities see volunteering (86.2%) and being politically involved (80.9%) as important aspects of American identity.

Rather than ask people if they see particular aspects of the incorporationist tradition as American norms, previous inquiries have asked respondents if they think immigrants should blend into the larger society *or* maintain their cultural traditions (Frendreis and Tatalovich 1997; Citrin et al. 2001). One problem with this format is that it fails to overtly tie the norms in question to the content of American identity. Another problem is that it does not allow respondents to endorse conflicting ideas about the role of immigration in shaping American identity. Though difficult to achieve in practice, many Americans believe a balance between assimilation and cultural maintenance can be reached and that such a balance uniquely characterizes the United States (Tyack 1999; Zolberg and Woon 1999; Citrin 2001; Schildkraut 2005a). The items in the 21-CAS address these problems. As with the other items, the content and wording was derived from existing scholarship and from qualitative research. The first item (carrying on the cultural traditions of one's ancestors) asks people whether keeping one's "hyphenated" self alive is a hallmark of Americanism, as is suggested by scholars like Walzer, Hollinger, and others, and as was articulated by focus group participants, including many native-born whites. The next item (respecting other people's cultural traditions) is designed to see whether people are wary of too much pressure toward assimilation, regardless of whether they maintain or shed signs of a distinct ethnic heritage. Incorporationism also recognizes that some amount of assimilation is necessary, albeit an amount that is difficult to specify; the third item (blending into the larger society) is designed to capture this recognition. The last item (seeing people of all backgrounds as American) is designed to capture the relatively new American norm of disentangling ethnicity from national identity. Table 3.1 suggests that support is highest for items that ask about respecting other people's choices and rejecting ascriptivism. Support is more equivocal for endorsing cultural maintenance or assimilation. That said, when "very" and "somewhat" important are combined, 72.7 percent say maintaining the cultural traditions of one's ancestors should be important to being American, and 73.4 percent say the same about blending into the larger society. The correlation between these items is 0.16; although they do not go hand-in-hand, they do not oppose one another either.

Finally, people were asked, for continuity with the GSS, if speaking English and having American citizenship should be important in making someone a true American. Both are widely seen as constitutive norms, yet arguments could be made for considering each one an element of more than one tradition. For instance, citizenship is a minimal boundary, one that nearly anyone can cross (liberalism), yet acquiring citizenship is both a step toward incorporation while also being a participatory act (incorporationism and civic republicanism). Likewise, a person might think a common language is essential for successful self-governance and, for practical reasons, that this common language should be English (civic republicanism) while another person might think that English is particularly important (ethnoculturalism). I rely on factor analysis (discussed in the following section) to guide which – if any – tradition is tapped by these items.[12]

HOW MANY "AMERICANISMS"?

Does the average American think that these normative elements of American identity "go together" the way academics do? Can internal contradictions be ignored such that a single measure of "Americanism" can be employed? Or is the range of constitutive norms too varied to use scales at all? Answering these questions will prove useful for deciding whether to use individual items or combined scales when testing the claim that a multicultural America has wrought a multicreedal America and when assessing the "multiple traditions" theory.

I used a combination of factor analysis and examinations of Cronbach's α to examine the extent to which the items tap into distinct conceptions of national identity.[13] The results (see Appendix B) justify three – rather than four – latent constructs, using rotated factor loadings of 0.4 as the cutoff and with several items failing to cohere well with any dimension. I then created summated rating scales for each of the three dimensions supported by the factor analysis. I added responses to each item and divided by the total number of questions on the scale the respondent answered. Then I constrained each scale to run from 0 to 1, in which 0 means the respondent said all items on the scale were "very unimportant," and 1 means the respondent said all were "very important."

One dimension, ethnoculturalism, contains all four ethnocultural items from Table 3.1 ($\alpha = 0.72$, mean = 0.30, s.d. = 0.26, average inter-item correlation = 0.40). Another dimension represents the "informed and involved" tenets of civic republicanism and consists of thinking that being informed about, and involved in, national and local politics, including volunteering, should be defining elements of American identity ($\alpha = 0.62$, mean = 0.78, s.d. = 0.19,

---

[12] The 2004 GSS shows that 83% of respondents say that speaking English and having American citizenship are very important elements of American identity, 12 and 7 percentage points more than respondents in the 21-CAS.

[13] This portion of the analysis used unweighted responses.

average inter-item correlation $= 0.20$).[14] The final dimension represents the self-perception components of civic republicanism and consists of thinking that having American citizenship, thinking of oneself as American, and feeling American should define American identity ($\alpha = 0.62$, mean $= 0.86$, s.d. $= 0.18$, average inter-item correlation $= 0.18$). I find two dimensions to civic republicanism, not one. The first represents how people act; the second represents how people think of themselves vis-à-vis the national community, with "having American citizenship" as a marker of identity.[15] This bidimensionality of civic republicanism is, to my knowledge, new to the literature.

Looking at the items that comprise the second civic republican factor, it seems related to the notion recently developed by Elizabeth Theiss-Morse that national identities should be thought of as social identities, consisting not just of a shared history or set of principles but, importantly, of a sense of belonging among group members (2009). Whereas Theiss-Morse's research concentrates on the dynamics of one's own sense of belonging, what is of interest here is one's belief that *all* Americans need to have this sense of belonging: Who is likely to feel this way? What implications does an adherence to this group-based understanding of American identity have on policy debates? Although Theiss-Morse might challenge using the term *civic republicanism* to describe this constitutive norm, the norm is certainly akin to the civic republican call for seeing political community as an important component of one's own identity.

For all three scales, the average inter-item correlation exceeds 0.15, as is recommended (Clark and Watson 1995). Bivariate correlations among all items (see Appendix B) show that items correlate within scales more than across them, suggesting construct validity (Paxton and Mughan 2006). In each of the three scales, item-rest correlations range from 0.30 to 0.56.

Even though most respondents support both liberal and incorporationist elements of American identity, those survey items do not cohere into scales that provide more information than the individual items on their own. Scholars recognize the ideological linkages between these concepts, but Americans seem to view them as distinct aspects of the national character. Does this finding puncture the multiple traditions thesis? Hardly. If anything, it suggests that the American people might perceive *more* traditions than the four outlined here. For instance, although "liberalism" unites political and economic freedom, ordinary citizens might be more likely to view these ideals distinctly while supporting both quite strongly. Likewise, Americans simultaneously recognize assimilation and the maintenance of cultural traditions as constitutive norms,

[14] Factor analysis (Table B.2 in Appendix B) suggests that "carrying on the cultural traditions of one's ancestors" might load onto this factor as well, with a loading of 0.45. This item was left off, however, because doing so yielded a higher Cronbach's α. A look at all diagnostics, combined with "theoretical sense" (DeVellis 2003) led to this decision. With all other factors, retaining the items that exceed the 0.4 factor loading yielded the highest α.

[15] The correlation between the "action" and "identity" scales is 0.28. To put this correlation in context, the correlation between the "identity" scale and the ethnoculturalism scale is also 0.28, while the correlation between the "action" scale and ethnoculturalism is 0.24.

but do not necessarily appreciate their theoretical union the way scholars do. Thus, in the remaining analyses, I examine the causes of liberal Americanism by treating economic freedom and political freedom separately, with "respecting American institutions and laws" left aside due to its aforementioned distance from the core elements of the liberal tradition. Likewise, though assimilation and carrying on the traditions of one's ancestors are central components of incorporationism, those questions do not represent a single construct, so I examine the causes of support for these constitutive norms through these two measures separately. I focus on these measures of incorporationism for the remaining analyses and leave the other two incorporationist items aside because the kept items have greater variation (Paxton and Mughan 2006) and make stronger normative demands.[16] In short, the constitutive American norms used in remaining analyses are captured through scales for ethnoculturalism, action-oriented civic republicanism, and identity-oriented civic republicanism, and through single items for economic freedom, political freedom, carrying on cultural traditions, and assimilation, for a set of seven constitutive norms.[17]

Importantly, separate factor analyses and Cronbach's α assessments for whites, blacks, Latinos, and Asians (results not shown) produces remarkably similar results across groups, with just a few differences to note. First, "being born in America" loads weakly on ethnoculturalism for black and Asian respondents, while "having American citizenship" loads weakly on identity-oriented civic republicanism for Asian respondents. Second, identity-oriented civic republican items overall have low factor loadings for Latino respondents. This is not to say, however, that Latinos do not endorse these constitutive norms. To the contrary, 64 percent of Latinos say that thinking and feeling American should be very important components of American identity, and 76 percent say the same about having American citizenship. Cronbach's α on identity-oriented civic republicanism for Latinos is 0.61, with an average inter-item correlation of 0.21 and item-rest correlations all more than 0.32. Together, these diagnostics suggest identity-oriented civic republicanism is a unique normative dimension of American identity for Latino respondents, but that its

---

[16] A more exploratory oblique factor rotation (results not shown) confirms that neither liberal item ("pursuing economic success" and "letting other people say what they want") loads onto any other latent factor nor does the incorporationist item on "blending into the larger society." "Carrying on the cultural traditions of one's ancestors" and "respecting other people's cultural differences" load weakly with action-oriented civic republicanism, similar to the varimax results.

[17] When all 18 American identity items are scaled together, the resulting α is 0.76. A high α, however, is not necessarily indicative of unidimensionality. Factor analysis is needed to shed light on how many dimensions can be justified (Cortina 1993; Clark and Watson 1995; Floyd and Widaman 1995; DeVellis 2003). As DeVellis writes, "A factor is considered interpretable to the extent that the items associated with it appear similar to one another and make theoretical and logical sense as indicators of a coherent construct" (115). In this case, the 3 factor model described here is more appropriate. A combination of factor loadings, a scree plot of eigenvalues, and theoretical and logical sense were used to arrive at this conclusion. Also note that the factor analysis confirms that "speaking English" fails to cluster with any broad conception of national identity.

components are not as strongly linked together as they are for other respondents. A similar pattern exists with action-oriented civic republicanism among black respondents. Lower factor loadings are combined with high support for each individual item (55% say volunteering should be very important, 76% say being informed should be very important, and 52% say being involved should be very important), along with a Cronbach's α of 0.57, an average inter-item correlation of 0.17, and item-rest correlations that range from 0.32 to 0.48. In sum, I find more similarities than differences across ethnic groups with regard to their overall attitude structure, but with weaker associations for identity-oriented civic republicanism among Latino respondents and action-oriented civic republicanism among black respondents and with less emphasis on nativity for black and Asian respondents.

Based on the full sample analysis, using a single measure of "Americanism" is not the way forward. But neither is using four neatly demarcated scales. In some cases, Americans link idea elements together the way academic reasoning suggests they "should" be linked although they do not in other cases. The lack of such linkages does not mean that the norms and values associated with each tradition are irrelevant. Each liberal norm, for example, is overwhelmingly endorsed as "American" by the public. Rather it means that we will gain more insight into opinion dynamics if we treat them on their own terms.

A MULTICREEDAL AMERICA?

The previous section shows that there is a great deal of consensus regarding the norms, values, and behaviors that constitute American identity. It also demonstrates the validity of the "multiple traditions" theory of American identity while highlighting some limitations regarding the extent to which the four theoretical constructs detailed match mass attitude structures. The next step is to investigate more thoroughly whether people of different backgrounds define American identity differently, paying special attention to Huntington's concern that, "a multicultural America will, in time, become a multicreedal America, with groups with different cultures espousing distinctive political values and principles rooted in their particular cultures" (2004, 340). The values and principles he revered involve a blend of liberal and ethnocultural norms and identity-oriented civic republicanism. He was concerned about the rise of incorporationism, and those who agree with him would no doubt find some of the patterns in Table 3.1 troubling. He also writes that "Mexican-Americans feel increasingly comfortable with their own culture and often contemptuous of American culture" (255). I examine here whether the incorporationist view of American identity is held primarily by the groups that concern him – the foreign-born and their descendants and Mexicans – and whether those groups are less likely to endorse economic and political freedom and the importance of seeing oneself as American. Although this investigation is framed around Huntington's writings, it is important to remember that observers on the left and the right have expressed similar concerns, and that rigorous social science scholarship has also highlighted the potential importance of shared norms for harmony and stability.

In addition to nativity, ancestry, ethnicity, and generation, I examine two more factors in this section: whether respondents identify with the American people and whether they belong to civic associations, both of which can be seen as whether respondents are "good" civic republicans, with the former tapping identity-oriented principles and the latter tapping action-oriented ones. Given the prominence of civic republicanism in how American identity is defined, it makes sense to consider whether endorsement is affected by one's own civic orientation. Moreover, recent work by Theiss-Morse (2003, 2005, 2009) shows that people who strongly identify with the American people are more likely to set exclusive and inclusive boundaries on American identity than people who weakly identify with the American people. Examining the causes of one's strength of identification is an important part of assessing the consequences of the nation's changing demography, but it is not the central focus here. Rather, such measures are included here because of their demonstrated role in shaping how boundaries are drawn.

Tables 3.2 and 3.3 show bivariate relationships between background characteristics and how people define the content of American identity (see Appendix A for original question wording and coding). For this analysis, I divided the ethnoculturalism scale and the two variants of civic republicanism into thirds and examined whether respondents ranked in the top third of each scale (Table 3.2). For the liberal and incorporationist items, I examined whether respondents said each item was very or somewhat important (Table 3.3). All results are statistically significant except for the few that are noted. In most cases, however, statistical significance does not correspond to substantive significance. The story across both tables is generally one of similarity more than it is one of difference.

With respect to race and ethnicity, blacks and Latinos are more likely than whites and Asians to endorse ethnoculturalism.[18] Latinos are more likely than whites to endorse action-oriented civic republicanism but less likely to endorse identity-oriented civic republicanism, suggesting a view in which "actions speak louder than words." Whites are less likely than everyone else to value the incorporationist norm of carrying on the cultural traditions of one's ancestors, which could be a sign that racial divergences might be on the horizon. Today, however, more than 60 percent of whites endorse this incorporationist view of American identity; that endorsement is noticeably less than all other racial groups, but it is still a majority. In no case does a majority of one racial group

---

[18] It has been suggested that this pattern results from the degree of religiosity in black and Latino communities (Citrin, Reingold, and Green 1990; Citrin et al. 1994; Schildkraut 2005a; Theiss-Morse 2005). A simple OLS regression (not shown) of each ethnocultural component on whether a respondent is black or Latino supports this suggestion. It shows that the coefficients on the racial dummy variables in the model for "being a Christian" far outweigh the size of the coefficients for any of the other three ethnocultural regression models and are almost three times the magnitude of the coefficients in the model for "being white."

TABLE 3.2. *Background Characteristics and American Identity (summated rating scales)*

	Ethnoculturalism	Civic Republicanism ("action")	("identity")	N (raw)
Race/Ethnicity				
White	6.5	62.0	82.4	1633
Black	17.0	76.7	80.7	300
Asian	5.1	62.3	68.2	299
Latino	12.7	67.7	75.7	441
Nativity				
Born in United States	8.0	63.1	81.7	2118
Not born in United States	10.6	73.5	75.4	554
Generation				
1st generation	10.6	73.5	75.4	554
2nd generation	8.5	57.6	71.3	164
3rd generation	5.1	59.1	79.2	178
4th+ generation	7.8	64.0	82.5	1726
Mexican				
Mexican, U.S. born	8.8	62.1	73.8^	123
Mexican, foreign born	16.1	76.3	73.7^	118
Rest of sample	8.1	64.4	81.2^	2431
Strength of identification				
High identifier	10.2	68.9	87.8	2035
Medium identifier	2.6	52.2	62.1	517
Low identifier	1.0	44.6	38.0	121
"Good" civic republican				
Belongs to civic associations	3.9	64.7^	80.6^	1183
Belongs to no associations	11.9	64.4^	80.7^	1466

Notes: Cell entries are percentage of respondents in top third of summated rating scale. All entries are statistically significant at p ≤ 0.05 except where noted (^). Weighted results. "Don't know" and "no answer" excluded.
Source: Twenty-First-Century Americanism Survey, 2004.

come to a different substantive conclusion about the constitutive norms of American identity than a majority of another racial group.

Looking at nativity and generation also reveals more similarities than differences. Like Latinos, immigrants are more likely than the native born to endorse action-oriented civic republicanism – hardly a cause for concern – and are less likely to endorse identity-oriented civic republicanism – more troubling from Huntington's perspective, though even here, 75 percent of the foreign born rank in the top third on this scale. Immigrants are less likely to endorse political freedom and more likely endorse the assimilationist and the diversity components of incorporationism. Thus, newer members of the polity are more likely to think that the blending and the maintenance of difference are sustainable and

TABLE 3.3. *Background Characteristics and American Identity*
(single survey items)

	Economic Freedom	Political Freedom	Maintaining Difference	Blending into Larger Society	N (raw)
Race/Ethnicity					
White	90.1^	90.1	67.1	72.1	1633
Black	92.5^	84.7	87.1	77.2	300
Asian	92.8^	82.8	78.7	77.8	299
Latino	92.1^	77.7	86.0	79.9	441
Nativity					
Born in United States	90.1	89.1	70.4	72.0	2118
Not born in United States	94.7	79.2	84.0	85.4	554
Generation					
1st generation	94.7	79.2	84.0	85.4	554
2nd generation	89.2	84.5	74.2	72.1	164
3rd generation	88.2	88.8	75.1	70.3	178
4th+ generation	90.2	89.5	69.8	72.0	1726
Mexican					
Mexican, U.S. born	91.5^	83.7	82.5	72.0	123
Mexican, foreign born	95.5^	60.9	91.4	88.6	118
Rest of sample	90.6^	88.7	71.5	73.5	2431
Strength of identification					
High identifier	93.3	89.5^	73.8	78.9	2035
Medium identifier	83.4	87.0^	67.2	61.7	517
Low identifier	78.0	87.7^	70.00	41.7	121
"Good" civic republican					
Belongs to civic associations	89.9^	88.8	68.1	71.6	1183
Belongs to no associations	91.7^	86.7	76.2	76.0	1466

Notes: Cell entries are percentage of respondents saying each item is very or somewhat important. All entries are statistically significant at p ≤ 0.05 except where noted (^). Weighted results. "Don't know" and "no answer" excluded.
Source: Twenty-First-Century Americanism Survey, 2004.

central to the idea of being American. It is important for future analyses to track whether this split between newer and older Americans becomes even more noteworthy over time or whether subsequent generations converge. That most of the differences in Tables 3.2 and 3.3 are between the first generation and everyone else suggests the latter scenario is most likely, but only time will tell. At present, strong majorities of the native born and the foreign born (and of each generational cohort) agree with each other.

Just less than 9 percent of the respondents say they (or an ancestor) are from Mexico; roughly half of them were born outside of the United States.

Tables 3.2 and 3.3 examine native-born and foreign-born Mexicans separately. As with race, nativity, and generation, the story is largely one of similarity. Foreign-born Mexicans are the most supportive of an action-oriented civic republicanism, the least supportive of political freedom, and the most supportive of both kinds of incorporationism. But again, well over a majority in each category agrees with the others.

To gauge if respondents identify strongly with the American people (i.e., if they are "high identifiers"), they were asked if they agree that "I feel strong ties to the American people" and "being an American is important to the way I think of myself as a person." These measures form an abridged version of the "strength of identification" scale used by Theiss-Morse (2009). They were combined into a 0 to 1 scale (Cronbach's $\alpha = 0.56$), in which 0 = strongly disagree on both items and 1 = strongly agree on both items. This scale was then divided into thirds (high, medium, low). Seventy-six percent of respondents are high identifiers, 19 percent medium, and 5 percent low.[19] Tables 3.2 and 3.3 show that, as Theiss-Morse has argued, the strength of one's identification is clearly associated with supporting a wide range of boundaries on American identity. The only exception is political freedom, with high, medium, and low identifiers equally likely to say that it constitutes an American norm. The differences between high and low identifiers are especially noteworthy with civic republicanism and assimilation. People who view their own identity as strongly tied to the collective are more likely than others to endorse such ties as important components of the identity. They are also more supportive of behaviors that reinforce such identification, such as community involvement and assimilation. These differences are the only cases across both tables in which a majority of one category differs with a majority of another.

Finally, respondents were asked if they belong to any civic associations and if so, how many. Forty-six percent of respondents say they belong to at least one civic association. Of those, 76 percent say they belong to more than one. Yet Tables 3.2 and 3.3 show that such civic activity fails to translate into substantively important differences with regard to how people define the content of American identity, even with civic republicanism, confirming that whether people value a particular ideal and whether they emulate it are not identical.

I find little support for concerns that different ethnic and immigrant groups define what being American means differently. Incorporationism does provide a more popular set of constitutive norms for the "new guard," but a substantial majority of the old guard endorses incorporationism as well. Whether this divergence portends a multicreedal America remains to be seen. Although there does not appear to be much support for Huntington's claim that non-Christians "have little alternative but to recognize and accept America as a Christian society" (101), one of the groups most likely to agree, ironically, is foreign-born Mexicans.

---

[19] Note that these questions were asked of American citizens only.

WHY PEOPLE DEFINE AMERICAN IDENTITY AS THEY DO

Examining if the differences in Tables 3.2 and 3.3 persist when the influence of other factors is controlled is the focus of this section. To see how individual-level characteristics shape how people define the content of American identity in a more rigorous fashion, I used ordinary least squares (OLS) regression analysis when the summated rating scales served as dependent variables (using the full 0 to 1 scales) and ordered probit analysis when the single-item norms served as dependent variables. Based on the previous section, I included among the independent variables race (with "white" as the omitted category), nativity, whether the respondent is of Mexican origin, and strength of identification with the American people (using the 0 to 1 scale). I omitted generation because nativity and generation produced such similar patterns, and most differences were between the first generation and everyone else. Likewise, I omitted whether respondents belong to civic associations because of the lack of noteworthy differences in Tables 3.2 and 3.3. Other independent variables include age, education, gender, political ideology, partisan identification, and whether English is the only language spoken in the home, with all nondummy variables recoded to range from 0 to 1.[20] Results are in Tables 3.4 (OLS) and 3.5 (ordered probit).[21]

As Table 3.4 shows, age, education, and strength of identification with the American people outweigh factors related to race or immigration in shaping support for ethnoculturalism, with older and less educated respondents and high identifiers more likely to show endorsement. Though as in Table 3.2, small yet statistically significant racial differences exist. Likewise, with action-oriented civic republicanism, age and strength of identification outweigh factors related to race and immigration for the most part, with older respondents and high identifiers more likely to endorse this tradition. Yet the difference between U.S.-born and foreign-born respondents from Table 3.2 remains, with foreign-born respondents and Mexican respondents more likely to endorse active citizenship as a constitutive American norm.[22]

The significant predictors of identity-oriented civic republicanism are small in magnitude, but the pattern is important given the centrality of identity-oriented norms to current debates about the impact of ethnic change

[20] The variable for partisan identification is a composite of questions 113–15 in Appendix A, in which 1 = strong Democrat; 2 = Democrat; 3 = leans Democrat; 4 = Independent; 5 = leans Republican; 6 = Republican; and 7 = strong Republican. This composite measure was then recoded to range from 0 to 1.

[21] I did not include household income because of the high refusal rate on that question. Including income does not affect the results in Tables 3.4 and 3.5, and income turns out to be statistically insignificant in nearly every case.

[22] The correlation between the Latino and Mexican dummy variables is 0.7. Fifty-four percent of Latinos in the sample have some Mexican ancestry. Running the models with only the Latino dummy variable (results not shown) renders the Latino measure significant with action-oriented civic republicanism (positive) and political freedom (negative), which replaces the significant coefficients for Mexicans. All other results are the same.

TABLE 3.4. *Antecedents of America's Ethnocultural and Civic Republican Traditions, OLS*

Independent Variable	Ethnoculturalism	Civic Republicanism ("action")	Civic Republicanism ("identity")
Age	0.22**	0.13**	0.06**
	(0.02)	(0.02)	(0.02)
Education	−0.28**	−0.05**	−0.05**
	(0.02)	(0.01)	(0.01)
Male	−0.002	−0.03**	−0.03**
	(0.01)	(0.01)	(0.01)
Born in United States	0.01	−0.06**	−0.02
	(0.02)	(0.02)	(0.01)
Black	0.16**	0.10**	0.03**
	(0.02)	(0.01)	(0.01)
Asian	0.06**	−0.02	−0.003
	(0.03)	(0.02)	(0.02)
Latino	0.07**	0.01	−0.01
	(0.03)	(0.02)	(0.02)
Conservative	0.09**	0.02*	0.06**
	(0.01)	(0.01)	(0.01)
Republican	−0.008	−0.01	0.02**
	(0.02)	(0.01)	(0.01)
Only English spoken at home	−0.04	−0.03	0.01
	(0.02)	(0.02)	(0.02)
Mexican	−0.02	0.05*	0.02
	(0.03)	(0.03)	(0.02)
"High identifier"	0.18**	0.17**	0.36**
	(0.03)	(0.02)	(0.02)
Constant	0.16	0.68	0.53
	(0.03)	(0.03)	(0.02)
R-squared	0.28	0.12	0.30
F	65.54	22.67	72.31
N	2044	2044	2044

Note: * $p < 0.1$; ** $p < 0.05$; standard errors in parentheses. Dependent variables recoded to range from 0 to 1, in which 1 = highest level of adherence. All nondummy variables recoded to range from 0 to 1.

Source: Twenty-First-Century Americanism Survey, 2004.

on American identity: Latinos, Asians, people of Mexican origin, and the foreign born are *not* significantly more or less likely than their white, U.S.-born counterparts to think that true Americans should think of themselves as American. The only powerful predictor in this model is strength of identification, with high identifiers more likely to endorse identity-oriented norms than low identifiers. One notable conclusion emerging from these results is the need to

examine the factors that alter a person's strength of identification.[23] Doing
so fully is beyond the scope of the analysis in this chapter, but a bivariate
examination finds few differences when it comes to race or nativity (also see
Pearson and Citrin 2006). Seventy-nine percent of whites are in the top third
of the "strength of identification" scale, compared to 78 percent of Latinos,
70 percent of Asians, and 65 percent of blacks – sizeable majorities in each case.
The foreign born were *more* likely than the native born to be in the top third
(80.9% vs. 74.7%), as were Mexicans compared to non-Mexicans (81.4% vs.
75.5%).

Table 3.5 shows that strength of identification and ideological conservatism
emerge as the strongest predictors of support for the norm of economic freedom
and opportunity. The foreign born, blacks, and Asians, are more likely than
the U.S. born and whites to say that pursuing economic success through hard
work should be an important boundary of Americanism. Latinos – Mexicans
included – do not differ from whites on this issue. This set of findings provides
a particularly compelling rebuke to the claim that immigrants and their descendants fail to accept the "Protestant work ethic" as an essential ingredient of
being American (see, e.g., Huntington, chs. 4, 8, and 9).

Political freedom stands out from all other components of American identity
in terms of the factors that dictate support. It is one of the only constitutive
norms to be more widely supported among the young, men, whites, and liberals
and to be unaffected by the strength of one's identification with the United
States. Overall support for defining American identity in terms of political
freedom is high, but at the margins, that support is driven by a unique set of
factors. Moreover, these results indicate it is not the case that some respondents
are simply more willing to agree with all of the items presented to them in the
survey. Respondents are able to make meaningful distinctions among the sets
of norms analyzed here.

Why don't political and economic freedoms "go together?" Why do they
have such different antecedents? Though these findings were not expected, it
is important to remember what Converse argued decades ago: how reality
is experienced can affect how people make sense of the world more so than
logic (1964). Logically, the classically liberal view of minimal government
intervention applies both to the pocketbook and the podium. Yet in our age,
conservatives generally defend the pursuit of economic gain while political
liberals are more likely defenders of speech rights, rights that have become more
salient during the "war on terror." That ideas are experienced together can
dictate the associations we make more so than logic, Converse argued, and the
results here support that view. Our long-standing political orientations shape
how we define American identity, and contemporary contestation between

---

[23] The strength of identification questions were asked of citizens only, which means only citizens
are included in the analysis in Tables 3.4 and 3.5. In separate models (not shown), the identification scale was omitted and was replaced with a dummy variable to distinguish citizens
from noncitizens. The coefficients on age, education, and ideology increase in magnitude. The
"citizen" dummy variable matters little. Other results remain the same.

TABLE 3.5. *Antecedents of America's Liberal and Incorporationist Traditions, Ordered Probit*

Independent Variable	Economic Freedom	Political Freedom	Cultural Maintenance	Assimilation
Age	0.39**	−0.30**	−0.48**	1.08**
	(0.14)	(0.13)	(0.12)	(0.12)
Education	−0.39**	0.13	−0.43**	−0.30**
	(0.10)	(0.10)	(0.09)	(0.09)
Male	−0.08	0.18**	−0.20**	−0.03
	(0.06)	(0.06)	(0.05)	(0.05)
Born in United States	−0.42**	0.01	−0.16	−0.46**
	(0.14)	(0.12)	(0.11)	(0.11)
Black	0.34**	−0.18*	0.71**	0.46**
	(0.10)	(0.09)	(0.09)	(0.09)
Asian	0.27*	−0.36**	0.21*	0.10
	(0.15)	(0.14)	(0.13)	(0.13)
Latino	0.05	−0.02	0.29**	0.30**
	(0.15)	(0.15)	(0.31)	(0.14)
Conservative	0.52**	−0.37**	−0.16**	0.12*
	(0.09)	(0.09)	(0.08)	(0.08)
Republican	−0.01	−0.13	−0.16**	0.21**
	(0.09)	(0.08)	(0.08)	(0.08)
Only English spoken	0.08	−0.38**	−0.29**	−0.14
at home	(0.15)	(0.14)	(0.13)	(0.12)
Mexican	0.11	−0.30*	0.19	−0.07
	(0.20)	(0.19)	(0.17)	(0.18)
"High identifier"	1.01**	0.07	0.68**	1.08**
	(0.14)	(0.15)	(0.13)	(0.13)
Cutpoint 1	−1.06	−1.64	−1.76	−0.66
	(0.21)	(0.21)	(0.19)	(0.18)
Cutpoint 2	−0.61	−1.10	−0.99	0.18
	(0.21)	(0.20)	(0.18)	(0.19)
Cutpoint 3	0.29	−0.33	0.09	1.27
	(0.21)	(0.20)	(0.18)	(0.19)
Chi-square	207.06	83.65	238.90	282.38
N	2029	1997	2016	1967

Note: * $p < 0.1$; ** $p < 0.05$; standard errors in parentheses. Dependent variables recoded to range from 0 to 1, in which 1 = highest level of adherence. All nondummy variables recoded to range from 0 to 1.

Source: Twenty-First-Century Americanism Survey, 2004.

conservatives and liberals appears to yield divisions over the relative centrality of economic and political freedoms to the very idea of American identity.[24]

Turning finally to incorporationism, the results show mixed support for the claim that Americans do not see cultural maintenance and assimilation as

---

[24] What of the finding that blacks, Mexicans, and Latinos seem less likely than whites to say political freedom is important? My suspicion is that such respondents might conjure up potentially

mutually exclusive constitutive American norms. Again, support for both is high, but at the margins, older respondents, conservatives, and Republicans have a harder time imagining such coexistence, choosing to prioritize assimilation (as indicated by the positive significant coefficient on assimilation and the negative significant coefficient on maintaining traditions). Likewise, younger respondents, liberals, and Democrats choose to prioritize the notion that true Americans should carry on the cultural traditions of their ancestors. Note that none of these latter categories of people draw explicit ire from Huntington or from contemporary critics of immigration reform.

The people most likely to think that we can "have it all" – people whom we might say are most supportive of the full range of incorporationist norms – are blacks, Latinos, and "high-identifiers." Those are the cases in which there are positive significant coefficients on both incorporationist items. There are also people that endorse one element of incorporationism while not being more or less likely than their counterparts to endorse the other (as indicated by a positive significant coefficient on one incorporationist item and an insignificant coefficient on the other). For instance, the foreign born are more likely than the U.S. born to endorse the normative demands of assimilation, but the U.S. born and the foreign born do not differ in their support for the maintenance of cultural traditions. Asians and people who speak a language other than English at home are more likely than whites and people who only speak English to support the maintenance of difference. Huntington and other critics of immigration might look to this result as support for their concerns, but they would have to acknowledge that Asians and whites, English speakers and non-English speakers, are equally likely to say that assimilation should be an important element of being a true American. Few characteristics seem to promote true incorporationist sentiment. But few characteristics promote only difference while diminishing assimilation (or vice versa) – and the ones that do map onto to traditional, long-standing political cleavages in the United States, such as ideology and partisanship, rather than new cleavages that result from immigration or ethnic change.

CONCLUSION

The central aim of this chapter was to provide a broad test of claims that the increasing cultural diversity in the United States in terms of race, ethnicity, ancestry, and nativity is undermining consensus on the meaning of American national identity. In short, I find little evidence to support this fear. It is important to remember, however, that contestation over group identities

---

threatening images of racist or discriminatory language when this survey question is posed. As Gibson and Gouws show, tolerance of speech rights becomes less revered in the presence of threat (2003). Understanding why an antecedent such as age would lead one to be more likely to endorse economic liberalism and less likely to endorse political liberalism demands further investigation beyond the scope of the present inquiry.

is a constant element of political life. The future may bring more contestation over how to reconcile multiple visions of American identity, and we should be equipped to gauge whether such contestation occurs. This study provides tools for such vigilance.

My analysis suggests that the primary lines of contestation at this point are the ones that are constant sources of political conflict in the United States: partisanship and ideology. Education and strength of identification with the American people also provide consistent dividing lines. Although Huntington said little about partisan threats to national identity, he did express concern that the educated elite reject his version of American identity. But he spent most of his energy on immigration and ethnicity. Though some racial and ethnic differences do emerge in this analysis, they are at the margins, and they fail to show one group directly opposing another.

The consensus documented here contradicts charges in the potentially inflammatory rhetoric that one finds so easily in media coverage of immigration debates. It should also be a welcome finding for scholars of democratic theory and social psychology who posit that shared meanings promote harmony and stability across ethnic lines. From the standpoint of social psychology, it is perhaps especially important to inject findings like these into public discourse in an attempt to dispel misperceptions. To the extent that commonalities among Americans from a variety of backgrounds are made salient, the pathologies of group dynamics can be subverted and group conflict can be diffused (Gaertner and Dovidio 2000; Transue 2007).

In testing claims about constitutive American norms, I also offer empirical evidence that supports the multiple traditions theory of American identity – with a caveat – and provide an in-depth look at the extent to which people consider civic republican and incorporationist norms to be part of what being American means. The caveat is that public opinion does not appear to be neatly organized into four distinct traditions even as the norms that comprise those traditions are widely endorsed. From a theoretical perspective, it makes sense that free speech rights and the social mobility provided by a free market economy would be grouped together as constitutive norms in the liberal tradition of minimal government. Although the norms of hard work and free speech are supremely endorsed by the American public, that same public does not necessarily view them as forming a cohesive liberal perspective regarding what it means to be American. Similar results emerged for civic republicanism and incorporationism. These multiple traditions have a long history in American political culture (some longer than others) and have been promoted at various times at all levels of government. The question of exactly how many dimensions there are to American identity is difficult to answer; it partly depends on whether we ask the theorists or the data. It is also important to remember that many of the questions asked here are new. Replications across time and space are needed to address this issue further.

What is clear is that most Americans think liberal and civic republican norms should dictate boundaries of American identity. They also think the

United States should be a society that converts the challenges of immigration into strengths and feel that Americans should form a common identity while preserving the diversity that makes America so different from all other countries. There are still Americans that think that the content of American identity should be white and Christian, though they are dramatically fewer in comparison to the levels of support found for other constitutive norms. Clearly, there are contradictions among these norms. Most obviously, ethnoculturalism and incorporationism are in tension. Less obvious contradictions also exist. The civic republican ideal, for instance, has been characterized as only achievable in homogeneous societies, which puts it in tension with incorporationism; it also makes demands on citizens that put it in tension with the individualism advanced by the liberal tradition (e.g., Smith 1988). Disregard for these contradictions is simply yet another area in which Americans of all stripes find common ground.

In addition to testing claims of immigration critics and assessing whether mass attitudes match the multiple traditions theory, this chapter also provides a snapshot of the norms and values Americans look to when they assess the meaning of their national identity, form expectations about how their fellow Americans will and should act, and try to determine appropriate responses to new political controversies. Such snapshots are essential for tracking how Americans will continue to define being American as today's immigrant population changes, immigrants bear children on American soil, and new waves of immigrants arrive.

In the end, we have a complex picture of how Americans define the content of American identity. But this complexity also brings insight. One important next step is for scholars to examine more fully the causes and consequences of the strength of one's personal identification with the United States and its people, because such identification emerged as a significant predictor of opinions here. Another important step is to look at how different normative assessments of American identity shape how people feel about ethnicity-related policy debates, such as whether government documents should be provided in multiple languages and whether racial profiling is an acceptable counterterrorism tactic. Such investigations teach us about the conditions under which different kinds of constitutive norms shape what people think policy debates are even about, let alone their preferred solutions. When we understand which aspects of American identity animate policy debates and drive opinions, we learn more about the kind of America that people want to preserve. The role of constitutive American norms in shaping preferences on such ethnicity-related policy debates is addressed in the next chapter.

4

Policy Implications of Multidimensional Americanism

A recent bill introduced in Congress to make English the official language of the United States received 130 cosponsors, which amounts to nearly 30 percent of the House membership. The bill's sponsor, Steve King (R-IA), filed a lawsuit in early 2007 against the secretary of state in his home state of Iowa for allowing non-English versions of election-related materials, such as voter registration forms, to be available online, charging that the practice violates the state's official-English law (Pfeiffer 2007). Given the presumably negligible cost of providing non-English forms over the Internet, Representative King's motivation clearly goes beyond concerns about the use of taxpayer dollars and instead has to do with the broader issue of the ability of non-English speakers to participate in the political process. King's own press release about the lawsuit simply contends that the forms violate the law, and it fails to note any cost-related concerns.[1]

Domestic conflicts have emerged in other ethnicity-related policy areas in recent years as well. Since 9/11, for instance, the American Civil Liberties Union (ACLU) and Amnesty International have issued reports decrying the use of ethnic profiling by law enforcement agencies in the United States in their efforts to combat terrorism. The ACLU report recounts the story of Muhammad Siddiqui, a Houston architect who was contacted by FBI agents who said they wanted to ask him questions. Siddiqui repeatedly told the agents, "I'd be happy to talk to you, but I'd like to have my attorney present," a request that was met with increasing levels of frustration by the agents, with one telling him that getting a lawyer would only make him look guilty and another pulling his coat aside to reveal his gun (American Civil Liberties Union 2004). Official Justice Department policy prohibits the use of racial or ethnic profiling in federal law

---

[1] Press release available at http://www.house.gov/apps/list/press/ia05_king/PRCulverMauroLawsuit 011007.html (accessed February 15, 2007).

enforcement, but activities related to the border and to national security are exempt.[2]

The primary goal of this chapter is to advance the study of how the norms associated with American national identity shape preferences on the policy debates invoked in these situations. The aim is to examine the relationship between conceptions of American national identity and what I call "boundary-related" policies. Policies such as language policy and domestic counterterrorism policy are "boundary related" because they call into question the territorial and conceptual boundaries of the nation. In terms of territorial boundaries, both types of policies are essentially products of immigration, and counterterrorism options in particular address the very security of the nation's physical space. In terms of conceptual boundaries, both policies call on us to consider the factors that determine whether a person is "truly" American and, as such, deserving of the full range of rights, opportunities, and access to government that come with membership in the American political community. Normative assessments about the boundaries of membership should therefore be key ingredients shaping how people evaluate such policies. To date, however, this effect has only been documented in a handful of studies, often using either a limited range of norms or regional data sets.

Investigating the relationship between identity content and policy preferences is worthwhile for several reasons. First, uncovering which constitutive norms shape preferences on which policies helps us to understand the power as well as the limits that such norms have. I am not only interested in examining opinions about national identity for their own sake but also because of their potential political consequences. Constitutive norms can be informal (such as a belief that Americans should feel American) but often become codified (such as requiring free speech protections). Moreover, they influence how other laws develop by shaping the policy alternatives that get considered and by helping lawmakers and citizens determine which state responses they deem appropriate. As Abdelal and colleagues write, "norms bias choice" (2006, 697). People will not support legislation that might be cast as "un-American." One can skim the *Congressional Record* for floor debate on virtually any type of issue and quickly see that rhetoric about what it means to be American is regularly invoked to justify the policies being advanced. Yet the particular aspect of American identity invoked will vary depending on the policy in question. In the present analysis, I examine if some aspects of American identity are chronically salient or if they only emerge as factors shaping policy views in particular contexts. If the latter, which is expected, we can gain valuable insight into what leads people to promote policies hostile to minorities. Moreover, we can learn how to minimize that hostility by, perhaps, heightening the salience of alternative constitutive norms. Research on framing has long shown that available and accessible beliefs stored in memory can be tapped to shape the considerations

---

[2] The policy guidelines are available at http://www.usdoj.gov/crt/split/documents/guidance_on_race.htm (accessed February 16, 2007).

that people bring to bear in the opinion formation process (Chong and Druckman 2007). My findings provide guidance regarding which alternative norms might be most fruitful in this regard. In short, it is not necessarily the case that we want to discourage the tendency to draw conceptual boundaries around the notion of American national identity. Nor is it the case that we should be concerned that such conceptual boundaries can influence policy views. Rather, we can unite our insights about the power and limitations of these boundaries in order to help us think about ways to promote and generate support for policies that foster inclusion, broaden access to government, and protect rights and opportunities all while building on popular norms.

Second, and related to the previous point, this investigation will provide more depth to our existing understanding of the dynamics of opinion formation regarding the policies. Such policy debates are becoming more common at every level of government (Hopkins 2007). In November 2006, for example, the town board of Pahrump, Nevada, one of the fastest-growing towns in the country, voted to make English its official language and to require that any resident flying a foreign flag must also fly an American flag. Reports suggest that considerable conflict followed in the form of vandalism, civil disobedience, the shouting of racial slurs on the streets, and hate mail (Friess 2006). Conflict and notoriety led the town board to repeal the law a mere three months after its passage (Friess 2007). The National Conference of State Legislatures reports that state-level legislative activity related to immigration has been rising dramatically in recent years, with more than 1,300 bills introduced in the states in 2008, up from 300 just four years earlier (Hagen 2009).

The changing demographics in the United States bring these policy debates to the fore. Members of the majority have increasing interactions with the minority as their communities diversify. Such experiences are not confined to the traditional receiving locations like California and New York either. The list of top ten states in terms of the percentage increase in the percentage of foreign-born residents from 2000 to 2007 includes South Carolina, North Carolina, Delaware, Wyoming, and Tennessee.[3] Even people who do not directly experience this diversity become familiar with its effects through media accounts of incidents such as those described throughout this book. This new reality can cause people to rally around valued aspects of their identity that they think might be threatened by diversity. The result is that people can become more likely to endorse attitudes and behaviors that are hostile to the outgroup (Branscombe et al. 1999).

Moreover, the policies under investigation can have profound effects on the nation's newest citizens and residents and on their opinions about their place in American society. When elected officials, for example, urge airport screeners to use more ethnic profiling, as Representative Pete King (R-NY), former chair of the House Committee on Homeland Security, did in August

---

[3] Demographics obtained from the Migration Information Source, http://www.migration information.org/DataHub/acscensus.cfm (accessed June 17, 2009).

2006 (Palmer 2006), Arab, Muslim, and Middle Eastern Americans surely become wary of American political institutions. A Justice Department study of Arab Americans concluded that many of them fear being a victim of ethnic profiling by law enforcement authorities more than they fear being the victim of a hate crime (Elliott 2006).

Finally, public opinion is often translated into policy, either through representative channels or ballot initiatives. Citizens have turned to initiatives more and more in recent years, particularly for ethnicity-related policies (Tatalovich 1995; Hero 1998; Sabato, Larson, and Ernst 2001; Schildkraut 2001; Ellis 2002). As recently as November 2006, 74 percent of Arizona voters opted to make English the official state language; in 2008, more than 80 percent of voters in Missouri did the same. Understanding the roots of support and opposition to such policies becomes all the more important when citizens undertake policy making directly. When we see which elements of American identity are brought to bear on these policy debates, we learn more about what people think such debates are about, and we learn about the type of America people seek to preserve through their preferred policy solution.

The measures developed in the previous chapter provide the tools necessary for this analysis. We have already seen that there is widespread consensus regarding some aspects of American national identity, such as economic liberalism, and ongoing debate about others, such as ethnoculturalism. The contestation generally falls along ideological lines more so than racial or ethnic ones. As such, of interest in this chapter is the relative influence of partisanship and ideology compared to measures of American national identity when all are included in models of policy preferences.

Also of interest is the role of incorporationism. As noted in Chapter 3, this aspect of American national identity has suffered from inadequate measurement in previous studies, leaving our insights into its role in shaping policy debates underdeveloped. Also noted in Chapter 3, not many Americans are *equally* likely to support assimilation and cultural diversity as true American norms, though many support both to some degree. Yet if they are both consistently strong predictors of views on boundary policies – with one leading to support for restrictions and the other to opposition – then this analysis will have reinforced my argument that scholars should continue to track whether stronger divisions emerge among the American public regarding the role of incorporationist norms in defining the meaning of American identity and whether these differences become a more substantial source of policy disagreement over time.

In the end, this chapter shows that using constitutive norms to place boundaries on American national identity does not automatically lead to preferences for policies that restrict the rights, opportunities, and access to government of Americans who do not fit the dominant cultural type. This finding is contrary to what some other research would lead one to conclude (Citrin, Reingold, and Green 1990; Theiss-Morse 2004). Rather, constitutive norms that have been traditionally overlooked can promote more inclusive preferences. For instance, thinking that active citizenship is an essential component of American identity generates opposition to some restrictive language policies. Likewise, thinking that political liberalism is an essential component of American identity generates opposition to some kinds of racial profiling. Thinking that true Americans should maintain the cultural traditions of their ancestors consistently generates opposition to restrictive language policies *and* racial profiling. This chapter also shows that conceptions of American national identity rival the influence of partisanship and ideology in shaping attitudes and that the nature of the policy can affect which aspects of American identity are brought to bear in opinion formation.

IDENTITY CONTENT AS A SYMBOLIC PREDISPOSITION

The theoretical approach that informs this analysis is symbolic politics theory. This theory contends that people develop attachments, or predispositions, toward socially constructed concepts that shape how they view the world (Elder and Cobb 1983). The meaning of the symbols and attachments to them are generated by political culture and reinforced through social interaction (Sears 1993). National identities are one of many symbolic predispositions. Partisan orientations and other group memberships are examples of other predispositions. These predispositions help people navigate their complex surroundings and provide language they can use to express their political views. In empirical studies, symbolic predispositions regularly turn out to be more potent influences on policy views than more tangible measures of self-interest, such as a person's financial situation or whether a person has a family member that might be affected by the policy in question (e.g., Sears and Funk 1990).

The extent to which a particular symbolic predisposition will affect policy attitudes is determined in part by how engrained a particular predisposition is for an individual and in part by external stimuli in the form of cues from the political climate, such as political rhetoric and the nature of issues (Sears 1993). As such, attitudes on policies that are inherently connected to the territorial and conceptual boundaries of the nation – or ones that are framed as such – might be especially likely to be affected by people's beliefs about such boundaries, especially when we recognize the important role that such boundaries play in helping people derive their own sense of self, as is highlighted by social identity theory (Citrin, Wong, and Duff 2001). Where the conceptual boundary of the nation encompasses a wide range of ideas, as it does in the United States, it is unlikely that all components will influence attitudes at any given time. Just as external cues can affect whether ideas about national identity will matter, so too can they affect which aspects of that identity matter (Citrin, Wong, and Duff 2001; Schildkraut 2005a). It is when we determine *which* aspects of the symbolic identity matter that we gain insight into what people think particular policies are about, and we learn about what it is about their national identity that they want to promote and protect through government action.

Considerable public opinion research has shown that the values associated with American political culture, such as individualism and the work ethic, shape a wide range of policy preferences (Feldman 1988; Feldman and Zaller 1992; Federico 2006; Jacoby 2006). But only a limited amount of work has examined the connections people make between those values and their definitions of being American. Yet how that linkage shapes preferences on contentious policies has been of interest to a growing number of scholars who recognize the distinct power that group identities can have over public opinion.

Previous scholarship has confirmed that ideas about identity content are cognitive tools people use to arrive at preferences on boundary-related policies (Citrin, Reingold, and Green 1990; Frendreis and Tatalovich 1997; Citrin et al. 2001; Citrin, Wong, and Duff 2001; Schildkraut 2005a). When measures of the content of American identity have been available, they have consistently and unambiguously turned out to be strong predictors of attitudes, with support for the measures in question leading to support for restrictions on immigration and on the use of languages other than English. Endorsing ethnoculturalism has also been shown to generate opposition to domestic spending programs aimed at aiding minority groups (Theiss-Morse 2006; though see Citrin, Wong, and Duff 2001 for null results on spending). Throughout these studies, the measures of the content of American identity consistently turn out to be as strong as, if not stronger than, factors such as partisanship, egalitarianism, and sociotropic economic concerns. As discussed in Chapter 3, however, the measures of American norms that scholars have been able to use thus far have been restricted to ethnoculturalism and vague measures of assimilationism, such as the importance of respecting America's institutions and laws. Civic republicanism, incorporationism, and political and economic liberalism have not been included. By using the broader set of norms developed in Chapter 3, we get a more comprehensive understanding of the power and limits of American national identity. Additionally, most existing studies use data sets that predate September 2001, which means they have been unable to study how definitions of American identity shape post-9/11 policy concerns, such as the use of ethnicity or religion in counterterrorism efforts.

Although quantitative analyses have relied on a constrained range of constitutive norms, qualitative approaches have been able to examine the influence of a wider range of norms on boundary-related policies. When citizens are given a chance to discuss American national identity in their own words, it becomes immediately clear that the civic republican responsibilities of active citizenship and the cultural challenges derived from our immigrant legacy coexist with liberalism and ethnoculturalism. It also becomes clear that this broader range of constitutive norms is brought to bear on discussions of public policy (Waters 1990; Conover, Crewe, and Searing 1991; Conover, Searing, and Crewe 2004; Schildkraut 2005a).

This line of research has also highlighted that the specific aspect of American identity that matters may depend on the nature of the policy. For example, focus group analysis suggests that civic republicanism is the main conception of American identity that shapes views on multilingual voting ballots whereas liberalism plays more of a role in helping people sort out their views on official-English policies (Schildkraut 2005a). Likewise, views on bilingual education are comparatively unaffected by conceptions of American identity relative to bilingual ballots and official English. With bilingual education, people tend to be primarily concerned with promoting whichever policy they deem most effective at helping students learn English, but they disagree quite strongly regarding which policy is most likely to achieve that end, a tension that renders concerns about national identity secondary (Schildkraut 2005a).[4]

Finally, focus group analysis has also shown that once political liberalism, civic republicanism, and incorporationism are taken into account, we see that some broadly supported American norms promote opposition to restrictive boundary policies instead of support. A civic republican concern for the quantity of political participation, for example, led to opposition to English-only ballots, while a liberal concern with the First Amendment led to opposition to making English the official language of the United States (Schildkraut 2005a). Because these American norms are broadly endorsed, heightening their salience when such policy debates arise could be an effective way to reduce the chance that exclusivist norms and attitudes prevail.

These qualitative insights are valuable as far as they go. But it is difficult to generalize their results, and it is impossible to isolate the independent influence of each attitudinal component the way that large-N quantitative inquiry is able to do. Additionally, as with the quantitative research, available qualitative investigations rely on pre-9/11 data, precluding the study of how conceptions of American identity shape newly salient boundary policies. In the remainder of this chapter, I seek to build upon the strengths of existing quantitative and qualitative scholarship while addressing their limitations. The Twenty-First-Century Americanism Survey (21-CAS) was specifically designed for this purpose. As documented in Chapter 3, it asks respondents to assess a wide range of norms associated with American national identity. Additionally, it asks respondents for their preferences on a variety of boundary policies related to language use and post-9/11 ethnic profiling.

In the analyses that follow, the key independent variables are the seven broad classes of constitutive norms developed and analyzed in the previous chapter. I expect that conceptions of national identity will play a significant role in shaping views on these policy areas, but that simply agreeing that a particular set of norms should be important in making someone a true American will not consistently lead to support for restricting language use or for ethnic profiling. The direction of influence will depend on the policy in question and on the norm being invoked. More details on specific hypotheses are discussed in the following sections.

---

[4] Note that some quantitative studies also indicate that ideas about American identity do not affect attitudes on bilingual education as much as they affect attitudes on other language policies (Citrin, Reingold, and Green 1990; Frendreis and Tatalovich 1997).

LANGUAGE POLICY

Recent reports suggest that Latinos often feel unwelcome in their communities. This feeling is partly due to local policy controversies, rhetoric of local leaders, perceptions of employment and housing discrimination, as well as conflicts over language usage and resources (Louie 2005; Deaton 2008). A national study by the Pew Hispanic Center in 2008 found that Latinos feel that their situation in the United States has been deteriorating. Many say that they have been stopped and questioned by the police about their immigration status, and a majority worries that they or someone they know may be deported (Lopez and Minushkin 2008). An earlier Pew study found that more Latinos feel that the mistreatment they receive in the United States is due to their language and accents than due to their appearance (Brodie et al. 2002). The issue of language is clearly a central aspect of contemporary debates about the implications of diversity for the country.

Debates about language use take on many forms. It is important to distinguish these different forms from one another when trying to understand public opinion because there may be specific aspects of the policies that lead to different patterns. As noted earlier, for instance, previous work suggests that conceptions of national identity might influence attitudes regarding official-English more than attitudes about bilingual education. Likewise, particular aspects of American identity might matter more for one type of policy and less for another. For example, focus group research has shown that civic republican concerns dominate discussions about bilingual ballots but not other language policy areas. Thus, the present analysis examines four distinct questions about language policy: whether English should be the official language, whether voting ballots should be only in English, whether local ordinances declaring that signs on stores and businesses must be partly in English are acceptable, and what type of instruction respondents think is best for students who do not know English.

One of the most prominent forms of language conflict in the United States involves the question of whether to make English the official language. Since 1981, several bills have been introduced in Congress each year to do just that. Though most of these bills have failed to make it out of committee, each chamber has voted to make English the official language in the recent past. The House did so in 1996, and the Senate did so when it approved an official-English amendment to its comprehensive immigration reform in 2006. Prominent national opinion leaders voice their support for restricting the use of other languages for government business. During the 2008 presidential primary campaign, for instance, former Massachusetts governor Mitt Romney warned New Hampshire residents that "we cannot be a bilingual nation like Canada," though he also offered a Spanish version of his campaign Web site (Montgomery 2007). During 2007, while considering his own possible presidential bid, former Speaker of the House Newt Gingrich regularly argued for the need to make English the official language and print election ballots only in English (Gingrich and Fonte 2007). In reality, however, most actual policy activity in this arena to date has taken place at the state and local level. According to U.S. English, a pro-official English citizen group, thirty states have declared English to be the official state language.[5] To gauge attitudes about official-English, respondents in the 21-CAS were asked, "Do you favor or oppose a law making English the official language of the United States, meaning most government business would be conducted in English only?" Seventy-seven percent said they favor this proposal.[6] This level of support is similar to that found in other national surveys such as the 2000 General Social Survey (GSS) (77.5%) and a 2006 survey by Fox News (78%).[7]

Whether to print multilingual election ballots is also a prominent language issue. Most congressional bills to make English the official language would repeal the sections of the Voting Rights Act that require bilingual voting assistance in limited situations. As with official-English, providing ballots only in English garners support from prominent commentators. As George Will recently wrote, for example, "by ending bilingual ballots, American law would perform its expressive function of buttressing, by codifying and vivifying, certain national assumptions and aspirations. Among those is this: The idea of citizenship becomes absurd when sundered from the ability to understand the nation's civic conversation" (2006). To measure attitudes on this issue, respondents were asked, "Do you believe that election ballots should be printed only in English or should they also be printed in other languages in places where lots of people don't speak English?" Only 37 percent said they think ballots should be printed only in English. Again, this figure is similar to that from the 2000 GSS (34%). The vastly different aggregate levels of support for official-English, on the one hand, and English-only ballots, on the other, indicates that people draw distinctions between language policies and that their opinions are not driven by an overarching "English-only" mentality.

In addition to debating official-English and ballots, several local governments have passed ordinances that require all, or part, of signs on stores and business to be in English. When enforced, these policies generate significant conflict at the local level, often involving lawsuits and charges of discrimination (Geller 1997; Lezin 1999a, 1999b). To my knowledge, attitudes about such policies have not been studied in any rigorous way. I was unable to find any existing survey question on this topic. In the 21-CAS, respondents were asked, "You may have noticed that in some neighborhoods, the sign on the front of a store or a business will be in a language other than English. Over the past several years, some cities and towns have adopted policies that require a certain percentage of the words on such signs be in English. Do you think you

---

[5] "States with Official English Laws," http://usenglish.org/view/13 (accessed June 10, 2009).

[6] Unless noted otherwise, all percentages refer to weighted data and are calculated after "don't know" and "no answer" responses have been dropped.

[7] 2000 GSS data found at http://sda.berkeley.edu/D3/GSS04/Docyr/gso4.htm (accessed February 7, 2007); Fox News data found at Lexis-Nexis.

would favor or oppose such a policy?" Sixty-six percent of respondents said they would favor a policy that required signs to include English.

Bilingual education is the final language issue studied here. In 1974, the Supreme Court ruled in *Lau v. Nichols* that limited-English proficient (LEP) students need to be able to participate meaningfully in the classroom and that schools that did not attend to their needs were in violation of the 1964 Civil Rights Act (*Lau v. Nichols*, 414 U.S. 563). Today, the federal government provides funding for bilingual programs through No Child Left Behind (NCLB). NCLB also requires states to test LEP children for reading in English after they have attended school in the United States for three consecutive years. States that do not meet their performance objectives for LEP students could lose some of their federal funding. But NCLB does not mandate a particular form of bilingual education. Such a mandate is expressly prohibited.[8] How the educational needs of language minorities are specifically met is determined at the state and local level.

Previous survey questions about bilingual education have been plagued by vague and inconsistent wording (Schildkraut 2005a). The policy labels offered in survey questions typically do not provide enough information to give respondents an accurate image of what exactly they are being asked to favor or oppose. Moreover, people have very different ideas about what "bilingual education" actually is, making it difficult to know what people are advocating when they say they are for or against it, especially when the survey question fails to offer a definition of bilingual education, a failing that is quite common. Using a modified version of the bilingual education question used in the 1994 and 2004 GSS, respondents in the 21-CAS were asked, "People have different ideas about how to teach non-English speaking children when they enter public schools. I am going to read a few of them. Please tell me which one comes closest to your view. First, all classes should be conducted only in English. Second, children should be able to take some classes in their native language just for a year or two. Or third, children should be able to take classes in their native language all the way through high school." Thus, rather than simply ask whether respondents favor or oppose "bilingual education," the question described three different possibilities for what might happen in the classroom and asked respondents which one they would prefer. These response options capture the three main approaches typically used in bilingual education programs (immersion, transitional bilingual education, and cultural maintenance) without obscuring preferences with vague or technical jargon.[9] Twenty-nine percent of the respondents said instruction should be only in English, 61 percent

---

[8] See Title III of NCLB at http://www.ed.gov/policy/elsec/leg/esea02/pg39.html (accessed June 10, 2008).

[9] Seventy-five respondents volunteered that all classes should be bilingual for all students. Those respondents are dropped from the bilingual education analysis because their answer invokes views about the type of education that English-speaking children should receive in addition to the type of education that LEP children should receive.

said that the native language should be allowed just for a year or two, and 10 percent said that the native language should be used all the way through high school. That a majority of respondents opted for a more forgiving approach than immersion further underscores the distinctions people make between various types of language-related policies.

Hypotheses

Overall, these patterns of opinions suggest that respondents support policies that allegedly aim to keep English the dominant language used in the public sphere while accepting some allowances for people that are not currently fluent in English. What role might the constitutive norms of American identity play in shaping these opinions? The hypotheses in this section are all derived from the expectations of symbolic politics theory, existing findings of the quantitative and qualitative studies discussed earlier, and normative underpinnings of each tradition discussed in Chapter 3.

The hypothesis for ethnoculturalism (comprised of thinking that true Americans should be white, be born in the United States, be Christian, and have European ancestors) is that this set of ascriptive norms will be a significant influence on attitudes for official-English, English-only ballots, and English signs, leading to *support* in each case because ethnoculturalism involves setting rigid cultural boundaries on group membership. For reasons already noted, ethnoculturalism – along with the other conceptions of American identity – is not expected to have much influence over attitudes about bilingual education.

The hypothesis for action-oriented civic republicanism (comprised of thinking that true Americans should be informed about, and involved in, national and local politics and should volunteer in their communities) is that it will lead to *opposition* to English-only ballots due to this tradition's emphasis on the responsibility of citizens to be informed and involved members of the polity. People with high scores on action-oriented civic republicanism are expected to oppose policies that could restrict the ability of some citizens to fulfill their duties. There is less reason to expect this notion of American identity to shape views on the other policies.

Identity-oriented civic republicanism (comprised of thinking that true Americans should feel American, think of themselves as American, and have American citizenship) has received less explicit attention from public opinion research to date. However, previous investigations have found that people who think it is important that true Americans "feel American" are more likely to say that current immigration levels should be decreased (Citrin, Wong, and Duff 2001; Schildkraut 2005a). Focus group research revealed that people who advocated making English the official language often invoked a perceived lack of a common American identity when explaining their views. These findings are in line with civic republican concerns about whether a certain degree of homogeneity is necessary to maintain a vibrant community of dutiful citizens who prioritize the common good. Finally, recall that this aspect of Americanism invokes the perspective that national identity should be thought of as a social identity in which a sense of belonging motivates subsequent attitudes and behaviors. Specifically, it prescribes a norm in which people view their own identities as being entwined with the group. Consequently, it is reasonable to expect that people who support this norm will look to language as a central unifying agent, especially in large "imagined communities" such as the United States (Anderson 1983). The fact that the policies in question might not actually help people learn English is beside the point. What is important is that these policies symbolize a commitment to the unifying power of a common language. The hypothesis for identity-oriented civic republicanism is thus the same as the hypothesis for ethnoculturalism: that it will be a significant influence on attitudes for official-English, English-only ballots, and English signs, leading to support in each case.

The hypothesis for political liberalism, which emphasizes rights such as free speech, is that it will promote opposition to official-English and English signs because both policies deal with a person's options for expression. The hypothesis for economic liberalism, conversely, is that it will promote support for official-English and English signs. At first glance, it is not immediately obvious that thinking that true Americans should pursue economic success through hard work would be related to language policy preferences at all. But many focus group participants who advocated making English the official language relied on notions of the work ethic when explaining their views, arguing that knowing English is a necessary condition for making the American Dream a reality (Schildkraut 2005a). This constitutive norm, it turned out, provided a framework through which people derived expectations about their fellow Americans, and they relied on that framework to help them navigate the issue of language diversity.

The hypothesis for the assimilationist aspect of incorporationism (whether true Americans should blend into the larger society) is the same as the hypotheses for ethnoculturalism and identity-oriented civic republicanism: that it will generate support for language restrictions, because adopting the most commonly used language of the country is a fairly obvious way in which such blending can occur and because respondents might think that restricting language use would presumably help advance that process. The hypothesis for the cultural maintenance aspect of incorporationism (that true Americans should carry on the cultural traditions of their ancestors) is that it will generate opposition to language restrictions because language is an unambiguous cultural marker that many Americans have tried to preserve or, if not, wish that they had. It should also be noted that both of these hypotheses reflect patterns revealed in focus group discussions (Schildkraut 2005a).

A final hypothesis to be tested, suggested earlier, is that all seven sets of constitutive norms will have a weaker, if not insignificant, influence on attitudes about bilingual education than on attitudes about the other policies under investigation. This hypothesis will test the argument that with bilingual education, most people share the same goal of wanting students to learn English but simply disagree over the best method for achieving that end.

Data Analysis

To test these hypotheses, probit models were run for official-English, English-only ballots, and English signs in which 1 equals the more restrictive preference, and an ordered-probit model was run for bilingual education, in which 1 equals immersion and 0 equals allowing both languages to be used all the way through high school. The additional independent variables used as controls can be broken down into several categories: demographics (age and education), acculturation (whether the respondent was born in the United States and whether English is the primarily language spoken at home), political orientation (partisan identification and liberal/conservative ideology), race/ethnicity (black, Latino, and Asian, with "white" as the omitted category), and tangible interests (perceptions of the national economy, the percentage of people living in the respondent's Zip Code that are Hispanic or Asian, and an interaction between that percentage and whether the respondent is white – in order to see if white respondents are influenced by residential diversity differently than nonwhite respondents; i.e., if whites become particularly restrictionist or welcoming when they live in diverse areas relative to nonwhites). All nondummy variables were coded to range from 0 to 1. All question wordings not described in the text can be found in Appendix A.

The results appear in Table 4.1. Overall, they show that conceptions of American national identity matter more consistently and often with greater magnitude than demographic characteristics, acculturation, and tangible interests. In short, the content of American identity is a powerful influence over attitudes on these boundary-related policies. The only close rivals of conceptions of American identity across all four models are partisanship and ideology, with Republicans and conservatives typically in favor of greater language restrictions. But the power of American national identity also has limits. As will be discussed in detail, the magnitude and direction of influence among the seven constitutive norms examined here varies in systematic and notable ways across issue types. This variation identifies what concerns people have about the issues under investigation and what aspects of American identity they want to protect. It also reveals which aspects of American identity have the potential to promote opposition to restrictive policies.[10]

---

[10] Given the power of "strength of identification" in Chapter 3 when it comes to influencing how people define what being American means, all models in Table 4.1 were also run with this measure as an independent variable. In all but the model for English signs, strength of identification was insignificant and did not substantively alter the other coefficients. For the "signs" model, people who feel strong ties to the American people are more likely than others to support ordinances that require the use of English. The general lack of significance of this measure suggests that people's views of what being American means are more powerful than

TABLE 4.1. *Determinants of Support for Restrictive Language Policies*

Independent Variable	Official Language	English-only Ballots	English Signs	Bilingual Education
Ethnoculturalism	0.11	0.43**	0.39**	−0.07
	(0.18)	(0.15)	(0.15)	(0.13)
Civic republicanism ("action")	−0.17	−0.35*	0.02	−0.39**
	(0.22)	(0.19)	(0.19)	(0.17)
Civic republicanism ("identity")	1.73**	0.92**	1.12**	0.83**
	(0.22)	(0.22)	(0.21)	(0.18)
True Americans should let other people say what they want, no matter how much they disagree	−0.13	0.01	−0.30**	0.09
	(0.13)	(0.12)	(0.12)	(0.10)
True Americans should pursue economic success through hard work	0.36**	0.23*	0.15	0.11
	(0.16)	(0.14)	(0.13)	(0.12)
True Americans should blend into the larger society	0.36**	0.28**	0.33**	0.17*
	(0.13)	(0.11)	(0.11)	(0.10)
True Americans should carry on the cultural traditions of their ancestors	−0.28**	−0.52**	0.33**	−0.57**
	(0.13)	(0.11)	(0.11)	(0.10)
Born in United States	−0.18	−0.07	−0.07	−0.32**
	(0.14)	(0.13)	(0.13)	(0.12)
Age	0.21	0.40**	−0.08	0.31**
	(0.19)	(0.16)	(0.16)	(0.14)
Education	−0.10	0.07	−0.40**	0.12
	(0.14)	(0.12)	(0.12)	(0.10)
Republican	0.50**	0.57**	0.11	0.32**
	(0.12)	(0.10)	(0.11)	(0.09)
Conservative	0.36**	0.23**	0.24**	0.10
	(0.11)	(0.10)	(0.10)	(0.09)
Speaks only English in the home	0.50**	0.29**	0.14	0.20
	(0.16)	(0.15)	(0.15)	(0.13)
Black	−0.37**	−0.29**	0.08	−0.05
	(0.14)	(0.13)	(0.13)	(0.11)
Asian	0.01	−0.16	0.14	0.03
	(0.21)	(0.19)	(0.19)	(0.17)
Latino	−0.43**	−0.29*	−0.24	0.02
	(0.18)	(0.18)	(0.17)	(0.15)
National economy getting worse	−0.01	−0.09	0.12	−0.09
	(0.09)	(0.08)	(0.08)	(0.07)
% Hispanic in Zip Code	−0.46*	−0.08	−0.21	−0.22
	(0.28)	(0.30)	(0.28)	(0.25)
% Asian in Zip Code	0.64	0.66	0.68	1.19**
	(0.62)	(0.61)	(0.60)	(0.53)
% Hispanic in Zip Code * white	0.12	0.52	0.21	0.81**
	(0.41)	(0.39)	(0.38)	(0.34)
% Asian in Zip Code * white	−0.07	−0.84	−0.69	−1.01
	(0.07)	(0.75)	(0.75)	(0.66)
Constant	−1.39	−1.78	−1.05	—
Cutpoint 1	—	—	—	−0.79
				(0.25)
Cutpoint 2	—	—	—	1.28
				(0.25)
Chi-square	357.25	324.83	219.04	193.44
N	1871	1941	1883	1916

Note: * p < 0.1; ** p < 0.05; standard errors in parentheses. Cell entries are probit or ordered probit coefficients, in which 1 = most restrictive preference.

Source: Twenty-First-Century Americanism Survey, 2004.

In order to assess each of the specific hypotheses and get a more intuitive interpretation of the results, it is useful to examine predicted probabilities in addition to probit coefficients. Table 4.2 shows the predicted probability that a respondent would opt for the most restrictive option for each dependent variable as the conception of American identity in question (across each row) changes from its minimum to its maximum value (from 0 to 1).[11] The results highlight which conceptions of American identity produce the most change and which ones actually lead to a change in the predicted outcome (i.e., changing from likely to oppose official-English to likely to support). Predicted probabilities are calculated only for significant conceptions of American identity from Table 4.1. The results show many cases in which the specific hypotheses were confirmed, as well as several in which they were not.

Turning first to ethnoculturalism, Tables 4.1 and 4.2 show that defining American identity ascriptively leads to greater support for language restrictions, but only with regard to ballots and signs. With ballots, going from the lowest to the highest value on ethnoculturalism changes the predicted policy preference, with a low ethnoculturalism score producing only a 34 percent chance of supporting English-only ballots and a high ethnoculturalism score producing a 51 percent chance. Both low and high ethnoculturalism scores are predicted to produce support for English signs, though a high score results in a considerably higher probability (63% vs. 76%). Contrary to expectations, however, ethnoculturalism was not a significant predictor of attitudes toward official-English. This lack of an effect is noteworthy given how much power ethnoculturalism has shown in previous studies. I suspect its underwhelming showing here is because there is much more to the role of conceptions of American identity in shaping views on official-English than ethnoculturalism but that previous research has been unable to account for that role adequately due to a lack of appropriate measures. Once such measures are available and other conceptions of American identity are controlled, the effect of ethnoculturalism diminishes, and a more complex image of how the American public assesses debates about language use emerges.

Action-oriented civic republicanism, as expected, generates opposition to English-only ballots and is not a significant predictor of official-English or English signs. Respondents clearly recognize that this aspect of being American is uniquely relevant to the one policy that explicitly invokes political participation, and they do so to a degree that changes the predicted preference. A low score on action-oriented civic republicanism produces a 50 percent chance of supporting English-only ballots whereas a high score generates only a 36 percent chance. The result is clear: the more a person thinks being American is

their own personal perceived connection to the polity when determining policy support on language issues.

[11] Predicted probabilities are calculated using CLARIFY, holding all nondummy variables constant at their means (King, Tomz, and Wittenberg 2000). Dummy variables were set to "white," "speaks only English in the home," and "born in the United States."

TABLE 4.2. *Predicted Probability of Supporting Restrictive Language Policy Option*

Independent Variable	Official Language			English-only Ballots			English Signs			English Immersion		
	o	1	Change	o	1	Change	o	1	Change	o	1	Change
Ethnoculturalism	—	—	—	0.34	0.51	0.17**	0.63	0.76	0.13**	—	—	—
Civic republicanism ("action")	—	—	—	0.50	0.36	−0.14*	—	—	—	0.37	0.23	−0.14**
Civic republicanism ("identity")	0.32	0.90	0.58**	0.14	0.44	0.30**	0.30	0.72	0.42**	0.09	0.30	0.21**
True Americans should let other people say what they want, no matter how much they disagree	—	—	—	—	—	—	0.75	0.65	0.10*	—	—	—
True Americans should pursue economic success through hard work	0.76	0.86	0.10**	0.32	0.40	0.08	—	—	—	—	—	—
True Americans should blend into the larger society	0.78	0.87	0.09**	0.32	0.43	0.11**	0.59	0.71	0.12**	0.22	0.29	0.07
True Americans should carry on the cultural traditions of then-ancestors	0.89	0.83	−0.06*	0.53	0.32	−0.21**	0.59	0.71	0.12**	0.39	0.20	−0.19**

Note: Cell entries equal probability of approving when independent variable equals o or 1, with all nondummy variables set to their means. * = $p < 0.1$; ** = $p < 0.05$.

Source: Twenty-First-Century Americanism Survey, 2004.

defined by active citizenship, the less likely she is to support restricting access to the ballot.

Identity-oriented civic republicanism, as expected, generates support for official-English, English-only ballots, and English signs. With official-English and English signs, it produces the most dramatic shifts in preferences of the entire analysis. A low score on identity-oriented civic republicanism produces only a 32 percent chance of favoring official-English while a high score produces a 90 percent chance, an impressive increase of 58 percentage points. Recall that the mean level of identity-oriented civic republicanism is 0.86, which means that this factor explains why official-English proposals are so popular for so many Americans. Nearly all Americans think it is important to think and feel American, and this belief is the strongest predictor of support for official-English.

It should be pointed out that identity-oriented civic republicanism is not merely a proxy for ethnoculturalism. Recall two findings from Chapter 3. First, the correlation between identity-oriented civic republicanism and ethno-culturalism is 0.28, practically the same as the correlations among the other identity content scales. Second, regression analysis showed that Latinos and Asians are equally likely as whites to endorse identity-oriented civic republi-canism while blacks are slightly more likely. In short, a genuine belief in the centrality of a common American identity is an important predictor of support for language restrictions, and beliefs about this common American identity are not concentrated among whites who prefer that the United States be a white, Christian nation.

Political liberalism is only significant in one model, and the model in which it is significant has to do with communication and speech: English signs. As predicted, a greater endorsement of this American norm depresses support for restrictions on speech. Likewise, economic liberalism generates expected support for official-English, though with a modest effect. In sum, political and economic liberalism are not as strongly related to language policy preferences as other American norms. Yet when such norms shape opinions, they do so in the expected directions and on the expected policies.

Both measures of incorporationism are significant in all four models and are significant in the expected direction in all cases but one. Thinking that true Americans should blend into the larger society increases support for official-English, English-only ballots, and having signs in English. Conversely, thinking that true Americans should maintain the cultural traditions of their ancestors generates opposition to official-English and English-only ballots. With ballots, the effect is substantial enough that it changes one's predicted preference: a person who thinks such maintenance is not important has a 53 percent chance of supporting English-only ballots while a person who thinks it is important has only a 32 percent chance.

The results for bilingual education are mixed. Ethnoculturalism, both forms of liberalism, and blending into the larger society fail to have a significant im-pact on the predicted likelihood of preferring immersion. Additionally, though identity-oriented civic republicanism increases the likelihood of preferring immersion, the magnitude of its influence is substantially lower than the magnitude of its influence over the other language policies. In these respects, the expectation that bilingual education would not be as influenced by conceptions of American identity as the other policies is met. But action-oriented civic republicanism and cultural maintenance each decrease the likelihood of supporting immersion, and the magnitude of their influence parallels the magnitude of their influence over attitudes for English-only ballots. It should be noted, however, that although focus group discussions revealed a lower propensity to invoke national norms when talking about bilingual education than when talking about other policies, the few times in which national norms were invoked tended to be civic republican and incorporationist rather than liberal or ethnocultural (Schildkraut 2005a), as was the case here.[12]

Summary

There are four main points to highlight from this analysis. First, ethnoculturalism matters, but its role is not as overwhelming or as consistent as some other constitutive American norms under investigation. Previous quantitative studies have given ethnoculturalism much attention – in part because they were bound by available measures – but there are clearly other symbolic normative concerns driving public opinion on language policies. Ascriptivist notions of American identity certainly drive some preferences for restrictions, but they by no means play the lead role here. If anything, the lead role behind support for language restrictions belongs to identity-oriented civic republicanism, a finding that arguably reveals a more positive image of how the American public feels about language diversity. As noted earlier, identity-oriented civic republicanism is not merely a proxy for ethnoculturalism. The normative underpinnings of this conception of what "true Americans" are like are grounded in the need for unity but not necessarily uniformity. Whether any of the policies in question will actually yield unity is questionable, but this motivation for policy support is not an obvious reason for concern. Though the policies are restrictive, an important motivation for supporting them is to promote and

---

[12] Other findings from Table 4.1 deserve brief mention. Being Republican, conservative, older, and acculturation tend to promote support for language restrictions. The ethnicity of the respondent matters erratically, with blacks and Latinos less likely than whites to support official-English or English-only ballots. The opinions of Asians are not significantly different from the opinions of whites. Notably, Latinos are not less likely than whites to support immersion over other forms of bilingual education. Perceptions of the national economy are insignificant in every model. Residential factors are largely insignificant, though white respondents who live in Latino neighborhoods are more likely to favor immersion than whites who live in white neighborhoods. Models were run that also included measures of respondents' perceptions of their neighborhood context (whether it was mostly Latino or mostly Asian). Only 14 white respondents felt that they lived in a mostly Asian neighborhood, and 57 felt that they lived in a mostly Latino neighborhood. Both measures were insignificant in every model.

protect a civic republican vision of American identity in which Americans prioritize their common enterprise over particularistic interests. Among those who fear that these policies would actually undermine harmony and even infringe on the rights and opportunities of language minorities, it is important to recognize this underlying concern among the American people.

Second, some constitutive American norms generate opposition to language restrictions rather than support. Action-oriented civic republicanism, political liberalism, and the cultural maintenance component of incorporationism are invoked to argue for a uniquely American rejection of language restrictions. Opponents of restrictive language policies can look to such widely endorsed norms in attempts to reframe policy debates in ways that build on existing consensus. As Chong and Druckman note, frames that coincide with one's existing predispositions are more likely to be successful than frames that contradict them (2007). As the analysis in Chapter 3 made clear, political liberalism and action-oriented civic republicanism are strong predispositions among people of all backgrounds.

Third, both components of incorporationism – blending and maintaining cultural traditions – matter regularly and in opposite directions. This finding reinforces the warning in Chapter 3 that scholars should continue to track whether stronger divisions emerge among the American public regarding the role of incorporationist norms in defining the meaning of American identity and whether these divisions remain a key source of policy disagreement. If they do, then concerns about the loss of consensus could gain more credibility.

Fourth, the type of policy involved can affect which American norm will shape preferences. Aggregate preferences differ substantially among the policies, as do the predictors of those preferences in several cases. The issue of English-only ballots, which invokes the image of active citizenship, is uniquely affected by action-oriented civic republicanism. The issue of English signs, in contrast, invokes the speech rights of business owners and is the only policy in which political liberalism is a predictor. Americans, in short, are capable of making meaningful distinctions between these various policies, and they draw upon different reservoirs of normative attachments to help shape their views.

9/11 PROFILING AND INTERNMENT

To develop further our understanding of how conceptions of American identity shape attitudes on boundary-related policies, I turn now to the issue of ethnic profiling. After 9/11, Americans found themselves debating whether they would be willing to give up some of their own civil liberties in exchange for greater national security. Though this debate has appeared from time to time throughout American history, it had been at least a generation since concern with the liberty-for-security trade-off reached such a prominent level. In addition to wondering if they would give up some of their own liberties, Americans also debated whether to demand that certain people – namely Muslims and people of Middle Eastern or Arab descent – give up more of their liberties than the rest of us. Although national newspapers and elected officials – including both houses of Congress and President George W. Bush – called on Americans not to take revenge upon innocent people and be tolerant and understanding of different cultures, public opinion polls revealed that many Americans were willing to reign in the civil liberties of Arab Americans and Middle Eastern immigrants. In one national survey conducted shortly after 9/11, for example, 66 percent of Americans said it would be acceptable for law enforcement officials to stop and search anyone who looked Middle Eastern in order to prevent another attack. In another survey, 31 percent said they would even support putting Arab Americans in camps until their innocence could be determined (Schildkraut 2002).

Though no policy as extreme as internment developed after 9/11, support for all kinds of ethnic profiling, including internment, has been high enough to warrant further investigation. Investigation is warranted for other reasons as well. First, Supreme Court rulings on Japanese internment as well as subsequent rulings on ethnic profiling near the U.S.-Mexico border suggest that the use of profiling in the name of national security would likely be deemed constitutional (Braber 2002; Harris 2003). Second, nonwhite Americans who think that they or their group have suffered discrimination can become alienated and withdraw from the very political process that has the potential to protect them (Schildkraut 2005b). Recent research suggests that many Latinos question whether police and the courts treat Latinos fairly. Among those Latinos who say they would be reluctant to report violent crimes to the police, fear of discrimination or other repercussions was the most common reason cited (Lopez and Livingston 2009). Third, elected officials and other prominent commentators have publicly advocated ethnic profiling. As noted earlier, Representative Pete King (R-NY) has urged airport screeners to use ethnic and religious profiling at airports (Palmer 2006). Michelle Malkin, a regular guest on Fox News, wrote the unambiguously titled *In Defense of Internment: The Case for Racial Profiling in World War II and the War on Terror* (2004). Given these realities, understanding public opinion regarding ethnic profiling is an important endeavor. Conceptions of American identity are likely to be strong players in this process because in the case of a foreign attack, the conceptual and territorial boundaries of the nation are clearly salient.

First, however, some key terms need to be defined. Ethnic profiling is when law enforcement authorities use racial or ethnic characteristics to determine which people to subject to heightened scrutiny in order to prevent crimes from occurring. Heightened scrutiny can range from interrogation to searches of one's person and/or property to arrests or even removal from the community, as in the case of Japanese internment during World War II. Profiling does not refer to the use of racial or ethnic characteristics to help catch a particular suspect once a crime has been committed and when police have at least one witness's description of a particular suspect (Harris 2003). Ethnic profiling in the name of combating terrorism can take on two forms: extreme and mild. Extreme profiling involves the physical removal or detainment of the profilees, an action akin to Japanese internment. Throughout this analysis, I use either the terms *extreme profiling* or *internment* to refer to this kind of policy. Mild profiling involves allowing law enforcement officials to use race, ethnicity, or religion for less severe tasks such as searches and interrogations. In this sense, mild profiling is analogous to the more familiar case of racial profiling in which black or Latino motorists have been disproportionately pulled over, with traffic violations serving as a pretext for police officers to search for drugs or weapons. Throughout this analysis, I use either the terms *9/11 profiling* or *mild profiling* to refer to searching or interrogating Arabs or Muslims solely because of their ethnicity, and I use *traditional profiling* to refer to the profiling of black and Latino motorists.[13] Unlike 9/11 profiling, support for traditional profiling has generally been low. In March 2005, a national survey by Princeton Survey Research Associates found that 75 percent of Americans say they disapprove of the practice.[14]

Unlike the boundary issue of language policy, attitudes about profiling have rarely been studied at all, let alone with attention to the role that conceptions of American identity play in shaping opinions. A literature search for public opinion on traditional profiling returned only two studies, both by Weitzer and Tuch (2002, 2005). Using two different national surveys, they note that overall support for profiling is low for blacks and whites, but that whites are less likely than blacks to think it is a widespread practice, and the race of the respondent was one of the strongest predictors of whether people approved of it. Other factors generating approval included living in a high-crime neighborhood and being personally afraid of crime. Having personal and vicarious experience with racial profiling also decreased approval.

Studies of 9/11 profiling are likewise small in number, but they show some important similarities with studies of traditional profiling as well as some differences. For instance, just as being afraid of crime generates support for traditional profiling, being afraid of another attack on the United States (sociotropic threat) and being afraid that one or one's family will be victims of an attack (personal threat) have each been shown to generate support for 9/11 profiling (Schildkraut 2002; Kim 2004; Huddy et al. 2005). Unlike studies of traditional profiling, however, the race of the respondent has thus far not proven to be a significant determinant of support for 9/11 profiling. Although studies of traditional profiling do not examine political attitudes, studies of 9/11 profiling find that Republicans and conservatives can be more supportive than Democrats and liberals (Schildkraut 2002; Huddy et al. 2005).

Despite these insights, there is still much we have to learn about the public's opinion about profiling. For example, existing studies only look at mild

[13] I do not use the term *mild* to suggest that such profiling is an inconsequential policy concern. Rather, *mild* is simply used as a contrast to the more extreme measure of physically removing people from their homes and placing them in camps.

[14] Survey results available at Polling the Nations, http://poll.orspub.com (accessed November 29, 2006.

profiling. No study looks at the one-third of people who have explicitly supported measures as extreme as internment. Moreover, no study looks at whether support for profiling is tempered when the profilee is expressly described as an American citizen or whether respondents would treat all people who look Arab or Muslim the same regardless of whether they are U.S. citizens. Such a distinction, however, could be significant given the central role of territorial and conceptual boundaries in the case of a domestic attack carried out by immigrants. Americans are likely to opt for treating citizens better than immigrants. Additionally, the conceptions of American identity that contribute to such attitudes might be different when the target is a citizen compared to when the target is an immigrant.

The 21-CAS used two split-sample designs when gauging opinions on extreme and mild forms of profiling in order to test (1) if the status of the profilee as an immigrant or as a U.S. citizen altered overall levels of support; (2) if the status of the profilee as an immigrant or as a U.S. citizen altered the type of American norm invoked to arrive at that opinion, and (3) if the factors that generate support for 9/11 profiling are similar to the factors that generate support for traditional profiling or if one type of profiling uniquely invokes the content of American identity. Regarding extreme profiling, half of the sample was asked: "If there were another terrorist attack in the U.S. with Arab or Middle-Eastern suspects, would you support or oppose allowing the government to hold Arabs who are U.S. citizens in camps until it can be determined whether they have links to terrorist organizations?"[15] Of those, 29.5 percent support internment and 70.5 percent oppose. The other half was asked the same question but with "Arab immigrants" replacing "Arabs who are U.S. citizens." Here 34 percent support internment and 66 percent oppose, which is a small but statistically significant increase in approval of 4.5 percentage points (p < 0.006). Note that this approval level is essentially unchanged from approval levels found immediately following 9/11.

For 9/11 profiling versus traditional profiling, roughly half of the respondents were asked: "It has been reported that some police officers stop motorists of certain racial or ethnic groups because the officers believe that these groups are more likely than others to commit certain types of crime. This practice is known as racial profiling. Do you approve or disapprove of the use of racial profiling by police?"[16] Twenty-three percent approve and 77 percent disapprove. The other half of the respondents were asked: "Since September 11th, some law enforcement agencies have stopped and searched people who are Arab or of Middle Eastern descent to see if they may be involved in potential

---

[15] This question wording was adopted from a *Time*/CNN poll taken shortly after 9/11, available at Polling the Nations, http://poll.orspub.com (accessed October 15, 2003).

[16] This question wording was adopted from a poll conducted shortly after 9/11 by the Kaiser Family Foundation, the Kennedy School of Government at Harvard University, and National Public Radio. The original survey is available at http://kff.org/kaiserpolls/loader .cfm?url=/commonspot/security/getfile.cfm&PageID=13879 (accessed October 15, 2003).

terrorist activities. Do you approve or disapprove of this kind of profiling?"[17] Here, 66 percent approve and 34 percent disapprove. The increase in approval of 9/11 profiling compared to traditional profiling is an impressive 43 percentage points (p < 0.000).[18]

These aggregate results show that support for 9/11 profiling is considerably higher than support for traditional profiling. People are even more likely to approve of placing people who fit the 9/11 profile into camps than they are to approve of disproportionately pulling over minority motorists. When it comes to such camps, support is higher when the profilees are immigrants instead of citizens.

Hypotheses

The hypotheses for how constitutive American norms might affect attitudes toward profiling are more exploratory than the hypotheses for language policy due to the low level of systematic attention attitudes about profiling has received. The hypotheses described in this section are derived, primarily, from the expectations of symbolic politics theory and theoretical underpinnings of the norms in question and, secondarily, from insights revealed in the analysis of language policies and assessments of the profiling policies.

Ethnoculturalism clearly promotes exclusion from the national community based on ascriptive characteristics, which could lead to a greater willingness to deny protecting the rights and liberties that come with membership for people who do not possess such characteristics. Thus, a high score on ethnoculturalism is hypothesized to lead to greater support for all forms of profiling, regardless of whether the profilee is an immigrant, citizen, or motorist.

It is not immediately clear that the norms associated with action-oriented civic republicanism would be relevant to opinions on profiling given the extent to which profiling calls into question the cultural boundaries of American identity and the potential restrictions on civil liberties rather than on active citizenship. Action-oriented civic republicanism is therefore not hypothesized to be a significant influence over attitudes toward any type of profiling.

Identity-oriented civic republicanism, however, presents an interesting case. One could argue that it is not obviously related to policy debates surrounding profiling and is therefore not expected to be especially relevant in this investigation. Yet given that this aspect of American identity calls on Americans to prioritize and promote their connection to the national group, it is possible that people with high scores on identity-oriented civic republicanism would think

---

[17] This question wording was also adopted from the poll conducted by the Kaiser Family Foundation, the Kennedy School of Government at Harvard University, and National Public Radio.

[18] All percentages exclude respondents who said "don't know." The percentages offering that response for each question were: interning U.S. citizens (9%), interning Arab immigrants (9%), 9/11 profiling (7%), and traditional profiling (6%).

that Arab Americans should "do their part" to help the cause of fighting terrorism, and that "doing their part" would involve giving up some of their liberties
for the safety of the collective. If so, then identity-oriented civic republicanism
could generate support for mild and extreme 9/11 profiling – and it might even
lead to greater support for profiling American citizens of Arab descent than
of profiling immigrants. It would not, however, necessarily influence attitudes
toward traditional profiling.

Political liberalism emphasizes the rights of people to be free from arbitrary
government intervention and provides a normative prescription to provide civil
liberties even in cases in which the majority of the community would prefer
restrictions. As such, the hypothesis for political liberalism is that people who
think that true Americans should let other people say what they want, no
matter how much they disagree with them will oppose all kinds of profiling
more than people who think that political liberalism is unimportant.

As with action-oriented civic republicanism, economic liberalism is not conceptually related to profiling in any obvious way. Economic liberalism is therefore not expected to be a significant influence over attitudes toward any type
of profiling.

Regarding incorporationism, it is likewise not immediately obvious that
thinking that true Americans should blend into the larger society would make
a person more or less likely to support ethnic profiling. Support for the notion
that true Americans carry on the cultural traditions of their ancestors, however,
is hypothesized to generate opposition to profiling because profiling entails
differential treatment based on ethnic markers, some of which exist due to the
very preservation of cultural traditions, such as wearing a *hijab* or speaking
Arabic. For similar reasons, this component of incorporationism is expected to
generate opposition to traditional profiling as well.

Data Analysis

Using the seven sets of constitutive American norms as key independent variables, I used probit analysis to predict opinions on each of the four profiling
questions. Based on the findings of earlier studies, I also examine the role of
the respondent's race, level of education, partisan identification, and political
ideology with the expectation that whites, people with lower levels of education, Republicans, and conservatives will be more supportive of all types of
profiling. In the three 9/11 profiling models (interning citizens, interning immigrants, and mild profiling), I also test whether personal threat and sociotropic
threat increase support for profiling.[19] Likewise, in the three 9/11 profiling
models, I test whether one's level of pride in being American influences support
because patriotism has been found to be a significant predictor of support for
restrictions on civil liberties after 9/11 (Davis and Silver 2004) and because

[19] The 21-CAS asks about fears of another attack, but does not ask about fears regarding crime.
Relevant measures of threat are therefore not available for the traditional profiling model.

studies point to patriotism as one reason why black and Jewish antidiscrimination organizations were largely silent on Japanese internment during World War II (Greenberg 1995). All question wordings not described in the text can be found in Appendix A. The results appear in Table 4.3.[20]

As with language policy, the results show that some conceptions of American identity, such as ethnoculturalism, are consistently strong predictors of opinions across the issue domain, often rivaling or surpassing the magnitude of more well-studied factors such as partisanship and sociotropic threat. Other conceptions of American identity, however, such as economic liberalism, are generally not significant. Table 4.3 also shows that when a conception of American identity influences support for internment, its effect is often stronger when the profilees are American citizens than when they are immigrants.

As before, it is useful to examine predicted probabilities in addition to probit coefficients in order to assess each of the specific hypotheses and get a more intuitive interpretation of the results. Table 4.4 shows the predicted probability that a respondent would approve of each type of profiling as the independent variable in question (across each row) changes from its minimum to its maximum value (from 0 to 1). Predicted probabilities are calculated only for the significant conceptions of American identity from Table 4.3. Table 4.4 also shows predicted probabilities for personal threat, sociotropic threat, and patriotism given the prominent role these variables have played in previous scholarship. The results show many cases in which the specific hypotheses were confirmed, as well as several in which they were not.

Tables 4.3 and 4.4 show that ethnoculturalism is a consistently strong predictor across all four profiling models. The powerful role of this conception of American identity was expected because these boundary policies call our attention to appearance explicitly. In both internment questions, moving from 0 to 1 on the ethnoculturalism scale changes the predicted preference from opposition to support. Notably, people who score a 1 on the ethnoculturalism scale are more likely to support interning Arab Americans (76%) than they are to support interning Arab immigrants (62%). The change in preference moving from 0 to 1 on ethnoculturalism is 68 percentage points for interning citizens and 47 percentage points for interning immigrants. On mild 9/11 profiling and traditional profiling, the effect of ethnoculturalism is more modest but still impressive in magnitude, increasing support by 14 and 16 percentage points, respectively.

Action-oriented civic republicanism, as hypothesized, is notably absent from Table 4.4 because profiling does not directly relate to active citizenship. It is significant in just one case: it generates opposition to random searches of people who look Arab or Muslim.

Identity-oriented civic republicanism is also notably weak here, in stark contrast to its prominent role in shaping attitudes regarding language policy.

---

[20] As with Table 4.1, all models in Table 4.3 were run with "strength of identification" included as an independent variable. As before, it is insignificant in every model.

TABLE 4.3. *Determinants of Support for Internment and Profiling*

Independent Variable	Intern Arab Americans	Intern Arab Immigrants	Profiling Arabs	Profiling Motorists
Ethnoculturalism	2.16**	1.34**	0.45*	0.49**
	(0.26)	(0.23)	(0.24)	(0.22)
Civic republicanism ("action")	0.12	0.03	−0.66**	−0.45
	(0.34)	(0.30)	(0.30)	(0.29)
Civic republicanism ("identity")	1.05**	0.62*	0.47	0.04
	(0.44)	(0.38)	(0.34)	(0.33)
True Americans should let other people say what they want, no matter how much they disagree	−0.50**	0.05	−0.31*	−0.07
	(0.19)	(0.18)	(0.18)	(0.18)
True Americans should pursue economic success through hard work	−0.05	0.37	−0.04	0.48**
	(0.24)	(0.24)	(0.21)	(0.22)
True Americans should blend into the larger society	0.13	−0.03	0.31*	0.49**
	(0.19)	(0.18)	(0.18)	(0.17)
True Americans should carry on the cultural traditions of their ancestors	0.04	0.21	−0.49**	−0.47**
	(0.18)	(0.17)	(0.17)	(0.17)
Age	0.31	0.26	0.09	−0.59**
	(0.26)	(0.25)	(0.24)	(0.25)
Education	−0.71**	−0.64**	−0.20	0.19
	(0.19)	(0.18)	(0.18)	(0.18)
Republican	0.38**	0.50**	0.72**	0.67**
	(0.16)	(0.16)	(0.16)	(0.18)
Conservative	0.02	0.46**	0.34**	0.08
	(0.16)	(0.16)	(0.15)	(0.15)
Black	−0.05	0.31**	−0.20	−1.13**
	(0.18)	(0.16)	(0.15)	(0.28)
Asian	0.27	0.13	−0.45*	−0.28
	(0.24)	(0.26)	(0.25)	(0.20)
Latino	−0.02	0.19	−0.20	−0.16
	(0.19)	(0.19)	(0.18)	(0.16)
Fear being victim of attack	0.51**	0.51**	0.19	—
	(0.18)	(0.17)	(0.17)	
Fear United States will be attacked	0.34*	−0.08	0.37**	—
	(0.20)	(0.18)	(0.17)	
Proud to be American	0.55	−0.19	0.77**	—
	(0.50)	(0.39)	(0.34)	
Constant	−2.89	−2.25	−0.52	−1.15
Chi-square	277.17	212.11	184.93	113.77
N	896	867	866	972

Note: * $p < 0.1$; ** $p < 0.05$; standard errors in parentheses. Cell entries are probit coefficients, in which $1 =$ support/approve.

Source: Twenty-First-Century Americanism Survey, 2004.

TABLE 4.4. *Predicted Probability of Approving of Internment and Profiling*

Independent Variable	Interning Arab Americans			Interning Arab Immigrants			9/11 Profiling			Traditional Profiling		
	0	1	Change	0	1	Change	0	1	Change	0	1	Change
Ethnoculturalism	0.08	0.76	0.68**	0.15	0.62	0.47**	0.67	0.81	0.14*	0.20	0.36	0.16*
Civic republicanism ("action")	–	–	–	–	–	–	0.85	0.66	–0.19**	–	–	–
Civic republicanism ("identity")	0.05	0.25	0.20**	0.13	0.29	0.16	–	–	–	–	–	–
True Americans should let other people say what they want, no matter how much they disagree	0.35	0.18	–0.17**	–	–	–	0.79	0.70	–0.009	–	–	–
True Americans should pursue economic success through hard work	–	–	–	–	–	–	–	–	–	0.14	0.26	0.12*
True Americans should blend into the larger society	–	–	–	–	–	–	0.64	0.75	0.11	0.15	0.29	0.14**
True Americans should carry on the cultural traditions of their ancestors	–	–	–	–	–	–	0.81	0.65	–0.16**	0.35	0.13	–0.22**
Fear of being a victim of attack	0.15	0.3	0.15**	0.21	0.38	0.17**	0.69	0.75	0.06	–	–	–
Fear United States will be attacked	0.16	0.25	0.09	0.28	0.25	–0.03	0.64	0.77	0.13*	–	–	–
Proud to be American	0.12	0.22	0.10	0.34	0.26	–0.08	0.45	0.73	0.28**	–	–	–

Note: Cell entries equal probability of approving when independent variable equals 0 or 1, with all nondummy variables set to their means. * = $p < 0.1$; ** = $p < 0.05$.

Source: Twenty-First-Century Americanism Survey, 2004.

This conception of American identity is associated with significant opinion change in only one case – interning Arab Americans. A low score on the identity scale yields a 5 percent chance of approval while a high score yields a 25 percent chance. As with ethnoculturalism, views on interning citizens are more powerfully affected than views on interning immigrants. This finding is consistent with the speculation that people who score highly on identity-oriented civic republicanism might be more likely than others to think that Arab Americans should willingly suffer the consequences of extreme profiling in order to protect the larger community.

Political liberalism only results in significant opinion change in one model, though it was hypothesized to be influential across all four. As with identity-oriented civic republicanism, political liberalism only produces significant opinion change on the question of interning Arab Americans. But as predicted, people who endorse this conception of American identity are less likely to support internment (18%) than people who do not (35%). As hypothesized, economic liberalism fails to influence either mild or extreme 9/11 profiling. It does, however, make support for traditional profiling moderately more likely.

Neither form of incorporationism – blending into the larger society or maintaining the cultural traditions of one's ancestors – affects attitudes toward internment. But thinking that cultural maintenance is an important element of American identity reduces the likelihood of support for mild 9/11 profiling (81% vs. 65%) and for traditional profiling (35% vs. 13%). Thinking that blending into the larger society is important makes support for traditional profiling more likely (15% vs. 29%). The hypotheses for incorporationism were thus partially confirmed. Significance was erratic, but when present it was in the expected direction.

Before concluding this section, it is instructive to compare the results for conceptions of American identity with factors that have been the focus of existing profiling research. First, as expected, Republicans and conservatives consistently support profiling more than Democrats and liberals. Second, the race of the respondent is largely insignificant. Black respondents are more supportive of interning Arab immigrants than white respondents, and they are less supportive of traditional profiling. Asian respondents are less supportive of 9/11 profiling. In all other cases, racial differences are insignificant, a pattern that is consistent with earlier studies of 9/11 profiling. Third, consistent with earlier studies, both sociotropic and personal threat increase support for profiling, but they do so erratically. Sociotropic threat only increases support for searches while personal threat increases support for both kinds of internment. Finally, pride in being American only generates support for profiling in the case of random searches.

Summary

There are seven main points to highlight from this analysis, the first four of which echo findings from the analysis of language policy. First, certain conceptions of American identity exhibit a strong influence over attitudes even after the influence of traditionally powerful factors, such as partisanship, education, and threat have been controlled. Many people believe that what the United States stands for was attacked on 9/11 just as much as U.S. territory was; thus paving the way for ideas about what the United States stands for to become a central player in shaping public opinion, just as symbolic politics theory would lead us to expect.

Second, features of the policy influence which American norm will become salient and influential. Identity-oriented civic republicanism, for example, is not nearly as much of a presence here as it was with language policy. Language policies that purportedly aim to enhance unity invoke identity-oriented civic republicanism whereas profiling policies that emphasize appearance invoke ethnoculturalism.

Third, it is not the case that simply agreeing that there are boundaries on the notion of American identity makes a person more likely to support a wide range of restrictive boundary policies. On the contrary, action-oriented civic republicanism, political liberalism, and the cultural maintenance component of incorporationism, when significant, promote opposition to restrictive policies.

Fourth, the internal tensions within incorporationism warrant monitoring. That tension is not as consistently evident with profiling as it is with language, but it is a factor in traditional profiling.

Fifth, the influence of ethnoculturalism over attitudes about extreme and mild profiling far surpasses that of other factors that we might expect to dominate, such as race, threat, partisanship, patriotism, and even political liberalism. Roughly 8.4 percent of the sample scores in the top third of the ethnoculturalism scale, which means that this substantial level of support for profiling, including internment, applies to a small, but nontrivial portion of the American population. The widespread endorsement of the normative prescriptions of political liberalism among the American public does surprisingly little to counter the support that ethnoculturalism generates, though it does have some potential as a successful counterframe, especially given its high level of support in the general population relative to ethnoculturalism.

Sixth, conceptions of American identity are more powerful influences over attitudes toward internment when the profilee is a citizen compared to when the profilee is an immigrant. Specifically asking about the treatment of one's fellow Americans seems to increase the relevance of conceptions of American identity when people are forming their views, especially with regard to ethnoculturalism and identity-oriented civic republicanism. This is yet another set of findings that underscore the idea that American identity is not a universally powerful influence over attitudes. Its influence is often context-specific. With regard to the particular asymmetry uncovered here, recent work by Theiss-Morse concurs: marginalized group members (those who differ from the majority in some way but are ingroup members nonetheless) can find that the rights that come with group membership become threatened when their marginalized status is made salient. Marginalized ingroup members are sometimes treated more harshly than outgroup members (Theiss-Morse 2009). In effect, marginalized ingroup members get punished for their difference, whereas outgroup members are expected to be different. Viewing American identity in ethnocultural terms and being asked about 9/11 highlight the marginality of American citizens of Arab descent, perhaps inducing this so-called black sheep effect. The extent to which this effect generalizes to other policies and conditions across time and space, however, still needs to be established further.

Finally, opinions about traditional profiling and 9/11 profiling seem to be driven by different sets of constitutive norms. People do not see both as invoking the same kinds of boundaries of American identity. Whereas ethnoculturalism and political liberalism dominate views on interning citizens, incorporationism dominates views on pulling over minority motorists.

CONCLUSION

In addition to confirming that a wide range of views on what being American means are important predictors of opinions on boundary-related policies, the analyses in this chapter highlight that people often rely on their views of American identity in reasonable and limited ways – generally (though not always) invoking ones that are particularly relevant to the policy at hand. Action-oriented civic republicanism, for instance, significantly generates opposition toward English-only ballots but does not affect views on official-English or English signs. Conceptions of American identity will, therefore, not always matter; their impact is conditional on what is seen to be at stake. The analyses here also showed that some very popular understandings of what being American means can be powerful forces leading people to reject restrictive policies. Having strong attachments to particular notions of what Americans "should" be like is not on the whole something to fear. Rendering certain constitutive norms salient has the potential to promote support for policies that are more inclusive.

This chapter also underscores that it would be wise for public opinion scholars to track the extent to which Americans define being American in incorporationist terms because this conception of American identity was often significant, with blending generating support for restrictions and cultural maintenance generating opposition. Incorporationism's place in the American psyche is by no means stable. As a national norm, it is relatively young compared to ethnoculturalism, liberalism, and civic republicanism. This dynamic and clearly potent set of concerns about the demands that the nation's immigrant legacy places on American citizens should therefore continue to receive scholarly attention along the lines it has received here. The question is whether more and more Americans over time will come to believe that we can and do "have it all" – healthy diversity plus a common core – or will the seeds of polarization revealed here and in Chapter 3 grow?

Turning now to the specific policies under investigation, these analyses confirmed that we gain more insight when we include a variety of measures of

American identity in our models than if we just focus on the presence or absence of ethnoculturalism. Americans see language conflict as primarily being about the challenges of finding unity in the face of diversity as revealed by the consistent power of incorporationism and identity-oriented civic republicanism. Americans rely on other national norms to help them interpret specific policy debates that might involve free speech, political participation, and, yes, ascriptiveness, but as a whole, the language issue is about how to achieve the right balance between conflicting American norms involving unity and difference. Recognizing that a significant source of support for restrictive policies is due to civic republican aspirations rather than ascriptivist ones is an important insight for analysts and activists alike.

What people seem to want is a common American identity, not necessarily a white, Christian identity. They fear that we are losing our sense of commonality and sense that restricting language use and fostering learning English rapidly will protect unity. The challenge facing policy makers is therefore to design language solutions that address this concern among the American public but that also protect the rights to speech and access that all citizens and residents possess. That so many Americans support political liberalism and civic republicanism – and that both temper support for language restrictions – suggests that policies framed with these American norms in mind have the potential to achieve public support while minimizing the kind of conflict that has visited Pahrump, Nevada, and other cities and towns across the nation. Decades of research in social psychology have shown that getting people to recognize what they have in common minimizes ingroup/outgroup divisions. The research here points to specific areas in which that might be possible with respect to debates about language use.

On the contrary, ascriptiveness is the main factor that leads people to be willing to resort to measures as extreme as internment as a response to terrorist attacks. For ethnoculturalists, people who do not fit the dominant cultural type do not automatically get the full range of rights that come with citizenship. Framing opposition to profiling in terms of political liberalism can temper support for internment and profiling, but the magnitude of its effect was considerably weaker than that of ethnoculturalism, especially with regard to internment. Nonetheless, support for political liberalism remains strong, and that support can be a valuable resource to draw upon as public policy debates unfold.

5

The Myths and Realities of Identity Prioritization

Previous chapters examined claims that our increasing racial and ethnic diversity is making the United States a place with less and less "there, there." Those examinations led to the conclusion that such claims are overblown. Few differences were found in how people from a variety of backgrounds define what being American means. Differences related to immigration, including nativity, were essentially gone with subsequent generations. By the time people are third- and fourth-generation American, they are, for the most part, equally likely to value the liberal, civic republican, and incorporationist underpinnings of American national identity. Even among people from Mexico, the target of the most vehement critics, most differences in how people define American identity were at the margins; the similarities between Mexicans and non-Mexicans were more noteworthy than their differences. For instance, 74 percent of foreign-born Mexicans agreed that true Americans should think of themselves as American and feel American compared to 73 percent of U.S.-born Mexicans and 81 percent of the rest of the sample. Moreover, the most striking differences between subgroups of Americans were partisan and ideological rather than racial or ethnic.

But there is more to the concerns raised by immigration critics about the consequences of our increasing diversity. Critics sound alarms not just about whether the newest Americans believe in core national values but also about the extent to which they live up to those values. The civic republican ideal of connecting one's own sense of self to the broader political community is especially relevant here. In particular, concerns arise over whether people do come to think of themselves primarily as American, or as American at all, even in combination with some other identity. The claim is that they do not, and that this lack of identification will in due time yield instability or worse. As Patrick Buchanan charges, "millions [of immigrants] bring no allegiance to America and remain loyal to the lands of their birth. And though they occupy more and more rooms in our home, they are not part of our family. Nor do they wish to be" (2006).

94

Many people have nostalgic views of immigrants at the turn of the century bravely leaving the old world for new opportunities in America. These poor huddled masses are admired not only for their courage but also for allegedly welcoming their new identities as Americans without looking back. As Buchanan writes when describing contemporary trends in illegal immigration, "This is not immigration as America knew it, when men and women made a conscious choice to turn their backs on their native lands and cross the ocean to become Americans" (2006). Lest Buchanan be dismissed as an extreme voice in American politics, it should be noted that the book from which these quotes were drawn landed him spots on news programs on CNN, NBC, and Fox, and the book, *State of Emergency*, reached number three on the *New York Times* nonfiction best-seller list in September of 2006.[1] Ordinary Americans likewise compare today's "bad" immigrants to yesterday's "good" immigrants when talking about immigration (Schildkraut 2005a). In short, the claim is that today's immigrants do not want to become American and fail to internalize their membership in their new national community. Moreover, it is argued that the descendants of immigrants also reject an American identity, a pattern that, in time, could result in substantial amounts of Americans who do not think of themselves as American (Huntington 2004).

In addition to pundits and commentators, political scientists, philosophers, and psychologists wonder about the role that national identity attachment plays in the vitality of democracies. Vigorous debates rage on about whether patriotism, love of one's country, and a strong sense of national identity are harmful or beneficial to individuals, groups, nations, and the international community. Both sides in this debate make valid claims. Having a strong attachment to one's country can lead to hostility toward outsiders and atypical ingroup members, feelings of superiority, diminished support for redistribution, and uncritical support for the policies and actions of one's government. At the same time, possessing strong national attachments can also lead to greater willingness to make sacrifices for the public good, obey laws and pay taxes, and engage in more civic-minded behavior (Druckman 1994; Schatz, Staub, and Lavine 1999; Furia 2002; de Figueiredo and Elkins 2003; Theiss-Morse 2003; Theiss-Morse 2004; Shayo 2009). Moreover, psychologists have shown that cooperation and group harmony are promoted when people recognize that they share an attachment to a common ingroup (Gaertner and Dovidio 2000).

In this vein, some political theorists maintain that a sense of common identity is essential in liberal democracies for a variety of reasons. Rogers Smith, for instance, writes that "if citizens feel that their most profound commitments go to a racial, ethnic, religious, regional, national, or voluntary subgroup, then the broader society's leaders may find that their government lacks adequate popular support to perform some functions effectively" (1997, 480), and that

---

[1] Information on Buchanan's media appearances was found at the Southern Poverty Law Center, http://www.splcenter.org/intel/news/item.jsp?aid=83 (accessed March 3, 2007). The book's best-seller ranking was found through Lexis-Nexis.

it is "politically necessary" to "constitute a people that feels itself to be a people" (474). He goes on to argue that liberal democratic societies such as the United States must devise a way to convince members of the "distinctive worth" of their membership because only when people possess such feeling can the very liberal principles that make the society of value be nurtured. He concludes that democratic societies need to do a better job of convincing its people that they are a people than they have done in the past; otherwise, particularistic and ascriptive myths of peoplehood, such as American ethnoculturalism, will be found more compelling and will win the day.

Other theorists, who have been labeled "liberal nationalists," claim that a shared sense of national identity is important for several reasons. First, it prevents alienation from political institutions. Second, it promotes political stability. Third, it leads to trust in one's fellow citizens, which makes people willing to rely on compromise as a way to settle political disagreement. Fourth, it generates a concern for the common good, which, in turn, leads to support for redistributive policies (see Mason 1999 for a review of liberal nationalist arguments). Communitarians, such as Michael Sandel, write of the importance of solidarity and loyalty to the political community in the maintenance of stable and vibrant democracies (1996). In short, several political theorists maintain that for the American political system – or any diverse democracy – to be governable, stable, and able to provide the opportunities of liberalism to all people, said people must feel like they are in it together.

Determining how to cultivate the benefits of strong national identities while mitigating the harms is an important political project, though not the one pursued here. For now I simply posit that there are valid reasons to believe it is desirable for all citizens, be they recent arrivals or Mayflower descendants, white or nonwhite, to view themselves as full and proud members of the national community and to think that being American is an important part of who they are. Additionally, the mere sentiment that today's immigrants reject the idea of being American can threaten stability, harmony, and cooperation. If that sentiment turns out to be misguided, it is important to correct it. If it turns out to be valid, then we need to investigate further to determine the specific political consequences.

In this chapter, the attention thus shifts from identity content to identity attachment. It is because of the potential benefits of having a citizenry that possesses strong attachments to the United States and today's climate of ethnic change and cultural tensions that I undertake this examination of who does and does not see themselves as Americans. I also examine whether the treatment people think their group receives from the larger society hinders the adoption of an American self-identification. In this inquiry, I pay particular attention to the analytical guidance offered by social identity theory, which explains how new group identities can emerge when people are treated by others as if they belong to that particular group (Tajfel and Turner 1986; Schmitt, Spears, and Branscombe 2003). This means that if people feel like they are treated as if they are not American, then they will become more likely to agree that they are not.

As Geraldo Rivera, who hosts a show on Fox News, recently put it, "We have created [an] environment in this country where the 46 million of us who have Latino roots now feel beleaguered, now feel besieged, now feel as if we are 'the other'" (Carroll 2009).

The analysis in this chapter examines some of the factors that have been shown to affect self-identification more thoroughly than previous studies have been able to do. The Twenty-First-Century Americanism Survey (21-CAS) has several unique benefits for these investigations. First, it distinguishes national origin (i.e., Dominican, Italian) from panethnic (i.e., Latino, Asian) identities; I say more on the importance of this distinction in the following section. Second, it can appropriately assess the role that perceptions of discrimination play in the self-identification process by using measures that separate national origin discrimination, panethnic discrimination, and individual-level discrimination due to one's race or ethnicity. Third, the survey asks the same questions of all respondents, which presents the ability to assess the identification process among non-Hispanic whites as well as to compare the self-identification process across nonwhite groups.

I find that concerns about the rejection of an American self-identification are exaggerated. A majority of the respondents chose "American" as their primary identity. Among those that did not, a majority still describe themselves as American some of the time. Regarding the factors that affect these identity choices, I find that acculturation tells a big part of the story, and that it does so in a way contrary to those who claim that experiences in the United States or the leaders of ethnicity-related interest groups encourage the rejection of an American identity (Miller 1998; Schlesinger 1998; Huntington 2004). Rather, the longer one's family has had an opportunity to integrate into mainstream American society and institutions, the greater the likelihood that he or she will identify primarily as American. I also find, however, that perceptions of discrimination are a key part of the story. Such perceptions are not a by-product of acculturation, but they do promote the rejection of an American identity. Perceptions of individual-level mistreatment are not as common as perceptions of group-level mistreatment, but they are more powerful in their influence over self-identification. Though the power of individual-level treatment I find is in line with other studies in this area (DeSipio 2002; Schildkraut 2005b), it goes against long-established findings in public opinion research more generally that group interest is a more powerful predictor of attitudes than self-interest (Sears and Funk 1990).

"I LIVE HERE, BUT THAT'S IT."

My interest in whether people adopt or reject an American identity was sparked by concerns similar to those noted regarding the importance of citizens in a diverse self-governing society sharing an attachment to the group and its enterprise. These concerns first came to me during focus group research I conducted in 1998 when one participant, Paloma, said, "I don't find that I fit in this country really like an American. When they ask me, 'What are you?' I don't say American. I say Dominican. I feel like . . . I was born here, but I don't feel that America includes me at all. I live here, but that's it."[2] The nods of agreement around the table led me to wonder how many other American citizens, descendants of immigrants, feel this way. Would such sentiments only become more prevalent as the nation's population continued to diversify? Patterns of self-identification and identity prioritization, I realized, were an important topic worthy of scrutiny, and not just for their own sake. Paloma's words and the larger questions they raised struck me so deeply because I felt that such sentiments must have serious consequences for American society. Common sense says that they should. People who think of themselves primarily as American surely feel more connected to American political institutions and feel a greater sense of obligation to American society than people who think of themselves primarily as Latino or Dominican, or so I thought. But is this common sense accurate? Are Paloma's feelings widespread? Do they portend a future with fewer and fewer Americans thinking of themselves primarily as American? Are the factors that drive differing patterns of identity prioritization troubling? To what extent does her rejection of an American identity stem from a feeling of victimization or marginalization? Among people who share Paloma's feelings, what are the political consequences? These are the questions that motivate the next two chapters.

Panethnic, National Origin, and American Identities

Three types of identities are under investigation here: one's national origin identity (i.e., Dominican, Polish, or Japanese), one's panethnic or racial identity (i.e., white, black, Latino, or Asian), and one's identity as American. It is important to distinguish panethnic and national origin self-identifications in studies such as this one. It has been noted that the labels "Hispanic" and "Asian American" are American creations that grew out of administrative bean-counting, marketing strategies by foreign-language media, and reactive self-perceptions among immigrants from Latin American and Asian countries (e.g., Espiritu 1992; Fox 1996; Rodriguez 1996). When a person is told she is Hispanic or Asian and when unique features of her national origin identity are glossed over, she can begin to see herself in terms of that new group identity (see Tuan 1998, ch. 6 for powerful examples). Social identity scholarship has long documented this process across a variety of identity types in a variety of cultures (Tajfel and Turner 1986; Branscombe et al. 1999; Schmitt, Spears, and Branscombe 2003). Time and again, people who initially lack unity become unified in the face of common experiences with larger outgroups. What may have begun as an artificial grouping can become a very real and deeply held part of one's self-understanding. As Yen Le Espiritu writes regarding hate crimes, "when manifested in racial violence, racial lumping necessarily leads to

---

[2] Name has been changed (see Schildkraut 2005a for details on the focus group methodology).

protective panethnicity" (1992, 11). Part of the concern among critics is that the experience of being nonwhite in America leads to an oppositional panethnic identity.

In an ironic twist, immigration critics now fear that the panethnic organizations that largely came into being in response to panethnic treatment have captured educational and political establishments and now foster oppositional panethnic identities (Miller 1998; Schlesinger 1998; Huntington 2004; Buchanan 2006). Arthur Schlesinger, for example, warned of "militant" and "extreme" separatists who deny a common American identity and foster ethnic conflict (1998). In short, self-identifying as Latino might be more troubling than self-identifying as Colombian or as Guatemalan because national origin identities might have more to do with maintenance of a prior life and simple acculturation – or lack thereof – rather than with anything overtly threatening to a broader American identity. Although it is possible that a national origin attachment could also be an oppositional by-product of life in America, or to particular experiences in local communities in which one national origin group is heavily concentrated, the conventional wisdom is that a national origin identification is less troublesome than a panethnic identification.

However, it might be the case that panethnic identities do not run as deep as national origin identities. People might rely on panethnic unity for strategic and instrumental purposes, such as garnering attention from elected officials or combating animosity, but fall back on their national origin attachments when the political imperative subsides (Sommers 1991; Espiritu 1992). As Lisa Lowe writes, "The grouping 'Asian American' is not a natural or static category; it is a socially constructed unity, a situationally specific position, assumed for political reasons" (1996, 82). The challenge facing panethnicity, writes Laurie Sommers, is that it needs to rely on "the most stereotypical common denominators as cultural symbols" (1991, 35), which makes it challenging for the concept to wield enduring appeal. Even the unifier of a common language can pose barriers. In her study of *Noticiero Univisión*, for instance, América Rodriguez describes just how much effort it takes for the show's journalists to appeal to Latino viewers from a variety of national origin backgrounds, including their efforts at cultivating and using "accentless" Spanish (1996). It is also said that panethnicity can exacerbate discrimination by perpetuating the notion that all group members are "the same" and therefore conform to particular stereotypes (Lowe 1996, 71).

It is thus possible that people acknowledge a panethnic attachment, but that the attachment does not compete with national origin, or even American, attachments when people are asked which identity best characterizes their own self-perception (Jones-Correa and Leal 1996; García 2003). If true, then panethnicity might not be as potent at the individual level as some observers fear. For these reasons, it is important to distinguish national origin and panethnic identities empirically so that we can see if they do have different root causes, and then go on to investigate if they have different attitudinal and behavioral consequences.

Some previous surveys allow respondents to choose an American identity, a "racial or ethnic identity," or a combination of the two (e.g., General Social Survey [GSS], Los Angeles County Social Survey [LACSS]). If they choose a "racial or ethnic identity," they are not given the opportunity to indicate whether the identity in question is a panethnic one or a national origin one. One important exception in this regard is the Pilot National Asian American Political Survey (PNAAPS), conducted in 2000–1 (Lien, Conway, and Wong 2004). In that survey, respondents are asked if they generally think of themselves as an American, an Asian American, an Asian, a hyphenated American (e.g., Chinese American, Korean American), or in terms of national origin (e.g., Vietnamese, Cambodian). Respondents who do not choose "Asian American" are then asked a "forced choice" question to assess if they "have ever" thought of themselves as such (229). The results of this unique and valuable measurement strategy are discussed in the following text. Another exception comes from the 2002 Kaiser Family Foundation/Pew Hispanic Center National Survey of Latinos (KFF/PHC). In that survey, respondents are asked if they have ever described themselves in terms of their national origin identity, their panethnic identity, or as American. Then they are asked which of those three they use to describe themselves first. A version of this format is used in the 21-CAS.

EXISTING FINDINGS ON IDENTITY CHOICES AND PRIORITIZATION

Previous investigations of self-identification have produced important insights. First, when given the option, most people tend to adopt an American identity and some other identity. Nonwhites are sometimes reluctant to say they are only American, but they are quite willing to say they are American and something else (Pearson and Citrin 2006). In the PNAAPS, 61 percent of respondents say they identify either as American (12%), Asian American (15%), or ethnic American (34%). The 2002 KFF/PHC survey had similar results, with a plurality of respondents (44%) identifying primarily with their national origin group, followed by American (32%). "Latino" was the least common primary identity chosen (22%) (Schildkraut 2005b). Finally, in laboratory studies, Devos and Banaji find no differences between white and Asian American participants in the extent to which they consider themselves part of the American ingroup (2005). In short, one consistent finding across studies is that although immigrants and nonwhite Americans hold on to national origin attachments, they generally see themselves as American as well.

Second, acculturation is formidable. Contrary to the fears of immigration critics, acculturation seems to increase rather than decrease the likelihood of adopting an American identity. Lien, Conway, and Wong (2004), for instance, find that English-language use and having most of one's education in the United States are strong predictors of whether Asian respondents choose an American identity over an ethnic identity. Additionally, they find that the greater the proportion of a person's life that has been spent in the United States, the greater the likelihood that he or she will identify as American instead of in national origin terms. Pearson and Citrin (2006) likewise report that "61 percent of third-generation Latino and Asian respondents to the [LACSS say they are "just American"], compared to just 20 percent of naturalized citizens and only 4 percent of non-citizen immigrants" (224). In their study of the children of immigrants, Portes and Rumbaut find that children born to immigrants in the United States are more likely than children brought to the United States by their immigrant parents to think of themselves as American (2001).

Third, as social identity theory would predict, perceptions that one is a victim of discrimination make a person less likely to adopt an American identification (Portes and Rumbaut 2001), a phenomenon also known as "reactive ethnicity." Lien, Conway, and Wong (2004) find that having experienced discrimination increases the likelihood that a person will identify in terms of their national origin only instead of as American, Asian American, or ethnic American, contrary to the view that discrimination promotes panethnicity. Their findings do, however, suggest that discrimination might promote panethnicity among the U.S. born and promote national origin identification among the foreign born. Likewise, DeSipio finds that having personally experienced discrimination makes a person more likely to think that people from various Latin American countries share a common culture (2002). Using perceptions of group interest as the dependent variable instead of self-identification, Chong and Kim find that more experiences with individual-level discrimination lead nonwhites to express higher levels of group-interested orientations (2006).

A NOTE ABOUT NON-HISPANIC WHITE AMERICANS

Typically, studies of self-identification focus on nonwhites only. Even if white non-Hispanic respondents are included in the survey, they are often not asked the questions about self-identification or about perceptions discrimination (as is the case with the 2002 KFF/PHC survey). But it is important to include non-Hispanic whites (hereinafter referred to as "whites") in our analysis as well. Moreover, when considering the self-identification process among whites, a different set of trajectories needs to be considered because the historical status of whites as the socially dominant group in American society complicates the processes described previously (Sidanius and Pratto 1999). In particular, panethnic ("white") and American identities are likely to "go together" for whites in a way that they might not for nonwhites (Cheryan and Monin 2005; Devos and Banaji 2005). This association between Americanness and whiteness continues a long tradition in American history in which immigrants – even European ones who are today considered to be white – have continually been portrayed as unfit for incorporation and a threat to America's superior white race (Higham 1963; King 2000; Gerstle 2001; Tichenor 2002). To the extent that "white" and "American" are seen as interchangeable, perceptions of discrimination among whites might heighten, rather than diminish, the likelihood that a person would think of him- or herself as American. Yet to my knowledge, no large-N survey research examines the extent to which white

Americans conflate racial and national identities or the extent to which whites perceive discrimination (either against whites or against themselves personally due to their race).

Some studies do, however, confirm that the identification process differs for whites than for nonwhites. Laboratory studies, for example, show that one's identity as "white" and one's identity as "American" are linked in a way that panethnic and American identities are not for Asians or blacks (Cheryan and Monin 2005; Devos and Banaji 2005). Other studies likewise suggest that ethnic and American identifications converge for whites more so than for nonwhites (Sidanius et al. 1997). Examining twenty-eight years worth of National Election Study (NES) data, Wong and Cho find that few of the factors that lead black respondents to feel close to blacks as a group affect whites similarly (2005). The only consistent predictor over time was education, with lower levels of education leading to a greater likelihood of white respondents feeling close to whites as a group. Wong and Cho also find that although roughly half of the white respondents report feeling close to whites as a group, such closeness does not influence attitudes toward affirmative action or other policies, leading the authors to conclude that "racial identity currently has very little significance in the political lives of White Americans" (716).

As for perceptions of discrimination, there is little beyond anecdotal evidence to suggest that white Americans in some parts of the country are increasingly likely to think that their status as a monolingual white person puts them at a disadvantage. As noted in Chapter 2, the *Sun-Sentinel* ran a series in 2003 on linguistic diversity. The Web-based version of the paper included a discussion board in which readers could share their views. Many of the postings from whites were very hostile toward linguistic diversity, often with people relating stories of how they had been denied a job because they were not Latino or did not know Spanish. Many were quite resentful and hate-filled, prompting the *Sun-Sentinel*'s editor to write an article about how unsettling the animosity was (Maucker 2003). As one commenter wrote, "I've lived in S. Florida for 20 [years], and I cannot wait to move out because of the Latin immigrant population. I feel displaced in my own country because so many people are speaking Spanish." Another wrote, "If I want a job, I have to learn Spanish, but if they want a job, without speaking English, they are hired!! Fed up and frustrated." Still another wrote, "I've been denied interviews because I'm not bilingual. How come the immigrants of the early 1900s were PROUD to learn to speak English and couldn't wait to learn. Now we have to cater to Hispanics? Give me a break." Such frustration was often expressed with cursing and epithets, as exemplified by one blogger who wrote, "They should have a big sign at every airport in the country saying 'if you don't speak English then get the f**k out.'"[3] How widespread is such sentiment? Where does it come from? Does it lead to more attachments to whiteness or to a strengthened sense

---

[3] Comments were found at http://www.sun-sentinel.com/news/local/special/sfl-508language message,0,5163917.graffitiboard (accessed May 8–12, 2003).

of Americanness? We do not know the answers to these questions because whites have traditionally not been asked the relevant survey items.

One of the most extensive examinations investigating the relationship between white Americans and their national origin attachments, conducted by Mary Waters, relies on interviews of white Catholics of European descent and concludes that ethnic identities for whites are largely symbolic in nature (1990). Such identities are not a significant day-to-day influence over their lives, but the psychological attachments can be deep and meaningful nonetheless. The role national origin plays in one's life is seen as largely a matter of choice, providing individuality and community. Are these national origin attachments among whites therefore harmless? Possibly not, suggests Waters, to the extent that the perception of choice might make it difficult for whites to recognize or understand the reactive nature of non-American identifications among nonwhites (also see Tuan 1998). This lack of understanding could then foster resentment toward nonwhites and fuel the very concerns described at the outset of this chapter (also see Alba 1990).

USING THE 21-CAS TO STUDY IDENTITY PRIORITIZATION

The 21-CAS has several features that benefit the analyses in this chapter. First, it distinguishes national origin and panethnic identities by asking about each one separately. Second, it assesses the role that perceptions of discrimination play in the self-identification process by using measures that distinguish national origin discrimination, panethnic discrimination, and individual-level discrimination due to one's race or ethnicity. Third, the survey asks the same questions of all respondents, which presents the ability to assess the identification process among whites as well as to compare the self-identification process across non-white groups. Fourth, by incorporating demographic data about each respondent's Zip Code, I am able to test whether living in an ethnic enclave inhibits "becoming American." In the sections that follow, I first examine the factors that influence whether a person thinks of him- or herself primarily as American, as a member of his or her panethnic group, or as a member of his or her national origin group. Then I examine the factors that influence one of the key causal variables – perceptions of discrimination.

Patterns of Identity Attachment

To establish one's national origin, respondents were asked, "What countries did your ancestors come from?" They were allowed up to three mentions. If they mentioned more than one, they were then asked, "Which of those countries do you identify with most?" Their answer to that question was used in all subsequent questions that refer to their national origin. To gauge identity prioritization, respondents were later asked three yes/no questions to see if they ever describe themselves in terms of (1) their national origin, (2) their panethnic group, and (3) being American. They were asked, "Do you ever describe yourself as _____?" The blank was first filled with the respondent's national origin. For example, if a respondent said her ancestors were from Italy, Ireland, and Poland, and if she said that she identifies with Italy most, she was asked, "Do you ever describe yourself as Italian?"[4] Next the blank was filled with the respondent's racial or panethnic group. If a respondent said she was white, she was asked, "Do you ever describe yourself as white?" Finally, all respondents were asked, "Do you ever describe yourself as American?" If a respondent said yes to more than one of these three questions, she was then asked, "Which one of those best describes how you think of yourself most of the time?" The response to this question is used to measure a respondent's primary identity.[5]

The analyses in this chapter and Chapter 6 concentrate on this particular measure of identity attachment instead of on a measure that focuses entirely on being American, such as the "strength of identification" scale discussed in Chapter 3, because it more appropriately captures the concerns that animate debates about immigration in American society today. Here, people are explicitly being asked to choose whether an American identity or some other national origin grouping describes how they think of themselves most of the time. The use of "most of the time" in the survey question is an attempt to capture the group to which one is most attached and the reality that identities also have a situational component. No identity is going to dominate one's self-perception all of the time; we all have multiple identities that might dictate our self-perception at any given time. At the heart of the debates that concern this research project is the possibility that alternatives to "American" are regularly being prioritized by immigrants and their descendants. The measure employed here allows this contention – and its possible behavioral and attitudinal implications – to be investigated in a way that other questions about attachments to Americanness that one finds in the literature do not.

Thirty-six percent of respondents said they describe themselves in all three terms, just under half (47%) said they use two of the three, and 10 percent said they use only one.[6] Of the entire sample, 78 percent chose American as their primary identity, 14 percent chose their racial or panethnic group, and 8 percent chose their national origin group. Of the 22 percent of respondents that did not choose "American" as their primary identity, 73 percent still sometimes describe themselves as American, leaving 6 percent that does not use "American" at all.

Table 5.1 shows bivariate breakdowns on identity prioritization, and it reveals few surprises. Whites, American citizens, people whose families have

---

[4] For a respondent that only named one country of origin, that ancestry was used to fill in the blank.

[5] Respondents who said yes to only one of the three yes/no questions were still asked which term describes how they think of themselves most of the time. The only respondents skipped were those who did not answer questions about their ancestry and/or race.

[6] Unless otherwise noted, all figures refer to weighted results, using population weights provided by the SESRC.

TABLE 5.1. *Identity Prioritization: "Which one best describes how you think of yourself most of the time?"*

	Panethnic	National Origin	American	n (raw)
White	7.8	2.8	89.4	1,589
Black	41.6	6.1	52.3	281
Asian	16.7	36.0	47.3	276
Latino	18.2	28.2	53.6	422
U.S. citizen	13.1	4.6	82.4	2,435
Not a U.S. citizen	26.2	56.1	17.8	249
1st generation	20.2	38.0	41.8	530
2nd generation	11.6	11.8	76.6	166
3rd generation	5.9	2.6	91.5	175
4th generation or more	13.6	2.2	84.2	1,765
Speaks primarily English at home	12.8	3.7	83.6	2,281
Speaks another language at home	23.6	43.9	32.5	404

Note: n = unweighted.

Source: Twenty-First-Century American Survey, 2004.

been American for generations, and people who mainly speak English in the home are overwhelmingly likely to identify primarily as American. All other groups are less so, though in no case does a panethnic identification achieve plurality. Moreover, a majority of Latinos and a plurality of Asians and first-generation respondents adopt "American" as their primary identity.[7] The only groups that are unlikely to see themselves primarily as American are people who speak a language other than English at home and people who are not citizens. In both of those cases, a national origin identification is most likely. Thus, most people in the United States describe themselves as American most of the time. With time, immigrants and their descendants seem increasingly likely to do so as well.[8]

---

[7] It is also worth noting that Latinos were the panethnic group most likely to choose only an American identity (17% vs. 8% for whites, 4% for blacks, and 6% for Asians).

[8] Recall from Chapter 2 that 201 respondents had their racial category recoded based on their open-ended responses and/or on their answer to the question on Latin origin or descent. For those respondents, the panethnic identity question and the panethnic discrimination questions used their original responses, not the recoded categories. For example, a person who identified racially as Chinese but was recoded as Asian in terms of panethnicity was technically asked about being Chinese twice: once for the panethnicity question and once for the national origin questions. All analyses in Chapters 5 and 6 were, therefore, rerun with such respondents dropped from the analysis. There are few noteworthy differences, though such differences are discussed in footnotes when appropriate. In Table 5.1, for instance, when only those who said that their race was Latino are included in the analysis, the percentage saying they think of themselves as American most of the time drops to 44.2% (still a plurality), the percent saying they think of themselves primarily as Latino increases to 23.4%, and the percent prioritizing the national origin group stays about the same. For Asians, the percentage prioritizing the panethnic group

All respondents were asked how important their chosen identity was to them, and more than 80 percent of all respondents who chose "American," regardless of race, said this identity was very important. The degree of importance among national origin and panethnic identifiers was substantially weaker. For instance, only 55 percent of Latinos who chose "Latino" as their primary identity said that being Latino was very important to them, in contrast to the 82 percent of Latinos who chose "American" and thought that being American was very important to them.

The next step is to examine these relationships more systematically and in a way that accounts for additional demographic and social factors. In particular, we need to examine whether all else being equal, perceptions of discrimination make people less likely to think of themselves in terms of an American identity and more likely to form bonds with coethnics or conationals. The worst fear of critics of immigration and multiculturalism is that nonwhites will increasingly reject an American identity in favor of an oppositional, or adversarial, panethnic orientation. A lesser fear is that they simply will stay focused on their country of origin.

A word about how perceptions of discrimination are measured and how they are distributed is therefore in order. Three types of discrimination perceptions were measured: against one's panethnic (or racial) group, one's national origin group, and oneself individually. For each of the two types of group-level discrimination, respondents were asked three questions: "In general, do you think discrimination against _____ is a major problem, a minor problem, or not a problem in schools? What about in the workplace? What about in preventing _____ in general from succeeding in America?" A respondent whose ancestors are from Japan would be asked the questions first with "Asian" filled in the blank and then with "Japanese."[9] Respondents' answers to the questions were combined to form two summated rating scales, one measuring the perception of panethnic discrimination ($\alpha = 0.84$), and the other measuring national origin discrimination ($\alpha = 0.91$).

Then respondents were asked three questions about individual-level discrimination: "Do you think you have ever been denied a job or promotion because of your racial or ethnic background? Do you think you generally receive worse service than other people at restaurants or stores because of your racial or ethnic background? Do you think your racial or ethnic background has made it difficult for you to succeed in America?" The wording here specifies the racial or ethnic background in order to rule out other attributions for mistreatment – such as gender or social class – but does not distinguish between one's panethnic or national origin background, as the more theoretically important distinction

---

decreases to 11.2%, the percentage prioritizing the national origin group increases to 42.5%, and the percentage choosing American stays about the same.

[9] These questions were derived from the 2002 KFF/PHC Survey of Latinos, which asked about the panethnic group only.

is individual level versus group level.[10] Again, respondents' answers to all three questions were combined to form a summated rating scale of individual-level discrimination ($\alpha = 0.64$).

All three scales were constrained to have a minimum of 0 (no discrimination) and a maximum of 1 (feels all scenarios in question are a major problem or have been personally experienced).[11] Exploratory factor analysis (available in Appendix C) confirms three distinct dimensions among the nine discrimination items. In line with much existing scholarship on the perception of discrimination (Crosby 1984; Fuegen and Biernat 2000; Kessler, Mummendey, and Leisse 2000; Sechrist, Swim, and Stangor 2004; Schildkraut 2005b), the perception of group-level discrimination was more common than the perception of individual-level discrimination. Panethnic discrimination was seen as the most common (mean = 0.37; s.d. = 0.33), followed by national origin discrimination (mean = 25; s.d. = 0.33), which was followed by individual-level discrimination (mean = 0.15; s.d. = 0.27). I provide a detailed examination of the factors shaping the extent of one's perceived discrimination later in this chapter.

Predicting Identity Attachment

One hypothesis I test – derived from existing scholarship and theory – is that measures related to acculturation will be strong influences among Asian and Latino respondents, with greater acculturation increasing the likelihood of identifying as American instead of panethnically or with one's national origin group. Another is that among those respondents who prioritize a national origin identity, it is expected that measures of acculturation will matter most, indicating that national origin attachments are largely derivative of the immigrant experience. Among those respondents who prioritize a panethnic identity, it is expected that perceptions of discrimination will matter most. Both group-level and individual-level perceptions of discrimination are expected to matter. At the group level, public opinion research has consistently shown group interest to be a powerful predictor of attitudes in a variety of domains (Sears and Funk 1990). Yet with regard to discrimination in particular, individual perceptions

[10] One could make the case that these measures are still group oriented in the sense that the attribution for mistreatment is one's membership in a particular group. That is certainly true, but that is also true of any type of treatment that would be characterized as discrimination. If a question simply asked if the respondent had ever been denied a promotion or received poor treatment in a store – questions that would undeniably ask an individual about purely individual-level treatment – the entire concept of discrimination would disappear from the measures. Yet discrimination is one of two key analytical concepts required for the present inquiry (the other being the type of discrimination in question: panethnic, national origin, or personal experience), which is yet another reason why the reference to one's racial or ethnic background is included in these questions.

[11] If a respondent answered only 2 of the 3 items on the discrimination scale in question, his or her answers to those two questions were summed and then divided by 2 instead of by 3.

can be especially potent (DeSipio 2002; Michelson 2003; Schildkraut 2005b). They are a uniquely powerful form of individual experience that shape political outlooks in ways that traditional measures of self-interest, such as the pocket-book, do not. Similar processes are expected for black respondents as well. For whites, however, discrimination might promote seeing themselves as American rather than as white.

Although it is plausible to argue that self-identification affects how people interpret the treatment of their group (in which case a panethnic identity would cause perceptions of discrimination rather than the other way around), the reactive ethnicity argument posited and documented in the literature concentrates on the causal arrow linking treatment to identity, hence the modifier "reactive." Panel data collected and analyzed by Portes and Rumbaut (2001) offer particularly compelling evidence to support this perspective. Moreover, panethnic labels such as Latino and Asian only exist in the United States and need to be learned. For the first generation in particular, the panethnic identifier logically cannot precede perceptions of treatment, which can form on a person's first day in the country. Many psychology experiments have confirmed that the manipulation of discrimination produces ties with the stigmatized group (e.g., Jetten et al. 2001), in line with the expectations of social identity theory (Tajfel 1982; Tajfel and Turner 1986). Simultaneous modeling by Branscombe and colleagues confirms that the "perceptions of discrimination lead to identification" argument is more powerful than the "identification leads to perceptions of discrimination" argument (Branscombe, Schmitt, and Harvey 1999; Schmitt and Branscombe 2002; also see Chong and Kim 2006). Once such identifications are in place, they can make the attribution of outcomes to discrimination more likely in ambiguous situations (Major, Quinton, and Schmader 2003). However, if a panethnic identity largely shaped perceptions of treatment rather than the other way around, then that identity should also have an independent influence on other political outcomes, such as feelings toward the U.S. government. I show in Chapter 6, however, that this influence largely does not exist.

I examine predictors of identity attachment for each panethnic category (Latinos, Asians, blacks, and whites) separately (results for the full sample can be found in Appendix C). The first set of independent variables consists of standard demographic measures (education, age, and gender). The second set consists of two items aimed at capturing acculturation: generation (first through fourth or more) and whether the respondent primarily speaks English in the home.[12] The third set consists of the three discrimination scales. Next, I added a variable measuring the percentage of residents in the respondent's Zip Code

---

[12] Citizenship is not included as an independent variable based on the arguments of de la Garza, Falcon, and Garcia (1996). According to these scholars, three factors reduce the utility of citizenship as an independent variable in this case: the high correlation between citizenship and nativity/generational status (here, 0.57 between citizenship and generation), the lack of eligibility of some immigrants for citizenship (a status that is not gauged in the 21-CAS), and the questionable ability of citizenship status to differentiate commitment levels to the United

that shares the respondent's panethnic category (e.g., for Latinos, I included the percentage of residents in the Zip Code that are Latino). This demographic information was included in order to examine the concern that living among coethnics could heighten a person's sense of solidarity with that group, thus making a panethnic identification more likely. I call this the "enclave critique." In the model with Asian respondents I also included a dummy variable for people of Japanese or Chinese ancestry (n = 151), because both national origin groups have a much longer history of immigration to the United States than other Asian groups (Lien, Conway, and Wong 2004). This history – which includes important events in American history such as the Chinese Exclusion Act, the building of the Transcontinental Railroad, and internment and military service during World War II – might result in unique effects that are not simply captured by a control for generational status.[13] Likewise, in the model for Latinos, I included a dummy variable for people of Mexican ancestry (n = 219). Given the prominence of Mexicans among Latinos in the United States, Mexican respondents may have a greater tendency to identify with the national origin group relative to other Latinos.

I investigated the relationship between these factors and self-identification using a multinomial logit model because the dependent variable consists of three nonordinal categories: American, panethnic, and national origin. The results appear in Table 5.2 (for Latinos and Asians) and Table 5.3 (for blacks and whites). The base category is "American," which means that the coefficients in each column should be interpreted as the impact of the independent variable on the likelihood of identifying as a member of one's national origin group or one's panethnic group versus as American. For example, the negative coefficients on age in Table 5.2 mean that older Latinos and Asians are less likely than younger Latinos and Asians to identify primarily with the panethnic group or the national origin group and are more likely to identify primarily as American.

Latinos. In the case of Latinos, identity attachment is primarily about acculturation. First-generation respondents are significantly less likely to identify as American than respondents in subsequent generations. Figure 5.1 displays the predicted probabilities for each identity choice across each generation (for a Mexican male who primarily speaks English in the home).[14] In the first generation, all identity types are equally likely, around 33 percent. But by the fourth generation, the probability of identifying primarily as American increases to 78 percent while the probabilities of identifying with the national origin group

States among native-born citizens, naturalized citizens, and immigrants who want to naturalize but have not yet done so.

[13] The correlation between the generation control and the Chinese/Japanese dummy variable (among Asian respondents only) is 0.09. The model was also run without the Chinese/Japanese dummy variable; all substantive results remain the same.

[14] Predicted probabilities are calculated using CLARIFY, holding all nondummy variables constant at their means for Latinos (King, Tomz, and Wittenberg 2000).

TABLE 5.2. *Determinants of Identity Prioritization, Latinos and Asians, Multinomial Logit*

Independent Variable	Latinos		Asians	
	Country of Origin	Panethnic	Country of Origin	Panethnic
Education	−0.55	−0.45	0.90	−0.20
	(0.52)	(0.68)	(0.63)	(0.76)
Age	−1.35*	−2.68**	−1.78**	−2.69**
	(0.82)	(0.98)	(0.91)	(1.14)
Male	−0.84**	−1.15**	−0.05	−0.29
	(0.30)	(0.37)	(0.33)	(0.44)
Generation (1st to 4th+)	−1.72**	−2.34**	−4.36**	−0.62
	(0.50)	(0.58)	(1.22)	(1.14)
Speaks primarily English at home	−1.28**	−0.73	−1.26**	−1.14**
	(0.43)	(0.47)	(0.36)	(0.52)
Perception of panethnic discrimination	−0.18	−0.84	−0.92	−0.75
	(0.64)	(0.81)	(0.88)	(1.29)
Perception of national origin discrimination	0.71	0.74	0.78	1.63
	(0.56)	(0.76)	(0.87)	(1.17)
Perception of individual-level discrimination	0.42	0.97*	1.42**	1.87**
	(0.47)	(0.52)	(0.62)	(0.80)
Mexican	0.29	0.53	–	–
	(0.32)	(0.40)	–	–
Chinese or Japanese	–	–	0.10	−0.53
	–	–	(0.33)	(0.46)
Percent Latino in respondent's Zip Code	−0.06	−0.53	–	–
	(0.59)	(0.73)	–	–
Percent Asian in respondent's Zip Code	–	–	−1.71	0.44
	–	–	(1.19)	(1.36)
Constant	1.10*	1.21*	0.94	−0.15
	(0.59)	(0.74)	(0.66)	(0.82)
N	361		235	
Chi-squared	113.05		61.59	

Note: ** $p < 0.05$; * $p < 0.1$. Standard errors in parentheses. All nondummy variables coded 0 to 1. Unweighted data. The base category is American.
Source: Twenty-First-Century Americanism Survey, 2004.

and with the panethnic group drop to 13 percent and 9 percent, respectively. More importantly, Figure 5.1 also shows that by the second generation, just under a majority of Latino respondents (49%) are predicted to identify primarily as American.[15] The other measure of acculturation in the model, speaking

---

[15] The model was also run with generational status as a series of dummy variables, with the fourth generation (or more) as the omitted category, in order to see if the straight-line model of acculturation implied by a single scale variable is misguided. For Latinos, the only significant dummy variable was that of the first generation, suggesting that the most noteworthy difference is between the immigrant generation and everyone else.

TABLE 5.3. *Determinants of Identity Prioritization, Blacks and Whites, Multinomial Logit*

Independent Variable	Blacks		Whites	
	Country of Origin	Panethnic	Country of Origin	Panethnic
Education	1.17	−0.45	−0.27	−0.40
	(0.91)	(0.49)	(0.58)	(0.41)
Age	−0.07	−1.34*	−2.60**	−3.08**
	(1.27)	(0.71)	(0.95)	(0.54)
Male	1.09**	−0.02	−0.60	−0.72**
	(0.55)	(0.28)	(0.38)	(0.24)
Generation (1st to 4th+)	−3.16**	−0.02	−2.77**	0.14
	(0.72)	(0.68)	(0.48)	(0.57)
Speaks primarily English at home	−0.54	−1.29	−0.44	−1.24*
	(1.26)	(1.07)	(0.53)	(0.69)
Perception of panethnic discrimination	0.29	0.19	−1.30*	−0.48
	(1.72)	(0.69)	(0.68)	(0.50)
Perception of national origin discrimination	−1.03	0.07	0.78	0.12
	(1.19)	(0.52)	(0.66)	(0.56)
Perception of individual-level discrimination	1.90**	0.64	1.67**	0.44
	(0.92)	(0.53)	(0.79)	(0.63)
Percent black in respondent's Zip Code	1.81	−0.01	–	–
	(1.14)	(0.51)	–	–
Percent white in respondent's Zip Code	–	–	−0.09	0.19
	–	–	(0.87)	(0.52)
Constant	−1.49	1.20	0.78	0.26
	(1.58)	(0.96)	(0.98)	(0.69)
N	253		1172	
Chi-squared	48.24		126.84	

Note: ** p < 0.05; * p < 0.1. Standard errors in parentheses. All nondummy variables coded 0 to 1. Unweighted data. The base category is American.
Source: Twenty-First-Century Americanism Survey, 2004.

primarily English in the home, likewise promotes an American identity over a national origin identity but is an insignificant factor in the American versus Latino model. Acculturation thus works as hypothesized with respect to national origin attachments, and it diminishes panethnic attachments as well, though only with respect to generational status.

Notably, perceptions of mistreatment are largely insignificant for Latinos. The only significant finding in this regard is that the perception of individual-level discrimination makes a Latino identity more likely than an American identity, underscoring the personal nature of reactive ethnicity. Figure 5.2 displays the predicted probabilities for each identity choice as the individual-level discrimination scale increases from 0 to 1 (using the same controls mentioned previously). Although the probability of identifying with the national origin

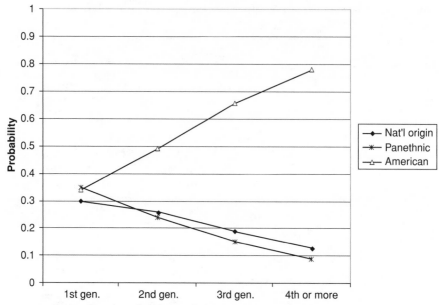

FIGURE 5.1. Predicted probabilities of identity prioritization for Latinos across generations. *Source:* Twenty-First-Century Americanism Survey, 2004.

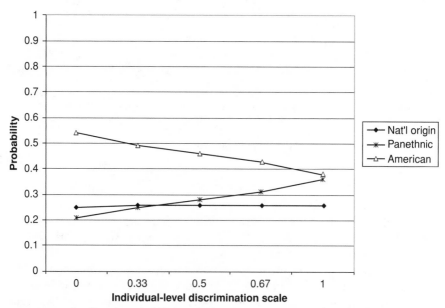

FIGURE 5.2. Predicted probabilities of identity prioritization for Latinos across perceptions of individual-level discrimination. *Source:* Twenty-First-Century Americanism Survey, 2004.

group stays flat at 26 percent, the probability of identifying as Latino increases from 21 percent to 36 percent. The probability of identifying as American, however, decreases from 54 percent to 38 percent.[16]

Though perceptions of personal mistreatment are not as common as perceptions of panethnic mistreatment, the former are a potent influence on panethnic identity prioritization, as hypothesized. Roughly 22 percent of the Latino respondents score at or above the midpoint on the individual-level discrimination scale, indicating that a nontrivial portion of the Latino population might be turned away from thinking of oneself primarily as American and driven to panethnicity due to the perception that one has personally been mistreated in the United States due to his or her race or ethnicity.

Finally, in direct contrast to some common critiques, being Mexican and living among other Latinos do not increase the likelihood of prioritizing either type of non-American identity.

Asians. As with Latinos, acculturation is a powerful influence over identity prioritization for Asian respondents. Speaking a language other than English in the home makes identifying primarily as Asian or with one's national origin group more likely than identifying primarily as American. One's generational status is an especially powerful force increasing the likelihood of identifying as American instead of with one's national origin group but does not influence the American versus Asian trade-off. Figure 5.3 displays the probability of a male non-Chinese/Japanese respondent who speaks primarily English in the home (with all nondummy variables held at their means for Asians) prioritizing each of the three identity types across generations. Moving from the first to the fourth generation impressively decreases the likelihood of identifying primarily with one's national origin group from 38 percent to 2 percent and increases the likelihood of identifying primarily as American from 49 percent to 83 percent. The probability of identifying as Asian stays at roughly 16 percent across generations.[17] Panethnicity is thus not acquired simply through time spent in the United States. The diversity of languages and national origins among Asian immigrants likely render the panethnic identity especially difficult to prioritize.

The results in Table 5.2 and in Figure 5.4 – which shows the probabilities associated with different identity choices while the perception of individual-level discrimination goes from 0 to 1 – indicate that only once perceptions

[16] Rerunning the model without people who initially identified racially as something other than Latino produces only one difference of note (besides a drop from n = 361 to n = 236), individual-level discrimination becomes an even more powerful determinant of panethnicity. The coefficient becomes larger and more significant.

[17] The model for Asians using generational dummy variables instead of a single generation variable shows that the most noteworthy difference is between the first generation and everyone else when it comes to choosing a national origin identity over an American identity. As in the model in Table 5.2, the generational dummies are insignificant in predicting panethnicity.

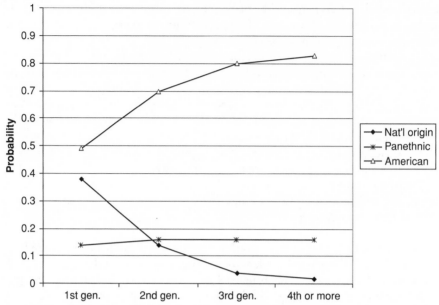

FIGURE 5.3. Predicted probabilities of identity prioritization for Asians across generations. *Source:* Twenty-First-Century Americanism Survey, 2004.

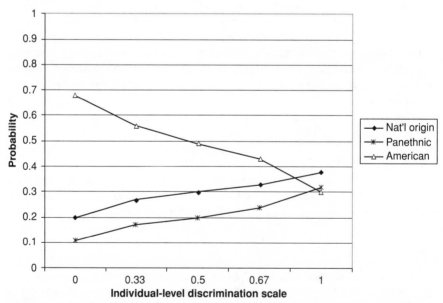

FIGURE 5.4. Predicted probabilities of identity prioritization for Asians across perceptions of individual-level discrimination. *Source:* Twenty-First-Century Americanism Survey, 2004.

of individual-level mistreatment emerge does panethnicity increase. When a person moves from 0 to 1 on the individual-level discrimination scale, his chances of identifying as Asian and with his national origin group increase, while his chances of identifying as American decrease precipitously from 68 percent to 30 percent. Although personal mistreatment makes panethnicity more common, it is important to point out that a national origin attachment is more likely than a panethnic one at every point on the discrimination scale in Figure 5.2. Roughly 22 percent of Asian respondents score at or above the midpoint on the individual-level discrimination scale, indicating that, as with Latinos, a nontrivial portion of the Asian American population might be turned away from thinking of oneself primarily as American due to the perception that one has personally been mistreated in the United States due to his or her race or ethnicity.

Finally, as with Latinos, "enclave living" fails to influence identity prioritization (also see Lien, Conway, and Wong 2004).

Blacks. For the majority of blacks, national origin ties are difficult to distinguish from panethnic ties because the overwhelming majority of blacks in the United States have been here for generations and are unable to specify a particular country of origin. Eighty-nine percent of black respondents in the 21-CAS are fourth generation or more, and when asked about where their ancestors are from, nearly all black respondents said either Africa (49%) or the United States (29%). Only six black respondents named a specific country in Africa. Thus, for many blacks, the process of prioritizing a national origin identity (African) over an American identity might be essentially the same as the process of prioritizing a panethnic identity (African American) over an American identity. The first column of the multinomial results for blacks (Table 5.3) should therefore be examined with such confounding in mind.

One would think that perceptions of discrimination are potent predictors of self-identification among blacks, but it turns out that only one measure mattered: perceiving individual-level discrimination makes black respondents more likely to think of themselves in terms of their national origin (African, for most respondents) than as American. Likewise, the closer a black respondent is to the immigrant experience, the more likely he or she is to identify with the national origin group than as American.[18]

Why don't perceptions of mistreatment register as determinants of panethnicity for blacks? Though not what I expected, I have two admittedly post hoc speculations. The first is that perceptions of discrimination against blacks are just so common that they yield little explanatory power in this sample. Fully 90 percent of the black respondents score at the midpoint or higher on the panethnic discrimination scale. Only eight black respondents scored a 0. The second is that perceptions of discrimination might have the power to lead

---

[18] Using generational dummy variables indicates that the significant difference here is between the first generation and everyone else.

blacks to reject even the "American" modifier on "African American" and instead promote seeing oneself primarily as just African.

Whites. The results for white respondents suggest that panethnicity and Americanness are interchangeable for many whites. First, only two variables are significant at the 95 percent level in the white versus American model, with older and male respondents less likely than younger and female respondents to identify primarily as American than as white. Second, no type of perceived discrimination affects whether whites identify as American or as white. Perceived discrimination against whites does, however, make whites less likely to identify with their national origin group (e.g., Polish, Italian, German) and more likely to identify as American. If whiteness and Americanness were distinct constructs, then panethnic discrimination would promote attachment to the panethnic group, but it does not. Perceiving mistreatment against whites evokes an American attachment not a racial one. Likewise, the perception of individual-level discrimination due to one's race or ethnicity would promote a sense of whiteness if whiteness and Americanness were distinct, but it does not. Instead, whites who perceive that their race or ethnicity has been a source of discrimination look to the more unique and useful marker of national origin. As Waters writes, whites look to the national origin group for a sense of individuality and commonality (1990). Moreover, whites who say they have felt this type of discrimination might be saying that they have felt ethnic mistreatment due to being Irish, Italian, and so forth, rather than mistreatment due to being white, in which case an increased attachment to that group makes sense from a social identity theory perspective (see Devos and Banaji [2005] for more about the cognitive connections between Americanness and whiteness, especially among whites).

It is important, however, to remember that the vast majority of whites in the sample identify primarily as American, regardless of their perception of any type of discrimination. Moving from 0 to 1 on the individual-level discrimination scale (for a male respondent who speaks English in the home) decreases the likelihood of identifying as American from 89 percent to 76 percent. Conversely, moving from 0 to 1 on the panethnic discrimination scale increases the likelihood of identifying as American from 87 percent to 92 percent. Although such shifts are noteworthy, so is the fact that so many Americans continue to identify as American at every level of perceived discrimination. The 21-CAS shows, in short, that the kind of resentment and perceived victimization displayed in the *Sun-Sentinel* discussion board are not as widespread as such anecdotes might have us believe, but that when such sentiments are felt, they have the potential to promote nationalistic sentiment (feeling American) rather than an explicitly white racial identity.

ADDITIONAL TESTS

As a complimentary examination, I ran a multinomial logit model predicting identity prioritization using the 2002 KFF/PHC survey of Latinos, which asked

TABLE 5.4. *Strength of Identification, by Race, OLS*

Independent Variable	Country of Origin		Latino/Hispanic	
	b	s.e.	b	s.e.
Perception of panethnic discrimination	0.24	0.30	1.32**	0.31
Perception of individual-level discrimination	−0.38	0.41	0.07	0.44
Generation (1st to 3rd+)	−2.35**	0.21	−1.10**	0.23
Speaks English well	−2.17**	0.51	−2.18**	0.55
Education	−1.00**	0.25	−0.56**	0.28
Age	−1.24**	0.35	−1.48**	0.41
Gender (1 = female)	0.26*	0.15	0.36**	0.16
Income	0.36	0.33	−0.10	0.37
Constant	0.16	0.27	−1.44**	0.32
N	1286		1286	
Chi-squared	363.09		363.09	

Note: ** $p < 0.05$; * $p < 0.1$. For all nondummy variables: mean = 0; range = 1. The base category is American.
Source: KFF/PHC 2002 Survey of Latinos.

respondents if they have ever described themselves as American, as Latino, or in terms of their country of origin, and then asked them which term they use to describe themselves first. The results, which appear in Table 5.4, largely replicate the findings from the 21-CAS. In particular, being past the first generation and claiming to speak English well both increase the likelihood of identifying primarily as American. The one discrepancy between the two data sets involves perceptions of discrimination. In the KFF/PHC survey, people who feel that Latinos as a group are discriminated against are more likely to identify as Latino than as American, although perceptions of personal mistreatment did not matter. In the 21-CAS, individual-level perceptions were the more potent form of discrimination for Latinos. Yet in both cases, the identity that was promoted was the panethnic one.

Finally, in order to account for the fact that many respondents said they do think of themselves as American at least some of the time, the analysis of the 21-CAS was rerun comparing respondents who *ever* think of themselves as American (n = 2,551) with respondents who *never* do (n = 238; results not shown). When run for the entire sample as well as for nonwhites only, the results replicate the findings in Tables 5.2 and 5.3. In particular, generation, language use, and the perception of individual-level discrimination all influence whether a person adopts or rejects an American identity.

SUMMARY

Thus far, there is little evidence to support the claims of immigration critics described at the outset of this chapter, and there is significant evidence to calm fears that immigrants and their descendants are unlikely to think of themselves as American or increasingly unlikely to do so as they spend more time here. Most respondents prioritize an American identity, regardless of their background. Immigrants and people who do not speak English have strong national origin attachments, but subsequent generations adopt an American identity rapidly. National origin attachments are affected by acculturation more than panethnic attachments for Latino, Asian, and black respondents, as expected. In some cases, panethnic attachments decrease with acculturation as well.

Research on acculturation consistently shows that immigrants and their descendants continue to learn English at great speed, and that people from the second generation forward are far more likely to speak only English in the home than they are to speak some other language. Such patterns of English acquisition hold across the three national censuses from 1980 to 2000 and may have even sped up during that time (Alba and Nee 2003; Citrin et al. 2007). Alba and Nee also find that the second generation tends to surpass the immigrant generation in terms of educational attainment and in the acquisition of professional and managerial employment (2003). Added to this socioeconomic data, I find little evidence that we need to be concerned about people living among coethnics. Even though 33 percent of Latino respondents live in Zip Codes that are 50 percent Latino or more, they are no less likely to reject an American identity than other Latinos. The percentage of coethnics in one's Zip Code is insignificant in every model in Tables 5.2 and 5.3. On the question of whether the rejection of an American identity is going to become more common as the nation continues to welcome new immigrants, the answer appears to be no.

But identifying as American is not just an innocuous process that happens with time and with English acquisition. The perception of individual-level discrimination consistently decreases the likelihood of identifying as American for Latinos, Asians, and blacks. For Latinos, such perceptions promote panethnicity, as hypothesized. For Asians, they promote panethnicity and national origin attachments. For blacks, they promote national origin (most likely "African") attachments. For whites too, the perception that one's ethnicity is a source of mistreatment increases attachments to that ethnicity. The only case in which group-level perceptions matter is for whites, who become more likely to identify as American if they feel that whites are mistreated.

Despite these statistically significant patterns, I find few substantively significant differences between panethnic and national origin identifications, except in the case of whites. However, I also ran the model of identity prioritization separately for the U.S. born and for the foreign born (results not shown) and found, like Lien, Conway, and Wong (2004), that perceptions of mistreatment lead the U.S. born to prioritize a panethnic identity whereas they lead the foreign born to adopt a national origin identity. In that sense, concerns that immigrants align with panethnic groups are inaccurate. Rather, perceptions of mistreatment for immigrants hinder broader group ties of any sort, keeping existing national origin ties strong. Instead, it is the U.S.-born children and grandchildren of immigrants who prioritize the panethnic group over being American in the face of discrimination.

In the end, experiencing life in the United States can both help and hurt the process of coming to see oneself primarily as American. On the one hand, acculturation promotes an American identity. On the other hand, being at the receiving end of discrimination in the United States can offset the gains made through acculturation. The question then becomes: to what extent are perceptions of discrimination promoted by the acculturation process, such as whether one is first or fourth generation, or whether one is able to interact with mainstream American society in English? This chapter has found that perceptions of individual-level treatment are particularly potent. The remainder of the chapter explores where such perceptions come from.

Predicting Perceptions of Discrimination

Because perceptions of individual-level mistreatment can offset the "Americanization" gains made through acculturation, it is important to investigate whether such perceptions stem from politically relevant phenomena related to debates about immigration. Although many studies examine the role that perceptions of discrimination play on a variety of personal and political outcomes, few studies examine their origins.

Some scholars speculate that socioeconomic background or economic perceptions might make perceptions of mistreatment more likely. Studies of "linked fate" investigate such claims in which the conventional wisdom that economic status should overcome a sense of racial group interest is challenged (Dawson 1994). It makes sense to think that perceptions of mistreatment would diminish as individuals in the group begin to experience economic and educational success. However, successful members of disadvantaged groups might be more likely than others to be aware of the limits of racial progress, either due to their educational attainment or through their own experiences in environments traditionally occupied by "the good old boys" in which they may encounter an ethnic glass ceiling. Thus, although economic perceptions and educational status might influence perceptions of mistreatment, it is not clear whether they render such perceptions more or less likely. Dawson (1994) found that blacks with higher levels of education were more likely than other blacks to think that blacks are economically subordinate to whites, suggesting the former. Yet little is known about how individual social mobility affects perceptions of discrimination among Latinos and Asians, although one study finds that higher-income Asians perceive more linked fate and that education enhances linked fate for Latinos (Masuoka 2006).

As for perceptions of the economy, sociotropic concerns (concerns about the nation as a whole) have traditionally been more influential over public opinion toward policies and groups than toward personal concerns. The power of sociotropic perceptions relative to personal ones not only holds true for general matters, such as presidential elections, but also for immigration-related public opinion, in which a pessimistic economic outlook is associated with a preference for reduced immigration (Citrin et al. 1997; Fetzer 2000). In the present analysis, thinking that the national economy is in trouble might make people think that discrimination is more common due to efforts by those with higher status to maintain their now-tenuous position. Likewise, people who are suffering economically might think that their situation is a product of mistreatment.

Some research speculates that time spent in the United States makes perceptions of discrimination more common (Michelson 2003), yet few studies provide an explicit test. Michelson, for example, finds that trust in government declines among Mexicans with acculturation but is unable to determine if the decline is because acculturation makes perceptions of discrimination more common or because, through acculturation, Mexicans become just like other Americans who typically distrust the federal government.

Psychologists have investigated whether some people are simply more likely than others to interpret situations, such as a poor grade or the denial of a reward, as resulting from discrimination than from some other factor. Much of this work focuses on the ambiguity of the particular situation (a factor that is manipulated experimentally) or on psychological factors such as depression, self-esteem, the need for approval, and the need for control rather than on politically relevant individual-level predispositions such as social class or immigration experience (Kobrynowicz and Branscombe 1997; Schmitt and Branscombe 2002; Sechrist, Swim, and Stangor 2004).[19] In these studies, in which the degree of ambiguity of the situation is a consistently powerful determinant of the attribution of outcomes to discrimination, the dependent variable is discrimination against the self, not the group.

PREDICTING PERCEPTIONS OF DISCRIMINATION

The analyses that follow are admittedly more exploratory than those in the previous section. The 21-CAS does not include measures of depression, self-esteem, the fear of being disliked, or other psychological variables that have been shown to shape discrimination perceptions. Rather, the goals are to see whether acculturation promotes perceptions of mistreatment and how acculturation compares to other potentially relevant predictors, such as personal and sociotropic economic concerns. I am interested in learning about where discrimination perceptions originate for whites as well as for nonwhites.

Before launching into the multivariate analysis, it is first useful to examine patterns of discrimination perceptions in the sample. Table 5.5 shows bivariate breakdowns along theoretically relevant characteristics. As with the full sample, the disjuncture between group-level and individual-level discrimination holds for all categories, and in every case, panethnic discrimination is seen

---

[19] This research reports that low self-esteem, depression, and the need for control make perceptions of discrimination more likely and that the need for approval makes such perceptions less likely.

TABLE 5.5. *Perceptions of Discrimination, Mean*

	Panethnic	National Origin	Personal	n (raw)
White	0.29	0.11	0.07	1,589
Black	0.74	0.61	0.46	281
Asian	0.47	0.42	0.24	276
Latino	0.57	0.49	0.25	422
U.S. citizen	0.39	0.26	0.15	2,435
Not a U.S. citizen	0.55	0.47	0.28	249
1st generation	0.52	0.43	0.24	530
2nd generation	0.47	0.33	0.14	166
3rd generation	0.32	0.19	0.15	175
4th generation or more	0.38	0.23	0.14	1,765
Speaks primarily English at home	0.38	0.24	0.15	2,281
Speaks another language at home	0.56	0.48	0.27	404
Employed	0.40	0.27	0.16	2,586
Unemployed	0.45	0.38	0.22	214
National economy gotten better	0.35	0.21	0.12	761
National economy stayed same	0.39	0.27	0.13	676
National economy gotten worse	0.44	0.32	0.21	1,308

Note: n = unweighted.

Source: Twenty-First-Century Americanism Survey, 2004.

as more common than national origin discrimination. Across all three types of discrimination, nonwhites perceive more discrimination than whites. Discrimination seems to level off after the first generation, and people who speak a language other than English in the home perceive more discrimination than people who speak only English. People who are unemployed or think that the national economy has gotten worse perceive more of all kinds of discrimination than people who are employed or are more optimistic about the national economy.[20]

I first examined predictors of perceptions of discrimination among the full sample. The results (in Appendix C) indicated that race was among the most powerful determinants, with Latinos, Asians, and blacks significantly more likely than whites to perceive all three types of discrimination. With race being such a significant predictor, it makes sense to analyze discrimination perceptions for nonwhites and for whites separately. The models for nonwhites have

---

[20] Re-creating Table 5.5 without people who initially identified racially as something other than Latino increases the mean level of panethnic discrimination to 0.61, the mean level of national origin discrimination to 0.54, and the mean level of individual-level discrimination to 0.27. Re-creating the table without people who initially identified racially as Asian increases the mean level of individual-level discrimination to 0.27 while the other levels of discrimination remain the same.

TABLE 5.6. *Determinants of Perceptions of Discrimination, Nonwhites, OLS*

Independent Variable	Against Panethnic Group		Against National Origin Group		Against Self Personally	
	b	s.e.	b	s.e.	b	s.e.
Education	0.05	0.04	−0.06	0.04	0.01	0.04
Age	0.04	0.05	0.08	0.06	0.19**	0.07
Male	−0.01	0.02	−0.01	0.03	0.03	0.03
Asian	−0.35**	0.04	−0.21**	0.05	−0.22**	0.05
Latino	−0.21**	0.03	−0.15**	0.03	−0.20**	0.34
Generation (1st to 4th+)	−0.02	0.04	0.02	0.04	0.06	0.04
Speaks primarily English at home	−0.11**	0.03	−0.11**	0.04	−0.10**	0.04
Unemployed	0.02	0.04	0.06	0.04	0.01	0.04
National economy gotten worse	0.10**	0.03	0.08**	0.03	0.10**	0.03
Constant	0.75**	0.04	0.63**	0.05	0.33**	0.05
N	734		668		735	
F	16.60		7.27		10.41	
R-squared	0.17		0.08		0.11	

Note: ** $p < 0.05$; * $p < 0.1$. All nondummy variables coded 0 to 1.
Source: Twenty-First-Century Americanism Survey, 2004.

three sets of independent variables. The first set consists of the standard demographic measures used earlier (education, age, gender, and race – with "black" as the omitted category). The second set consists of the two acculturation measures used earlier (generation and whether the respondent primarily speaks English in the home). The third consists of one individual-level economic consideration (whether the respondent is unemployed) and one sociotropic economic consideration (whether the respondent thinks the national economy has gotten worse during the past year, stayed the same, or gotten better). Note that educational attainment, though listed here as a demographic control, is also a measure of socioeconomic status theorized to shape discrimination perceptions for class-based reasons. As before, all nondummy variables are coded to range from 0 to 1. The models for each type of discrimination perception are estimated using ordinary least squares (OLS). The results appear in Table 5.6.

Perhaps the most noteworthy finding is that acculturation does not promote perceptions of discrimination. Generational status is insignificant across all three models, and speaking English, which integrates one into mainstream American society, consistently lowers the likelihood of thinking that oneself or one's group is mistreated.[21] Thinking that the national economy is

---

[21] Generational status just barely achieves significance at the 90% level when the models predicting national origin and individual-level discrimination in Table 5.6 are rerun without respondents who were recoded for panethnicity. The coefficient in both cases is positive, suggesting that this aspect of acculturation might lead to greater perceptions of discrimination for some people. The coefficients on the primary languages spoken at home, however, remain negative and

suffering does promote perceptions of mistreatment across the board. Perhaps poor economic conditions result in ambiguous situations that enable attributions to discrimination to become more likely. Being unemployed, however, is insignificant. Education is also insignificant, though it was plausibly theorized to potentially have either a positive or a negative effect. Not surprisingly, blacks perceive more discrimination than Latinos or Asians.

It is also noteworthy that the sizes and the magnitudes of the coefficients in Table 5.6 are similar across all three models. This suggests first – along with the findings from the previous section – that panethnic and national origin identities might be more similar than is typically acknowledged. The more theoretically interesting distinction thus far remains comparing perceptions about how the group is treated versus perceptions about how oneself is treated. It also suggests that despite the different role group- and individual-level perceptions play with regard to identity prioritization, and despite the differing levels of these types of discrimination perceptions, they are driven by the same sets of factors.

Additional models were run predicting perceptions of discrimination for Latinos, Asians, and blacks separately (results not shown). The general trends discussed thus far remain. For Latinos, people of Mexican ancestry were not different from other Latinos when it comes to perceiving discrimination against Latinos, but Mexicans were more likely to think that their national origin group is mistreated than other Latinos. Replication using the 2002 KFF/PHC survey (results not shown) also yielded similar results, with acculturation reducing panethnic discrimination (and not influencing individual-level discrimination), and a pessimistic economic outlook increasing group- and individual-level perceptions of mistreatment.[22]

For Asians, acculturation reduced perceptions of group-level discrimination and was insignificant for individual-level discrimination. Sociotropic concerns increased perceptions of individual-level but not group-level discrimination. Replication using the PNAAPS (which has a measure of individual-level discrimination only) confirms that acculturation does not generate perceptions of mistreatment (results not shown). In that replication, the U.S. born were less likely than the foreign born to report mistreatment and language use was insignificant.[23]

Analyzing discrimination perceptions for blacks yielded the only case in which evidence emerges to support the linked-fate contention that education promotes awareness of the group, its history, its treatment, and experience with the limitations of progress. Higher levels of education resulted in a greater likelihood of perceiving panethnic and individual-level discrimination. Here

insignificant in all three models. When all three models are rerun with generational dummy variables, all dummy variables are insignificant at the 95% level in each model.

[22] Independent variables used in this replication were education, age, gender, generational status, language spoken at home, perception of personal economic situation, and whether the respondent is unemployed.

[23] Independent variables used in this replication were age, education, gender, whether the respondent was born in the United States, and whether the respondent primarily speaks English.

TABLE 5.7. *Determinants of Perceptions of Discrimination, Whites Only, OLS*

Independent Variable	Against Panethnic Group		Against National Origin Group		Against Self Personally	
	b	s.e.	b	s.e.	b	s.e.
Education	−0.17**	0.02	−0.16**	0.02	−0.02	0.01
Age	0.05*	0.03	0.002	0.03	−0.07**	0.02
Male	0.01	0.02	−0.02*	0.01	0.04**	0.01
Generation (1 to 4+)	0.01	0.03	−0.02	0.03	−0.02	0.02
Speaks primarily English at home	0.01	0.05	−0.01	0.04	−0.02	0.04
Unemployed	0.004	0.03	0.001	0.03	0.02	0.02
National economy gotten worse	−0.01	0.02	0.01	0.01	0.03**	0.01
Percent white in respondent's Zip Code	−0.05	0.03	−0.02	0.03	−0.04**	0.02
Constant	0.36**	0.05	0.25**	0.05	0.14**	0.04
N	1537		1193		1545	
F	6.54		7.42		5.46	
R-squared	0.03		0.05		0.03	

Note: ** p < 0.05; * p < 0.1. All nondummy variables coded 0 to 1. Unweighted data.
Source: Twenty-First-Century Americanism Survey, 2004.

too, however, the sense of one's own treatment and the treatment of the group were also tied to perceptions of the economy. In all three models, thinking the economy is doing worse led to more perceptions of discrimination.

Thus, although there are some minor differences when each ethnic group is analyzed separately, the general picture still holds, with acculturation either being insignificant or making perceptions of discrimination less common, and with a pessimistic economic outlook making such perceptions more common.

Table 5.7 shows the results for models run with white respondents only. Here the percentage of residents in the respondent's Zip Code that is white was added to the model in order to examine if living in a diverse area makes the traditional majority feel like it is losing out. In the group-level models, the only notable predictor is education, with higher levels reducing the likelihood of perceiving mistreatment. At the individual level, however, a different picture emerges. Younger and male respondents perceive more individual-level discrimination than older and female respondents. People who think the national economy has gotten worse also see more individual-level discrimination, as do whites who live in Zip Codes with lower percentages of whites. Individual employment status is insignificant.[24]

---

[24] For whites, using generational dummy variables shows that the first generation is more likely than other generations to perceive national origin discrimination and individual-level discrimination.

Although there is difficulty predicting why some whites feel that whites as a group are mistreated, the individual-level model suggests that there is some truth to the image of the angry white male who feels under siege amid increasing diversity. The case of hostile South Floridians posting rants about bilingualism in response to a *Sun-Sentinel* report might be generalizable after all.

SUMMARY

The central finding of this section is that acculturation does not promote feelings of victimization. Though I recognize that panel data would enable this claim to be made more forcefully, the evidence from this and other cross-sectional surveys consistently shows that when controlling for other factors, one's generational status has no impact on perceptions of discrimination, and becoming integrated into mainstream American society through the use of English makes perceptions of treatment better not worse. Simply being a member of a non-white panethnic group renders all three types of discrimination perceptions more common, but few distinctions within each panethnic group were found.

One consistent finding is that the fate of one's group and of oneself is often seen as tied to the fate of the national economy. A person's sense of how the national economy is doing, however, is a perception that is not racially tinged. In the 21-CAS, whites were more likely than nonwhites to think the national economy has improved, but a plurality of whites, blacks, Asians, and Latinos all felt that it had gotten worse.

Together, these findings lead me to conclude that perceptions of discrimination are driven more by the factors established in the psychological literature (and not measured here), such as the ambiguity of the situation and self-esteem, than by the politically relevant factors explored here. It is quite possible that difficult economic times generate the kind of ambiguous situations that lead people to become more likely to attribute negative outcomes to discrimination. This possibility cannot be tested here but is worth contemplating in future research. It could also very well be the case that perceptions of discrimination, particularly at the individual level, are driven by actually experiencing discrimination, and the fact remains that nonwhites are simply more likely to have such experiences than whites. Actual discrimination, however, is impossible to measure in a public opinion survey.

CONCLUSION

Despite finding no evidence to support the claim that people are increasingly reluctant to think of themselves first and foremost as American and despite finding that the adoption of an American identity is promoted primarily by acculturation, I do not end this chapter ready to dismiss the concerns that immigration critics, democratic theorists, and social psychologists raise. Their concerns regarding self-identification are instrumental in nature. Identity attachment matters, it is argued, because it affects one's relationship to American political institutions and to other Americans. Whether this argument is true still needs to be assessed, and such an assessment is the focus of Chapter 6.

Moreover, though national origin and panethnic attachments seem to operate similarly so far, the two non-American identity types might not be similar in their effects. The conventional wisdom is that they are not, with panethnic attachments creating more of an oppositional and adversarial stance toward American society than national origin attachments. This possibility also needs to be assessed. The main case thus far in which those identities are not similar is with respect to whites. For whites, perceptions of panethnic-level mistreatment are not widespread, but when present, they create a nationalistic response more than attachment to whiteness.

I am thus only partially ready to answer some of the questions raised by Paloma's assertion that she does not feel American even though she was born in the United States. One question was whether Paloma's feelings are widespread. In terms of simply thinking of oneself as American, I find that there are certainly large numbers of people out there who do not, but the majority does. Of those that do not, they become increasingly likely to do so as they learn English, and their children and grandchildren are significantly more likely to do so as well. Moreover, a majority of people that do not think of themselves primarily as American still think of themselves as American some of the time. Regarding the question of whether the patterns of identity attachment portend a future with fewer and fewer Americans thinking of themselves primarily as American, I therefore conclude that the answer is no, at least when looking at the power of acculturation.

Another question Paloma's comment raised was whether factors that drive differing patterns of identity prioritization are troubling. Regarding this question it is important to point out that Paloma attributes her lack of American identity to the fact that she doesn't feel like America includes her. Her lack of American identification is paired with, indeed caused by, feelings of mistreatment. In this respect, her sense of herself in relation to mainstream American society is generalizable. Perceptions of individual-level mistreatment promote the rejection of an American identity.[25] But such rejection does not happen with exposure to U.S. society in the traditional assimilationist sense. Regardless of how far removed one is from the immigrants in the family, experiencing

---

[25] Future research should investigate two additional questions related to the measures of perceptions of discrimination employed here so that we can gain a more nuanced understanding of how discrimination influences identity choices and other political attitudes and behaviors. First, does the impact of perceptions of discrimination weaken – or perhaps strengthen – as the number of perceived discriminations increases? Figures 5.2 and 5.4 suggest that each additional perception brings added changes in self-identification. But the question of just how many perceived slights need to occur before politically relevant consequences emerge (or diminish) is worth pursuing further. Second, are some types of individual-level mistreatment more influential than others? For example, does being denied a job have more politically relevant consequences than receiving poor service in a restaurant? The 21-CAS questions can allow these questions to be pursued, but the modeling permutations required are extensive and are not pursued here.

mistreatment due to one's race or ethnicity encourages the rejection of an American identity. But the social and political factors that drive such perceptions do not appear to sound alarms.

Among Latinos and Asians in the sample, 14 percent and 15 percent respectively score at or above the midpoint on the individual-level discrimination scale and identify primarily as something other than American. Whether those percentages are large or small, I leave up to the reader to decide. My own assessment is that they are large enough that we should continue to monitor such patterns over time, and that we should explore whether those people do have more of an oppositional stance toward American political institutions than others. That brings me to the question of what the political consequences are among people who share Paloma's feelings. Does the identity choice matter? Or is it the perceptions of mistreatment? Or is it the combination of the two? These questions are addressed in the next chapter.

6

Does "Becoming American" Create a "Better" American?

Recent debates about immigration reform have focused on many topics, including the economic impact of illegal immigration, language policy, national security, guest-worker programs, and earned citizenship. One other prominent concern has been the question of American identity. Immigrants and their supporters at rallies have been praised as showing native-born Americans what active citizenship – a key constitutive American norm – is all about (Meyerson 2006). But they have also been chastised for not "becoming American." These charges were perhaps most vocal when a group of musicians released a Spanish interpretation of the national anthem. As one newspaper columnist wrote, it signaled "an invitation to separatism and a fractured national identity now finding voice among Mexican illegal immigrants and their advocates" (Farmer 2006). One editorial noted that "the mere fact that [the anthem] is in Spanish is a protest against assimilation."[1] Even President Bush, who was advocating immigrant-friendly reforms at the time, spoke out against the Spanish anthem. Critics also pointed to the presence of Mexican flags at immigration rallies in order to underscore their concerns. Some blamed activists or the federal government rather than immigrants. As one columnist wrote, "New immigrants are not expected to learn our history, master our common language, or even demonstrate loyalty and commitment to the United States" (Wilson 2006). Others, though, blamed immigrants. Recall Bob Lonsberry, the talk-radio host who argued to listeners that Latinos make choices that keep them oriented toward their ethnic identity and away from an American identity. Regardless of whether the instigator is the government or immigrants, the consequences allegedly hurt the nation as a whole, which will suffer if commitment and loyalty disappear. The goal of this chapter is to assess whether prioritizing a panethnic or national origin identity over an American identity promotes

---

[1] From an editorial at *Investor's Business Daily*, "Star Spanglish," May 1, 2006, available at http://www.investors.com/editorial/IBDArticles.asp?artsec=20&artnum=3&issue=20060501 (accessed May 24, 2006).

alienation from the American political community in the form of reduced trust and a diminished sense of obligation and patriotism.

This chapter picks up where the previous one left off, asking: How much do we need to be concerned about identity attachments? Does a person of Latino descent who primarily identifies as Latino, or as Mexican, feel more alienated from law enforcement or the federal government than a person of Latino descent who primarily identifies as American? Does that same person feel less of a sense of obligation to the United States and the American people? Is that person less patriotic? Or are perceptions of treatment what really matter? Or is it the joint presence of a particular identity type and a sense of victimization that should concern us?

This chapter relies on insights from research about group consciousness and social identity theory in order to develop hypotheses about how identity prioritization and perceptions of discrimination might affect trust and obligation and to provide explanations for the mechanisms driving these processes. The analysis reveals that the impact of identity choices on trust and obligation is conditional on how people feel they or their group is treated. Identity choices largely have no impact. Instead, perceptions of group-level and individual-level discrimination are more damaging. In some cases, the damaging effects of discrimination can be mitigated by identifying with the aggrieved group. In other cases, the damaging effects of discrimination are actually activated by such identification. Absent perceptions of discrimination, one's primary self-identification is often of little consequence. When such perceptions are present, a non-American identification can be beneficial with regard to trust and detrimental with regard to obligation. These findings raise important questions about when – and whether – the adoption of an American self-identification is desirable.

TRUST, OBLIGATION, AND IDENTITY

Trust in political institutions is generally defined as a belief that leaders will do (or are doing) right by the community and its interests (Smith 2003) and the extent to which people think the government's performance is living up to their expectations (Hetherington 2005). It has been shown that trust affects compliance with political and legal processes, particularly in cases in which people dislike the outcomes of those processes (Tyler and Huo 2002; Tyler 2006). Trust affects whether people support policies aimed at reducing inequality (Miller 1995; Hetherington 2005). It is argued that trust plays a role in sustaining our willingness to take risks on behalf of the community (Smith 2003) and accept compromise as a means of resolving conflict (Miller 1995).

Trust in law enforcement, in addition to trust in the federal government, is an important factor to investigate when debating the impact of immigration and ethnic change on the connections people forge with the American political system. Race and immigration are central factors in policy debates about post-9/11 antiterrorism efforts. In addition, efforts to enlist local law enforcement agencies to locate and apprehend illegal immigrants are becoming more common across the nation. Referred to as 287(g) programs (in reference to the 1996 addition to the Immigration and Nationality Act that authorizes them), these partnerships allow Immigration and Customs Enforcement (ICE) to train local law enforcement officers in the enforcement of immigration law. Between July 2002 and April 2008, forty-seven partnerships were approved by ICE. These partnerships are not limited to border communities. Arkansas, Georgia, Massachusetts, Ohio, and Tennessee each have at least one 287(g) program. As word of these programs spread, so has their popularity. As of May 2008, there were more than ninety requests for such partnerships pending.[2]

Obligation refers to the duties of citizenship, what we "owe" to our compatriots and to our political institutions in exchange for the privileges and rights conferred by membership in the political community. It is generally agreed that compliance with the law is where our obligations start, though many Americans also feel that they have a duty to devote some time and resources to the common good. Some argue that fulfilling such obligations is necessary in order to protect the ability of a self-governing society to provide rights and privileges in the first place. William Galston, for instance, argues that a sense of obligation is essential in a society that provides people with so many individual-level benefits, such as freedom, prosperity, and stability. He writes that these benefits "do not fall like manna from heaven; they must be produced, and renewed, by each generation. . . . There remains an injunction to do one's fair share to uphold the institutions that help secure these advantages" (2003, 179). Likewise, Christopher Wellman writes that "the state cannot exist and perform its functions without the collective sacrifice of its citizens" (2001, 233).[3] In more practical terms, people with a greater sense of civic duty are more likely to participate in politics and thus embody the ideal of the active citizen (Campbell et al. 1960; Abramson, Silver, and Anderson 1987).

Concerns about whether immigrants develop a sense of obligation lead observers to center their attention on identity choices and national attachment as essential ingredients. It is not just conservative or nativist observers who voice such concerns. Noah Pickus, for example, advocates a strong sense of national attachment and warns that "a shared national identity that is capable of binding citizens requires more than just a commitment to abstract and general principles. It requires some felt sense of communal obligation, some feeling of responsibility derived in part from a perception of a shared history and fate" (1998, 111). He promotes a naturalization process that acknowledges the nation's failures and highlights the role that citizens have played in challenging the country to live up to its ideals (Pickus 2005). Doing so, he argues, would cultivate the psychological attachment to the United States on the part of

---

[2] Information about the 287(g) program can be found at http://www.ice.gov/partners/287g/Section287_g.htm (accessed June 17, 2008).

[3] Also see Epstein (1984), Miller (1995), and Sandel (1996).

naturalized citizens, which would, in turn, enhance commitment. This perspective is hardly extreme or nativist. He warns against a "brittle and timid" defense of American identity (2005, 160). Along similar lines, progressive commentator Thomas Geohegan argues that new citizens should be required to register to vote and should "prove to us [that they are] going to read a paper, follow current events, and take up the responsibilities of democratic self-government" (2007). Pickus and Geohegan, along with more extreme observers, like Huntington (2004) and the columnists quoted earlier, are all animated by worries that commitment and obligation are getting short shrift among today's newcomers. Such commentators and scholars therefore center on identity choices for instrumental purposes. Without seeing themselves as American, they argue, people will not trust the American political system nor will they be loyal or committed to it.[4]

Such discourse, however, is often devoid of empirical analysis (Weaver 2003). What, if anything, does social science research tell us about these matters? As it turns out not a whole lot. For the most part, the role that race, ethnicity, and identity play in shaping trust and obligation has been somewhat neglected. Studies of trust among Americans have tangentially mentioned that blacks are sometimes less trusting than whites or simply include racial dummy variables as controls but fail to comment further (Owen and Dennis 2001; Richardson, Houston, and Hadjiharalambous 2001; Keele 2005). Unlike trust, opinions about the obligations of citizenship have not received much attention at all from empirical social science scholarship, let alone with respect to identity and diversity. When they have, the focus has generally been on whether people feel they have a duty to vote or pay taxes, but not on whether they feel they have other obligations, such as volunteerism or serving in the military. Pride in being American, which I treat here as a specific type of obligation, has received more attention from public opinion scholarship, though the extent to which it is affected by the factors under investigation here has only recently received attention.

Group Consciousness and Social Identity Theory

Two theoretical approaches guide the analysis in this chapter: group consciousness theory and social identity theory. These broad approaches are the main frameworks employed in the handful of empirical studies of the political consequences of group identities. Notably, both go beyond investigating whether objective membership in a particular group shapes individual-level political outcomes and instead concentrate on the conditions under which the psychological processes associated with group membership become influential and the ways in which such influence plays out. In both theories, the perception of threat plays a key role in activating the power of identities.

---

[4] See Sandel (1996) for a more general argument on the importance of commitment, solidarity, and obligation.

Group consciousness theory posits that objective group membership must be paired with both a psychological attachment to, or self-identification with, the group and a sense that the group membership is politicized before the identity will affect political attitudes and behavior (Miller et al. 1981; Conover 1988; Conover and Sapiro 1993; McClain et al. 2009). Politicization can involve the perception of threat in the form of discrimination against one's group and against oneself individually (Schildkraut 2005b; McClain et al. 2009). It can involve perceptions of deprivation relative to other groups in society along with the view that the political system – and not individual attributes – is to blame for such deprivation (Miller et al. 1981). It can also involve feelings of linked fate (Dawson 1994), or a sense that the group is worth fighting for (García Bedolla 2005). When politicized, identification with one's ethnic group can generate political activity and minimize the otherwise alienating effects of perceptions of discrimination (Miller et al. 1981; Schildkraut 2005b). It does so by providing a psychological resource – or psychological capital (García Bedolla 2005) – that facilitates engagement with the political system. People with politicized identities feel that a change in the system – and not in themselves – is necessary for improved status (Miller et al. 1981). Importantly, they believe such change is possible, but only if they engage with the system. In contrast, people who perceive mistreatment, yet do not feel close to the aggrieved group, lack this mobilizing resource and withdraw.

Social identity theory also highlights the important role that perceptions of threat can play in determining whether group identities affect subsequent attitudes and behavior. This theory posits that the need to maintain a positive group image is so powerful that group identification can promote ingroup bias and/or outgroup derogation (Theiss-Morse 2003). Moreover, the perception of threat heightens the need to see one's group positively and exacerbates these tendencies. This is not to say that social identity theory maintains that outgroup derogation automatically follows from group attachment and threat; some derogation is more accurately characterized as a product of ingroup promotion rather than outgroup hostility (Ellemers, Spears, and Doosje 1999; Oakes 2001; Turner and Reynolds 2001).

Social identity research has demonstrated that "the mere perception of belonging to a social category is sufficient for group behavior," as measured by "intergroup discrimination in social perception and behavior or intragroup altruism" (Turner 1982, 23). Studies have documented ingroup bias with respect to helping behavior and that this bias is enhanced by the perception of group threat (Dovidio and Morris 1975; Hornstein 1976; Hayden, Jackson, and Guydish 1984; Flippen et al. 1996). As Branscombe and colleagues explain, "when outgroup based threats to the ingroup's value in the form of discrimination and devaluation are severe enough . . . we would expect that most ingroup members would behave in [a] defensive fashion; closing ranks following explicit group-based exclusion allows devalued group members to protect their well being" (1999, 47). Thus, whereas group consciousness theory predicts little power for group identification absent a politicizing agent, social identity theory contends that a psychological identification with a group can sometimes be enough to lead people to close ranks around the ingroup. Both theories are in agreement, however, in noting that attachments to group identities are especially powerful when politicized by a perception of threat.

The question is whether the power of such politicized identities will lead to more or less engagement with the broader national political community. Here, the two theories generally provide complimentary expectations, though not in all cases. Much like the group consciousness literature, some social identity scholarship has been concerned with understanding when people in disadvantaged groups will become more likely to engage in actions aimed at improving their status. Such scholarship argues that collective action is more likely when a person identifies with the disadvantaged group, a person perceives that the group is disadvantaged, group boundaries are seen as impermeable (as is typically the case with race and ethnicity), "cognitive alternatives to the status quo" can be imagined (Spears, forthcoming), and the group's lower status is perceived as illegitimate (Tajfel and Turner 1986; Ellemers and Barreto 2001; Wright 2001). These conditions set the stage for the psychological capital described in the group consciousness literature to emerge. They create conditions in which people become empowered, confident in their own abilities, and motivated by a feeling of common cause shared with other group members. In this respect, social identity theory and group consciousness theory generate similar expectations with regard to actions that could yield group-specific gains, such as voting or protest. Both theories would lead us to predict higher rates of political participation among ethnic minorities in the presence of a politicized identity. They might also lead us to expect a greater sense of trust in the political system among those with politicized identities than among those who perceive discrimination but do not identify strongly with the aggrieved group. After all, the very ability to imagine an alternative to the status quo implies that one believes that the political system is responsive to pressure from collective action. The psychological capital that politicized identities provide sustains such beliefs. At a minimum, at least, we might expect that politicized identities can inoculate people against the loss of trust in the political system that can otherwise result from the belief that one's group is disadvantaged.

When it comes to a sense of obligation to that system and the people who make up the national community, however, engagement is predicted to decline among those with politicized identities, at least according to social identity theory. Social identity scholarship has repeatedly demonstrated that an attachment to a particular identity paired with the perception that the identity is threatened leads to withdrawal from prosocial interactions with the outgroup (also see Gaertner and Dovidio 2000). In existing psychological studies, measuring prosocial behavior has generally involved experimental manipulations that assess a subject's willingness to answer a call for help; in the present study, the relevant form of prosocial behavior is to perceive that one has various obligations to the broader community rather than just to one's specific ethnic group. Thus, when it comes to cooperation, altruism, and a sense of obligation to the national community, social identity theory suggests that identifying with a narrower group such as Latinos or Mexicans could lead to disengagement when that identity is paired with a perception of discrimination. As Branscombe noted, attachment plus the perception of threat leads people to close ranks around their ingroup. Though this process has not yet been tested with regard to one's sense of obligation to a larger group such as the national community, it implies that one would be less willing to make the sacrifices that the obligations under investigation here require when an attachment to a subgroup and the perception of threat to that group are present. In contrast to social identity research, research on group consciousness has typically only focused on collective action outcomes and not on prosocial behavior, leaving us with little in the way of expectations regarding how a politicized identity might affect one's sense of obligation to the national community.

Finally, it is important to bear in mind that social identity theory suggests that identification with the group might be enough to influence one's relationship to politics, whereas group consciousness theory explicitly rejects this possibility. In the present context, this aspect of social identity theory would lead us to expect that ethnic minorities might be less likely to feel as though they have obligations to the national community if they do not think of themselves as part of the American ingroup, just as immigration critics contend. Both theories agree that a psychological attachment to the group is necessary for the identity in question to become politically consequential. Whether it is sufficient is not only a matter of debate across these theoretical approaches but also within some elements of social identity theory (Turner 1999).

To sum up, the expectations for the present inquiry, as informed by group consciousness theory and social identity theory, are the following: With regard to trust in institutions, American identifiers who perceive discrimination against their panethnic or national origin group or against themselves should be more alienated (i.e., have lower levels of trust) than non-American identifiers who perceive discrimination. With regard to obligations to the national community, it is the non-American identifiers who perceive discrimination who are expected to withdraw. In both cases, perceptions of discrimination activate the ability of identity attachments to become politically consequential. On their own, such attachments should have no (or comparatively less) predictive power.

Existing Research Linking Identity, Discrimination, and Political Outcomes

Little research to date has examined whether the influence of politicized identities goes beyond voting or protest and carries over to trust in government, trust in law enforcement, or one's sense of obligation to the national community. The few that exist have shown that identity attachment on its own can be relatively innocuous with respect to trust in government and law enforcement (Tyler and Huo 2002; Schildkraut 2005b). Other factors related to group consciousness and social identity have been examined with respect to trust. These include descriptive representation, acculturation, and perceptions of discrimination. Studies find, for example, that trust among blacks in their local government increases when their city has a black mayor (Howell and Fagan 1988; Rahn and Rudolph 2005). Contrary to the concerns of immigration critics, Mexican Americans have more confidence in the executive branch and Congress than non-Hispanic whites (Weaver 2003), and Latinos trust the federal government more than other ethnic groups (Pearson and Citrin 2006). But this heightened trust might be conditional upon acculturation. Melissa Michelson argues that Mexican Americans might start out with higher levels of trust, but that acculturation (measured by language use) actually dampens trust rather than boosts it (2003). She also finds that perceptions of discrimination reduce trust. On the one hand, she concludes, Mexicans simply become just like other Americans when they assimilate, as the low levels of trust among native-born whites have troubled social scientists for years. Being distrustful, she notes, "is part of being American" (2003, 928). On the other hand, she speculates that acculturation might promote familiarity with discrimination, which also reduces trust.[5]

Other studies have likewise found that perceptions of personal discrimination reduce trust in the federal government among Latinos (Schildkraut 2005b), and that personal experiences with discrimination diminish trust in local government among Asian Americans (Lien, Conway, and Wong 2004).[6] Perceptions of discrimination also reduce trust in law enforcement (Weitzer and Tuch 2004). Likewise, Californians who report having had positive or "procedurally fair" interactions with police and the courts are more likely to have favorable views of law enforcement. Nonwhites, however, are less likely than whites to report positive or fair experiences (Tyler and Huo 2002).

With regard to obligations, Elizabeth Theiss-Morse finds that whites who identify strongly with "the American people" are more likely than whites who identify weakly with the American people to think that they have various obligations, such as donating to charities and volunteering in their communities (2006, 2009). Adding stress to the mix can enhance this tendency to look out for one's own group but not for others (Dovidio and Morris 1975). Using panel data, for instance, Putnam found that the 9/11 terrorist attacks led to a short-lived increase in civic behavior, such as volunteering and working on a community project (Putnam 2003).

---

[5] Wenzel provides similar findings in his study of Mexican Americans in south Texas (2006), in which acculturation (measured by language use) reduces trust in the federal government but has no effect on trust in the local government. He posits that trust in local government is unaffected because local government in south Texas often provides descriptive representation for Mexican Americans. As for trust at the national level, he is unable to discern if acculturation matters due to increasing perceptions of discrimination or due to Mexican Americans becoming "just like other Americans." My findings in Chapter 5 suggest that the latter scenario is more likely. His study did not include perceptions of discrimination.

[6] More objective measures of acculturation, such as language use and proportion of one's life spent in the United States, do not affect trust in local government in the study by Lien, Conway, and Wong (2004).

In sum, existing scholarship about how identity choices and perceptions of threat shape trust and obligation, though small in volume, is united in finding that perceptions of threat or mistreatment are powerful. Both group-level and individual-level mistreatment have been shown to matter. At the same time, identity attachment, the concept animating immigration critics and scholars of democratic theory, is often innocuous. It can neutralize the negative effects of discrimination in some areas, yet it can exacerbate alienation in other areas.

To date, however, most studies in this area have looked only at group identification or mistreatment. They have not tested whether the interactive dynamic proposed by group consciousness theory and social identity theory plays out with respect to trust and obligation. Moreover, most group consciousness research has focused primarily on African Americans. Applying its insights to other groups, such as Latinos and Asians, might be more complex due to the different histories of these groups and due to the extensive diversity encompassed by panethnic labels (Junn and Masuoka 2008; McClain et al. 2009). Additionally, many findings in social identity regarding prosocial behavior come from laboratory studies that manipulate stimuli and not from survey data gathered in the context of actual entrenched intergroup situations. The studies described thus far also lack the means to distinguish between types of non-American identifications, generally contrasting an American identification with only a panethnic or a national origin identification. Whether panethnic and national origin identifications play the same role in shaping political outcomes is largely unstudied, yet as noted in Chapter 5, a panethnic identity might be a more politically potent form of identification than enduring ties to one's country of origin.

The present study is able to address these limitations through use of the Twenty-First-Century Americanism Survey (21-CAS), which, in addition to the identity attachment and discrimination questions discussed in Chapter 5, contains questions about trust in institutions, obligations to the American people, and pride in being American. Trust in government and law enforcement is gauged by asking respondents, "How much of the time do you think you can trust [the government in Washington/law enforcement] to do what is right . . . just about always, most of the time, some of the time, or never?" "Just about always" is coded as 1, "never" as 0. Most respondents said that they trust government only some of the time (57%) and trust law enforcement most of the time (53%).

Obligation is measured by offering respondents a list of possible obligations and asking them to indicate if they think each one is an obligation they owe to other Americans. "Yes (1)," "no (0)," and "it depends (0.5)" were accepted responses. The obligations under investigation here are giving money to charities, volunteering in your local community, and serving in the military.[7] Overall, Americans feel that they have all three obligations: charity = 57 percent;

---

[7] Questions about obligations were adopted from Theiss-Morse's Perceptions of the American People Survey, 2002.

volunteer = 72 percent; military service = 45 percent (a plurality).[8] Patriotism, a form of national obligation, is discussed later in the chapter. Bivariate examinations of the mean levels of trust and the percentage of respondents saying yes to the obligation questions by ethnicity, identity attachment, perception of discrimination, and more, can be found in Appendix D.

PREDICTING TRUST AND OBLIGATION

Trust

Over the years we have learned that trust is affected by one's level of generalized trust (beliefs about whether people tend to be fair and trustworthy or whether they tend to look out for themselves and take advantage of others); approval ratings of Congress and the president; beliefs about the fairness and equity of the political process; and partisanship, with people being more trustful of government if their own political party is in the majority (Brehm and Rahn 1997; Citrin and Luks 2001; Hibbing and Theiss-Morse 2001; Keele 2005). As far as factors related to ethnicity, identity, and immigration are concerned, the main factor affecting trust has been perceptions of discrimination rather than identity attachment. Thus, as noted, non-American identities are not expected to lead to mistrust. On the contrary, a non-American identity might mitigate the mistrust generated by perceptions of discrimination.

Three ordered probit models were run to predict each form of trust: whites only, blacks only, and Latinos and Asians. Latinos and Asians were analyzed together for several reasons. First, together these groups comprise well over a majority of contemporary immigrants. Second, Latino and Asian respondents yielded similar patterns underlying identity prioritization in Chapter 5. Moreover, studies have shown that there are minimal differences among Asians of different national origins with respect to trust (Lien, Conway, and Wong 2004), "Hispanics from different national origin backgrounds express relatively similar political views" (Claassen 2004; also see Schildkraut 2003), and Latinos and Asians "bear similar underlying structures of ethnicity" (Lien 1994). Third, analyzing Latinos and Asians together yields more precise standard errors due to the increased sample size. Except where noted, running the models in this chapter for Asians and Latinos separately yielded similar results.

Each model has five sets of independent variables (with all nondummy variables coded to range from 0 to 1). The first set consists of standard demographic and attitudinal measures: education, age, partisanship, and generalized trust (in which 1 = most people can be trusted, and 0 = you can't be too careful).[9] The

---

[8] "It depends" was a volunteered response. For donating to charity, volunteering, and serving in the military, the percentage of respondents who said "it depends" was 9.6%, 6.4%, and 11.8%, respectively.

[9] I did not include household income because of the high refusal rate on that question. The 21-CAS does not have measures of approval ratings of Congress or attitudes about the fairness of the political process. See Appendix A for question wording not described in the main text.

second set captures acculturation: generation (first, second, third, or more) and whether the respondent primarily speaks English in the home. The third set consists of identity choices (American, panethnic, or national origin), with "American" as the omitted category. The fourth set consists of perceptions of discrimination against one's panethnic group, one's national origin group, and oneself personally (see Chapter 5 for measurement description). The fifth set consists of interactions between each type of identity choice and discrimination. These interaction terms reflect the concept of a politicized identity. They go beyond mere objective membership in a group by capturing both identification (attachment) and beliefs about social standing, a combination that is essential for group consciousness to emerge. Group identification on its own (measured here by asking respondents which group characterizes how they think of themselves most of the time) is "a psychological sense of belonging or attachment to a social group" (McClain et al. 2009, 476). Only by interacting this measure with perceptions of discrimination can we compare people who are and are not attached to the ethnic group (or to being American) under different degrees of politicization, as social identity and group consciousness theories maintain we should. It moves the debate beyond whether attachment does or does not affect political engagement by shifting our attention to the conditions under which such effects might be more or less likely to emerge.

For the model with black respondents, only the identity and discrimination measures relating to panethnicity were included, and for blacks and whites, speaking only English was dropped due to its failure to achieve significance in earlier tests. In all cases, the model for whites is considered to be the baseline, as most of what we know about trust and obligation comes from studying whites. The particular role of identity and discrimination in shaping the opinions of whites is of less theoretical interest in this chapter.

Trust in Government

The results for trust in government appear in Table 6.1. Bear in mind that due to the interaction terms, the coefficients on identity choices should be read as the effect of that identity choice on trust when perceptions of discrimination equal 0 (i.e., when they are absent). Likewise, the coefficients on the different types of discrimination should be read as the effect of each type of discrimination on trust for American identifiers (i.e., when the panethnic and national origin identification dummy variables both equal 0). The coefficients on the interaction terms, in turn, indicate if the effect of identity attachment is different when the various perceptions of discrimination are present and if the effect of discrimination is different for non-American identifiers than it is for American identifiers (Brambor, Clark, and Golder 2006).

Table 6.1 shows that trust in government for whites works much like most existing research on trust would expect: Republicans and people with more generalized trust are more trusting of government (note that the Republican party controlled the executive and legislative branches when the 21-CAS was

TABLE 6.1. *Trust in Government, by Race, Ordered Probit*

Independent Variable	White b	s.e.	Black b	s.e.	Asian and Latino b	s.e.
Education	−0.28**	0.13	−0.14	0.25	−0.33*	0.19
Age	0.23	0.17	0.45	0.38	0.02	0.26
Republican	1.13**	0.10	−0.19	0.33	0.74**	0.16
Generalized (interpersonal) trust	0.23**	0.08	0.46**	0.18	0.04	0.12
Generation (1st to 4th+)	0.04	0.14	0.21	0.34	−0.53**	0.16
Speaks primarily English at home	–	–	–	–	−0.21*	0.13
Latino	–	–	–	–	0.44**	0.13
National origin self-identification	−0.23	0.22	–	–	−0.08	0.21
Panethnic self-identification	0.25	0.18	0.02	0.44	−0.58*	0.34
National origin discrimination	0.31	0.21	–	–	0.19	0.24
Panethnic discrimination	−0.17	0.16	−0.43	0.48	−0.59**	0.24
Individual-level discrimination	−0.05	0.27	−0.69**	0.34	−0.12	0.25
National origin × national origin discrimination	−0.89	1.02	–	–	0.11	0.37
National origin × individual discrimination	1.50	1.05	–	–	0.07	0.37
Panethnic × panethnic discrimination	−0.60	0.42	−0.88	0.63	1.19**	0.53
Panethnic × individual discrimination	−0.90	0.84	1.03**	0.50	−0.36	0.47
Cutpoint 1	−1.14	0.21	−1.41	0.45	−1.89	0.24
Cutpoint 2	0.93	0.20	0.66	0.44	0.01	0.23
Cutpoint 3	2.32	0.21	1.69	0.47	1.32	0.24
Chi-square	165.35		32.46		75.66	
N	1006		228		463	

Note: ** $p < 0.05$; * $p < 0.1$. All nondummy variables coded 0 to 1. Unweighted data.
Source: Twenty-First-Century Americanism Survey, 2004.

conducted), and people with higher levels of education are less trusting. No measures of identity choice or perceptions of discrimination are significant nor are the interaction terms. For blacks, generalized trust promotes trust in government, and individual-level discrimination diminishes trust in government. Identifying primarily as black has no impact absent perceptions of discrimination, but it mitigates the damaging effects of individual-level discrimination.

Discrimination hurts trust in government only for blacks who identify primarily as American (see the interaction term for panethnic identity and perception of individual-level discrimination).

To get a better sense of the magnitude of the relationship between individual-level discrimination and self-identification for blacks, I turn to predicted probabilities. Figure 6.1a shows the probability that a black respondent trusts the government "most of the time" as his identification changes from American to black and his perception of individual-level discrimination changes from 0 to 1.[10] Figure 6.1b shows the probability that a black respondent "never" trusts the government under the same conditions. The figures indicate that American identifiers are considerably more trusting than black identifiers when discrimination is absent, but that they become more likely than black identifiers to "never" trust government when discrimination is present. The probability that a black American identifier never trusts government is only 0.08 when discrimination is absent, but it jumps to 0.23 when discrimination is present. Conversely, the trust levels among blacks who identify as black are actually enhanced, though modestly, when that identity is politicized.

For Latinos and Asians, education and being a Democrat lower trust while generalized trust raises trust in government. The model also shows that Latinos are slightly more trusting of government than Asians. Moreover, as Michelson found, acculturation seems to lower trust, as indicated by the negative coefficients on generational status and language use.[11] But as with blacks, discrimination and identity also play a complicated role. Here, panethnic discrimination diminishes trust rather than personal discrimination. But as with blacks, this effect only applies to people who identify primarily as American. Identifying as Latino or Asian (but not as a member of one's national origin group) neutralizes the damaging effect of discrimination.[12]

Predicted probabilities of trusting government "most of the time" and "never" are displayed in Figures 6.2a and 6.2b for Latinos and in Figures 6.3a and 6.3b for Asians.[13] These figures show that among American identifiers, perceptions of panethnic discrimination decrease the likelihood of trusting government "most of the time" by more than 10 percentage points for Latinos and

---

[10] Predicted probabilities are calculated using CLARIFY, holding all other variables constant at their means for blacks (King, Tomz, and Wittenberg 2000). I predicted "most of the time" instead of "just about always" because so few respondents of any kind said that they trust the government "just about always" under any condition.

[11] Running models for Latinos and Asians separately indicates that the impact of generational status is driven by Latinos.

[12] Rerunning the model without people who initially identified racially as something other than Latino or Asian produces only one difference of note (n = 463 vs. n = 346): panethnic discrimination, on its own, fails to achieve significance. However, the interaction between a panethnic identity and panethnic discrimination remains positive and significant, meaning that the politicized identity continues to offset alienation and promote engagement.

[13] Predicted outcomes are calculated using CLARIFY, holding all other variables constant at their means for Latinos and Asians, with "speaks English at home" held constant at 1, while changing panethnic discrimination from 0 to 1.

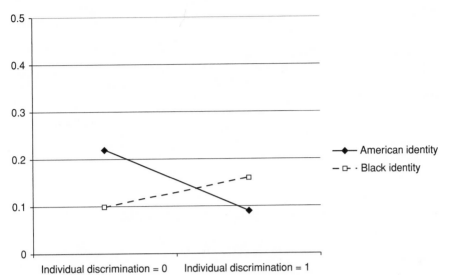

FIGURE 6.1a. Predicted probabilities of blacks trusting government "most of the time" as individual-level discrimination and identity prioritization vary. *Source:* Twenty-First-Century Americanism Survey, 2004.

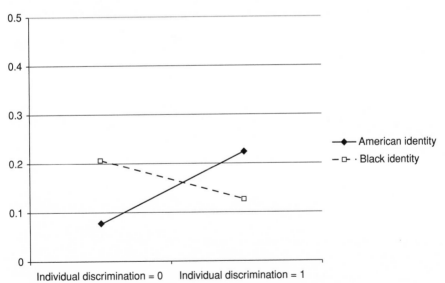

FIGURE 6.1b. Predicted probabilities of blacks trusting government "never" as individual-level discrimination and identity prioritization vary. *Source:* Twenty-First-Century Americanism Survey, 2004.

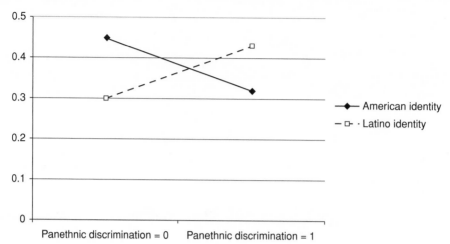

FIGURE 6.2a. Predicted probabilities of Latinos trusting government "most of the time" as panethnic discrimination and identity prioritization vary. *Source:* Twenty-First-Century Americanism Survey, 2004.

Asians. At the same time, such perceptions provide psychological capital for panethnic identifiers, whose likelihood of trusting government "most of the time" is roughly equivalent to the levels of trust exhibited by American identifiers who do not perceive discrimination. The change in the likelihood

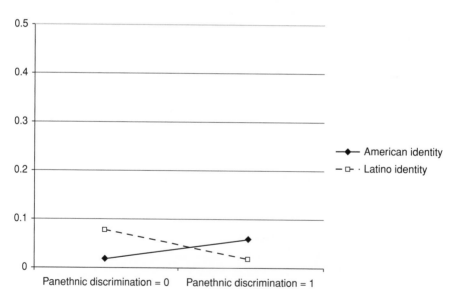

FIGURE 6.2b. Predicted probabilities of Latinos trusting government "never" as panethnic discrimination and identity prioritization vary. *Source:* Twenty-First-Century Americanism Survey, 2004.

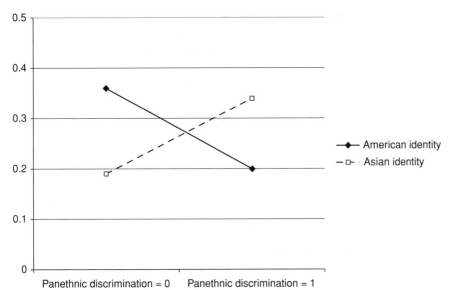

FIGURE 6.3a. Predicted probabilities of Asians trusting government "most of the time" as panethnic discrimination and identity prioritization vary. *Source:* Twenty-First-Century Americanism Survey, 2004.

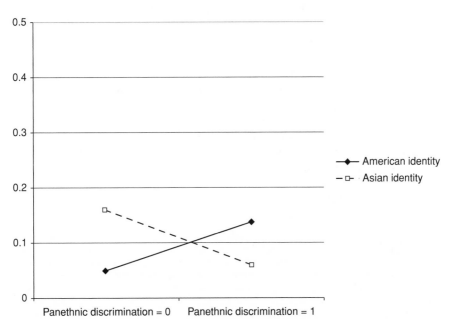

FIGURE 6.3b. Predicted probabilities of Asians trusting government "never" as panethnic discrimination and identity prioritization vary. *Source:* Twenty-First-Century Americanism Survey, 2004.

of trusting government "never" as identity and discrimination vary is not as dramatic, but the figures tell a similar story: trust among American identifiers is lowered in the face of panethnic discrimination while trust among panethnic identifiers is enhanced. It is important to note as well that a panethnic identification for Latinos and Asians does reduce trust in government when perceptions of discrimination are absent (see Table 6.1), indicating that the concerns of immigration critics cannot be dismissed completely.

Clearly, the role that identity attachment plays in shaping trust is more complicated than it is typically cast. For blacks, Latinos, and Asians, having an American identification is only beneficial if perceptions of discrimination are absent. Unfortunately, such perceptions are not absent. Twenty-two percent of black respondents score at or above the midpoint on the individual-level discrimination scale and identify primarily as American. Likewise, 25 percent of Latino and Asian respondents score at or above the midpoint on the panethnic discrimination scale and identify primarily as American. Thus, a nontrivial portion of the population would have its level of trust in government raised if it were to identify primarily with the panethnic group instead of as American.[14]

Trust in Law Enforcement

The results of the ordered probit analyses for trust in law enforcement appear in Table 6.2. They show that the complicated relationship between identity attachment and discrimination previously described for blacks, Latinos, and Asians does not apply when our attention shifts from government to law enforcement. Perceptions of individual-level discrimination diminish trust for blacks, Latinos, and Asians, and self-identification does nothing to alter this effect (as indicated by the insignificant interaction terms).[15] Likewise, the perception of panethnic discrimination diminishes trust for whites, but identifying as white does nothing to mitigate that impact. Again, it is helpful to turn to predicted probabilities in order to illustrate the magnitude of these effects (no figures shown). The probability that a Latino respondent who identifies as American will trust law enforcement "just about always" drops from 0.21 to 0.08 when the perception of individual-level discrimination changes from 0 to 1. For Asians, it drops from 0.12 to 0.04. Changing one's primary self-identification has no impact on these results.

[14] In separate analyses (not shown), I used the PNAAPS to predict trust in local government. Using the original model by Lien, Conway, and Wong (2004) as a starting point, I added measures of self-identification (American, Asian American, Asian, national origin) and interacted them with perceptions of individual-level discrimination. In that model, the interaction between an Asian identification and discrimination was positive and significant, confirming that this panethnic identification can neutralize the negative impact of discrimination on trust for Asian Americans.

[15] Rerunning the model for blacks without respondents who were recoded for panethnicity (n = 229 vs. n = 236) results in one difference of note: panethnic discrimination and individual-level discrimination reduce trust in law enforcement. Yet as in Table 6.2, none of the interaction terms are significant.

TABLE 6.2. *Trust in Law Enforcement by Race, Ordered Probit*

Independent Variable	White b	s.e.	Black b	s.e.	Asian and Latino b	s.e.
Education	0.05	0.13	0.38	0.27	−0.23	0.20
Age	0.35**	0.17	0.83**	0.39	−0.03	0.28
Republican	0.81**	0.09	−0.10	0.30	0.28*	0.17
Generalized (interpersonal) trust	0.23**	0.08	0.11	0.18	0.37**	0.11
Generation (1st to 4th+)	−0.09	0.14	0.02	0.31	−0.51**	0.17
Speaks primarily English at home	–	–	–	–	−0.21*	0.13
Latino	–	–	–	–	0.36**	0.13
National origin self-identification	−0.65**	0.20	–	–	0.02	0.19
Panethnic self-identification	−0.22	0.18	−0.22	0.49	−0.31	0.41
National origin discrimination	−0.16	0.21	–	–	0.02	0.27
Panethnic discrimination	−0.42**	0.17	−0.77	0.50	−0.20	0.26
Individual-level discrimination	−0.37	0.27	−0.87**	0.35	−0.62**	0.28
National origin × national origin discrimination	−1.43	0.92	–	–	−0.04	0.37
National origin × individual discrimination	2.88**	0.85	–	–	−0.04	0.39
Panethnic × panethnic discrimination	0.27	0.51	0.42	0.69	0.014	0.62
Panethnic × individual discrimination	0.14	0.62	0.09	0.47	0.13	0.53
Cutpoint 1	−2.19	0.23	−2.05	0.50	−2.39	0.27
Cutpoint 2	0.38	0.21	−0.15	0.47	−0.68	0.24
Cutpoint 3	1.35	0.21	1.27	0.47	0.86	0.24
Chi-square	126.54		33.79		57.60	
N	1010		229		468	

Note: ** $p < 0.05$; * $p < 0.1$. All nondummy variables coded 0 to 1. Unweighted data.
Source: Twenty-First-Century Americanism Survey, 2004.

Other findings in Table 6.2 show that Latinos are again more trusting than Asians, and both measures of acculturation again reduce trust.[16] Whites who

---

[16] As before, the main substantive difference when running models for Latinos and Asians separately is that the effect of generational status is driven by Latinos. In this case, the impact of generalized trust is also driven by Latinos. Running the model dropping people who initially identified as something other than Latino and Asian (n = 350 vs. n = 468) produces the same results as in Table 6.2 except the measure of language use loses significance.

identify with their national origin group instead of as American are less trusting of law enforcement, but this effect goes away if those same respondents think they have personally been mistreated due to their race or ethnicity. Exploring the dynamics of self-identification and discrimination among whites clearly merits further investigation but is not the main concern of the present inquiry.

In sum, perceptions of personal discrimination and panethnic discrimination are powerful. When it comes to trust in government, the expectations of group consciousness theory and social identity theory are borne out: identifying with the aggrieved group can inoculate people against alienation. But the impact of discrimination on trust in law enforcement is too powerful; identifying with the aggrieved group offers no protection for blacks, Latinos, or Asians. Finally, because perceptions of discrimination are controlled, acculturation likely decreases trust in the federal government and in law enforcement due to the increasing similarity with native-born whites that acculturation promotes rather than due to an increasing likelihood of perceiving mistreatment. This interpretation is bolstered by the findings in Chapter 5 that acculturation did not influence the perception of discrimination.[17]

Obligation

Although there is little research on public opinion about the obligations of membership in the American political community, there is research about whether people actually fulfill varied obligations, the factors that distinguish volunteers from nonvolunteers, and community-level characteristics that might promote volunteerism (e.g., Eckstein 2001). Scholarship regarding whether we fulfill the duties of citizenship have blossomed in recent years thanks to a surge of interest in social capital (Putnam 2000), and these studies tell us that people often fall short of the ideal. Some studies suggest that people who say they have obligations are likely to carry those obligations out (Lee, Piliavin, and Call 1999), yet others show that most people acknowledge the duties of citizenship while also admitting that they shirk them (Hibbing and Theiss-Morse 2002). Yet for the most part, examinations of people's thoughts about obligations, regardless of whether they live up to them and whether race, ethnicity, and identity matter, are rare.

The types of obligation under investigation here are to donate to charity, volunteer in one's community, and serve in the military. As noted earlier, research

---

[17] Both trust models for Latinos and Asians were also run with generational status as a series of dummy variables, with the fourth generation (or more) as the omitted category, to see if the straight-line model of acculturation implied by a single scale variable is misguided. For trust in government, the first and third generations were significantly more likely than the fourth generation to trust government, with the first being most likely. There was no difference between the second generation and the fourth generation. No group trusted government more than the first generation or less than the fourth. For trust in law enforcement, the first generation was more trusting than all of the others. The second and third generations were not significantly different from the fourth.

on group consciousness has not examined this kind of prosocial behavior; it has focused on collective action in pursuit of group specific gains. Whether the power of politicized identities to inoculate against the alienating effects of discrimination in the realm of collective action carries over into the realm of making sacrifices to the broader community remains to be tested. Social identity scholarship suggests that panethnic or national origin identifications, when paired with perceptions of discrimination, would make one's sense of obligation to the broader community less likely. Attachment plus the perception of threat is expected to lead people to "close ranks" around the aggrieved group.

I again use ordered probit models in this analysis. The models are identical to the models used to predict trust but with three changes. First, generalized trust is removed. Second, gender is added because of scholarship suggesting that women are more sympathetic to the disadvantaged than men and possess an "ethic of caring" (Conover 1988), and because men are more likely to serve in the military.[18] Third, action-oriented civic republicanism is added. Recall from Chapter 3 that this measure captures the belief that "true Americans" should do volunteer work in their community, be informed about local and national politics, and be involved in local and national politics ($\alpha = 0.62$; mean $= 0.78$ on 0 to 1 scale). It is expected that people who think American identity is uniquely defined by active citizenship are more likely to feel that they personally have obligations to the United States and the American people.[19] The results appear in Table 6.3. For ease of presentation, standard errors are not reported in this table but can be found in Appendix D.

The strongest and most consistent relationship revealed across all models is the power that action-oriented civic republicanism plays in shaping whether people feel that they personally have obligations to other Americans. Recall from Chapter 3 that Latinos, Asians, and non-English speakers are as likely as English-speaking whites to define the meaning of American identity in civic republican terms, and that blacks are slightly more likely. To the extent that Americans of these diverse backgrounds are more or less equally likely to think that being American means living up to an ideal of active citizenship, they also share a similar attitude structure when it comes to whether they feel they personally have specific obligations.

With regard to the main causal variables of this chapter, self-identification absent perceptions of discrimination only matters twice: whites who identify as white are less likely to say they should volunteer in their communities, and blacks who identify as black are less likely to say they should serve in the military. Perceptions of discrimination for American identifiers are relatively inconsequential. Blacks are more likely to say that they should volunteer in their

---

[18] According to the U.S. Census Bureau, the membership of the armed forces in the United States is 15% female. See http://www.census.gov/Press-Release/www/releases/archives/facts_for_features_special_editions/006232.html (accessed June 9, 2006).

[19] Bivariate correlations between this civic republican definition of American identity and obligations to donate, volunteer, and serve in the military are 0.22, 0.32, and 0.25, respectively.

TABLE 6.3. *Obligation to Give Money to Charities, Volunteer, Serve in Military, by Race, Ordered Probit*

Independent Variable	Donate			Volunteer			Serve		
	White	Black	Asian/Latino	White	Black	Asian/Latino	White	Black	Asian/Latino
Education	0.31**	0.10	0.26	-0.02	-0.43	0.23	-0.71**	-0.50*	-0.54**
Age	0.54**	0.15	0.67**	-0.001	0.34	0.41	1.81**	2.62**	1.43**
Male	-0.18**	0.04	-0.11	-0.21**	-0.32*	0.004	0.26**	0.78**	0.15
Generation (1st to 4th+)	-0.26*	-0.30	0.38**	0.01	-0.22	0.21	-0.33**	-0.11	-0.44**
Speaks primarily English at home	–	–	-0.34**	–	–	-0.13	–	–	0.02
Civic republican Americanism	1.75**	1.54**	0.79**	2.51**	2.29**	1.51**	1.11**	1.53**	1.51**
Latino	–	–	-0.17	–	–	-0.19	–	–	-0.07
National origin self-identification	-0.16	–	0.02	-0.24	–	0.27	-0.22	–	-0.03
Panethnic self-identification	-0.02	0.38	0.41	-0.55**	-0.60	-0.06	-0.26	-0.77*	0.06
National origin discrimination	0.04	–	-0.05	0.18	–	-0.16	-0.07	–	0.09
Panethnic discrimination	-0.14	0.17	0.02	0.03	-0.41	0.14	0.25*	-0.95**	-0.22
Individual-level discrimination	-0.07	0.22	0.05	-0.05	0.90**	0.26	-0.10	-0.14	0.07
National origin × national origin discrimination	0.57	–	0.07	-0.11	–	-0.80**	0.63	–	-0.35
National origin × individual discrimination	0.19	–	-0.32	0.79	–	-0.11	-0.21	–	0.01
Panethnic × panethnic discrimination	-0.20	-0.25	-0.86*	1.05**	1.24*	0.17	0.20	0.39	-0.13
Panethnic × individual discrimination	2.10**	-0.09	0.58	-0.41	-0.71	0.39	0.48	-0.26	0.11
Cutpoint 1	0.92	0.80	0.38	0.85	0.55	0.48	0.84	1.01	0.86
Cutpoint 2	1.20	0.99	0.69	1.12	0.66	0.66	1.18	1.31	1.14
Chi-square	116.40	15.01	35.23	157.69	29.83	46.75	218.39	91.28	95.70
N	1168	271	604	1167	272	605	1157	268	598

Note: ** $p < 0.05$; * $p < 0.1$. All nondummy variables coded 0 to 1. Unweighted data.
Source: Twenty-First-Century Americanism Survey, 2004.

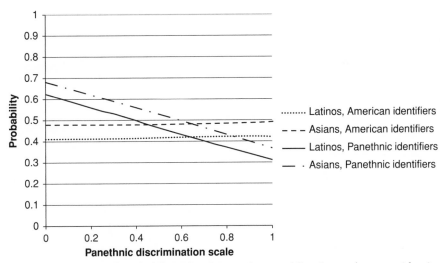

FIGURE 6.4. Predicted probability of saying one has an obligation to donate as identity and panethnic discrimination vary. *Source:* Twenty-First-Century Americanism Survey, 2004.

communities when they feel they personally have been mistreated due to their race, and they are less likely to say they should serve in the military when they feel that blacks have been mistreated.[20] Identifying primarily as black instead of as American does nothing to mitigate – or exacerbate – these relationships.[21]

Perceptions of discrimination on their own do not affect whether Latinos or Asians feel they personally have obligations to donate, volunteer, or serve, but such perceptions do become consequential when paired with a Latino or Asian identity. Contrary to the positive impact that politicized identities have on trust, the joint presence of discrimination and attachment to a non-American identity here reduces one's sense of connection to the American ingroup. For donating to charity, the relevant level of analysis is panethnicity. For volunteering in the community, it is the national origin group.

Figure 6.4 shows the predicted probability of thinking that one has an obligation to donate to charity as one's identity choice (American vs. panethnic) and that the perception of panethnic discrimination varies for Latinos and Asians. It shows that those who identify as Latino and Asian actually have a higher likelihood of saying that they have an obligation to donate than American identifiers when perceptions of panethnic discrimination are absent. But once such perceptions are present, the sense of obligation among these

---

[20] Though unexpected, it is possible that panethnic mistreatment promotes the belief among blacks that one owes it to other Americans to volunteer in the community due to the prevalence of residential segregation in the United States. When black respondents hear "the community," they may think of a largely black community.

[21] When the models are rerun without blacks who initially identified racially as something other than black, identifying panethnically loses significance in the military model.

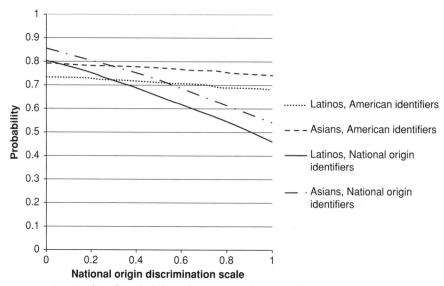

FIGURE 6.5. Predicted probability of saying one has an obligation to volunteer as identity and national origin discrimination vary. *Source:* Twenty-First-Century Americanism Survey, 2004.

panethnic identifiers drops considerably and ends up lower than the sense of obligation among American identifiers.[22] A Latino respondent who identifies as Latino but does not perceive discrimination has a 62 percent chance of saying he or she has an obligation to donate to charity. When the same respondent thinks Latinos are mistreated, that probability drops to 31 percent – a precipitous drop of 31 percentage points.

Figure 6.5 shows the predicted probability of thinking that one has an obligation to volunteer in one's community as one's identity choice (American vs. national origin) and that the perception of national origin discrimination varies for Latinos and Asians. Similar to the findings for the obligation to donate, those who identify with their national origin group have a slightly higher likelihood of saying they have an obligation to volunteer than American identifiers if perceptions of national origin discrimination are absent. But once such perceptions are present, the sense of obligation among these national origin identifiers drops dramatically and ends up quite a bit lower than the sense of obligation among American identifiers.[23] An Asian respondent who identifies with his national origin group but does not think that the group is mistreated has an 85 percent chance of saying that he has an obligation to volunteer in his community. When the same respondent thinks his national origin group is mistreated,

[22] This result falls just short of significance at 90% (p = 0.13) when the model is rerun without people who were recoded for panethnicity (n = 441 vs. n = 604).

[23] This relationship also achieves 90% significance for serving in the military when the model is rerun without people who were recoded for panethnicity (n = 436 vs. n = 598).

that probability drops to 54 percent – again, a drop of 31 percentage points. The politicized non-American identity turns Latinos and Asians away from the American community.

Twelve percent of Latino and Asian respondents identify primarily as Latino and Asian and score at or above the midpoint on the panethnic discrimination scale, and 23 percent of Latino and Asian respondents identify primarily with their national origin group and score at or above the midpoint on the national origin discrimination scale. In short, the number of people affected by the phenomenon depicted in Figures 6.4 and 6.5 is large enough that it should not be ignored.

Other results from Table 6.3 show that acculturation can be a mixed blessing. For Latinos and Asians, the longer one's family has been in the United States, the more likely a person is to say that she or he has an obligation to donate to charity but she or he is less likely to say that one has an obligation to serve in the military.[24] Gender works largely as previous scholarship would expect: white women are more likely than white men to say that they have an obligation to volunteer and donate, but white men are more likely to say that they have an obligation to serve in the military. Likewise, black women are more likely than black men to say that they have an obligation to volunteer, and black men more likely than black women to say that they have an obligation to enlist. There are no significant gender differences among Latinos and Asians.[25]

PATRIOTISM

There are vigorous debates in the literature over the different manifestations of patriotism, how to measure its variations, and whether certain types – such as "blind" patriotism – are more worrisome than others – such as "constructive" patriotism (Schatz, Staub, and Lavine 1999).[26] Other research debates center on the similarities and differences between patriotism and nationalism (de Figueiredo and Elkins 2003; McDaniel and Nooruddin 2008). But regardless of their specific conclusions regarding these debates, most scholars who have studied patriotism recognize that one form consists of pride in being a member of the country in question, a dimension sometimes referred to as "symbolic" patriotism (Huddy and Khatib 2007). For that reason, and because many contemporary debates about immigration center on such pride – such as the debates about singing the national anthem in Spanish, pride in being American

---

[24] Models with generational dummy variables indicate that the generational differences are between the first generation and everyone else in both cases. All generational dummy variables remain insignificant in the volunteerism model.

[25] There are no substantive differences between Latinos and Asians when the obligation models are run separately for each group, though some relationships from Table 6.3 fall just short of significance at the 95% or 90% levels.

[26] "Blind" patriotism does not allow room for criticism and is characterized by an unquestioning loyalty to the nation. "Constructive" patriotism, however, is motivated by a desire to improve the nation and therefore permits criticism (Schatz, Staub, and Lavine 1999).

is analyzed here. When the Spanish anthem was released in the spring of 2006, defenders claimed that it was a vehicle to communicate American ideals to newer residents who were not yet fluent in English and thus help instill commitment to, and pride in, those ideals. Critics, however, said the anthem was sacred and that translating it (and changing some lyrics in the process) was an insult to the very ideals embodied in the song as well as a direct renunciation of commitment to the United States (Montgomery 2006).

As noted earlier, pride in being American is often discussed as bound up with the set obligations citizens may or may not have to the national community and their compatriots. Existing public opinion scholarship on such pride examines the consequences of different forms of patriotism (Sullivan, Fried, and Dietz 1992; Schatz, Staub, and Lavine 1999; de Figueiredo and Elkins 2003; Huddy and Khatib 2007) but devotes less attention to the causes of national pride. Some studies note that age and ideology play a role, with older respondents and conservatives generally exhibiting more pride than younger respondents and liberals (Davis 2007; Huddy and Khatib 2007). Some studies have also found that African Americans tend not to be as proud as whites (Sidanius et al. 1997; Davis 2007; Huddy and Khatib 2007).

Regarding factors relating to identity and immigration, Davis found that being born in the United States is associated with higher levels of patriotism (2007), and Citrin and colleagues found that native-born Hispanics exhibited more patriotism than whites (2007). Using a measure of identity choice that lets respondents identify as American, a member of an ethnic group, or both, they also found that levels of pride in being American were high across all three types of identifiers, and that the main difference was between those who opted for an ethnic identity only and everyone else. In particular, "just ethnic" identifiers had lower levels of pride than "just American" identifiers or people who identified as both (Citrin et al. 2007). On the one hand, this finding gives evidence to support the contention that not identifying as American could have negative consequences for the political system – to the extent that pride in being American is a virtue (a matter of ongoing academic debate). On the other hand, it is important to point out that Citrin also finds that "just ethnic" is the least common identity chosen, and that the likelihood of choosing it decreases across generations (Pearson and Citrin 2006).[27]

Similarly, de la Garza and colleagues found Mexican Americans to have more pride in being American than Anglos, and that the extent to which one consciously thought of oneself as Latino (instead of as white) did not matter (1996). They also found that the least acculturated respondents, in terms of language use and nativity, were actually more patriotic than the most acculturated. Sidanius, however, found that for nonwhite students, an ethnic identity and symbolic patriotism were negatively correlated whereas the reverse was true for whites. In a national rather than student sample, this pattern held for blacks but not for Latinos (Sidanius et al. 1997). The study of symbolic

[27] Citrin's studies did not include perceptions of discrimination.

patriotism by Sidanius is the only one I have found that includes perceptions of discrimination among the independent variables (using individual level only). He found that experiences with discrimination led to lower levels of patriotism for Latino students.

This collection of findings, along with the findings detailed so far in this chapter, leads to the expectation that discrimination hurts pride in being American, and that identity attachment, absent perceptions of discrimination, is unlikely to have much of an impact over pride except perhaps among blacks. Yet the psychological mechanisms discussed earlier might lead us to expect that attachment to a non-American identity could inoculate people against the alienating effects that perceptions of discrimination bring by producing a psychological resource that interrupts the loss of pride that American identifiers experience in reaction to discrimination. However, it is also possible that, as with obligations, pride will be diminished even further when non-American identities are politicized in an effort to close ranks around the mistreated group. The analysis in this section is thus more exploratory than the analyses in previous sections.

To measure patriotism, respondents were asked if they strongly agree (coded 1), somewhat agree, somewhat disagree, or strongly disagree (coded 0) with the following statement: "I am proud to be an American." This question was asked only of respondents who were American citizens; noncitizens are therefore not included in this section. Overall, 84 percent of respondents said they strongly agree, and only 1 percent said they strongly disagree. This high level of patriotic sentiment is in line with findings from other national and regional surveys, such as the National Election Study (NES), the General Social Survey (GSS), Gallup polls, and media polls (Schildkraut and Furia 2003; Citrin et al. 2007).[28] Bivariate comparisons of the mean level of patriotism across relevant variables can be found in Appendix D.

The multivariate analysis of patriotism uses an ordered probit model similar to the models in Table 6.3 but without action-oriented civic republicanism. The results appear in Table 6.4. As with other studies, older respondents are consistently more proud to be American than younger respondents. For Latinos and Asians, familiarity with English also promotes pride, though generational status is insignificant.[29] In line with Citrin's findings, identity choice does not matter for blacks, Latinos, or Asians. A person of Mexican ancestry who identifies primarily as Latino or as Mexican is just as patriotic as a person of Mexican ancestry who identifies primarily as American.[30] The only case

---

[28] From 1983 to 1990, at least 90% of the American population consistently considered itself to be very or somewhat patriotic (Schildkraut and Furia 2003).

[29] Using generational dummy variables instead of the straight-line measure did not change the results. All generational dummy variables were insignificant.

[30] When models were run separately for Latinos and Asians, the substantive results on identity choice and the interactions remain the same, while the effects of education, age, language use, and panethnic discrimination are driven primarily by Asians. The coefficients in the Latino model are of the same sign but fail to achieve significance.

TABLE 6.4. *Proud to Be American, by Race, Ordered Probit*

Independent Variable	White b	White s.e.	Black b	Black s.e.	Asian and Latino b	Asian and Latino s.e.
Education	−0.90**	0.17	−1.09**	0.30	−0.52**	0.26
Age	1.28**	0.22	1.27**	0.59	0.60*	0.35
Male	−0.16*	0.09	0.02	0.20	−0.01	0.14
Generation (1st to 4th+)	0.23	0.17	0.52	0.42	−0.12	0.21
Speaks primarily English at home	–	–	–	–	0.37**	0.16
Latino	–	–	–	–	0.43**	0.18
National origin self-identification	−0.04	0.29	–	–	−0.12	0.31
Panethnic self-identification	−0.68**	0.18	−0.39	0.55	−0.14	0.52
National origin discrimination	−0.03	0.25	–	–	0.57*	0.34
Panethnic discrimination	0.91**	0.24	−0.79	0.57	−0.69*	0.41
Individual-level discrimination	−0.49	0.31	−0.34	0.41	−0.12	0.39
National origin × national origin discrimination	1.12	0.88	–	–	−0.02	0.53
National origin × individual discrimination	−1.94**	0.65	–	–	−0.04	0.55
Panethnic × panethnic discrimination	0.34	0.60	−0.28	0.80	0.30	0.70
Panethnic × individual discrimination	0.68	0.84	0.96*	0.54	0.19	0.77
Cutpoint 1	−2.49	0.29	−2.90	0.61	−2.31	0.37
Cutpoint 2	−1.80	0.25	−2.40	0.61	−1.99	0.33
Cutpoint 3	−0.87	0.25	−1.40	0.61	−0.67	0.23
Chi-square	144.51		24.77		32.98	
N	1150		261		403	

Note: ** $p < 0.05$; * $p < 0.1$. All nondummy variables coded 0 to 1. Unweighted data.
Source: Twenty-First-Century Americanism Survey, 2004.

in which identity prioritization matters is for whites who identify primarily as white. Such people are less patriotic than whites who identify primarily as American.

Perceptions of discrimination matter for Latinos and Asians but not for blacks. Latinos and Asians who think that their panethnic group is mistreated are less patriotic. No identity type mitigates this impact, similar to the findings from the trust in the law enforcement model.[31] Black respondents, however, respond as group consciousness theory would expect: identifying as black and perceiving individual-level mistreatment yields a positive coefficient, suggesting that the group identification provides a psychological resource that prevents discrimination from generating alienation.[32]

A WORD ON VOTING

The 21-CAS asked respondents if they had voted in the 2000 presidential election. The percentages of people saying they did are suspiciously high, indicating that overreporting is a problem on this measure. For instance, 83 percent of Latino citizens and 80 percent of Asian citizens said that they voted. Yet according to the November 2000 Current Population Survey, approximately 45 percent of Hispanic citizens and 43 percent of Asian citizens voted in the 2000 election.[33] Nevertheless, I ran a model for Latinos and Asians (not shown) in order to test whether identity choices and perceptions of discrimination affect this most basic act of "good" citizenship in the ways that group consciousness theory and social identity theory would predict (recall that both theories contend that collective action for group-specific gains is likely among the highly identified when the identity is politicized).

The results showed that these theories predict voting behavior quite well. Panethnic and national origin identifiers, absent perceptions of discrimination, were less likely than American identifiers to report having voted. Likewise, people who perceived discrimination against the national origin group were less likely to have voted but only among those respondents who identified as American. When a national origin identity and the perception of national origin discrimination were present, the likelihood of voting rebounded, as did the likelihood of voting when a panethnic identity and the perception of panethnic discrimination were present.[34] Thus, in the absence of discrimination, immigration critics may be correct: prioritizing a non-American identity might lead to alienation in the case of voting. But perceptions of discrimination are rarely absent. In terms of actual magnitude in the real world, a non-American identity

[31] Perceptions of discrimination fail to achieve significance when the model is rerun without people who were recoded for panethnicity.

[32] Rerunning the model for blacks without people who were recoded for panethnicity (n = 270 vs. 261) bolsters this interpretation: panethnic discrimination achieves significance, reducing patriotism, but its effect is completely neutralized by the interaction between panethnic discrimination and a panethnic identity.

[33] Data available at http://www.census.gov/population/www/socdemo/voting/p20–542.html (accessed June 17, 2008).

[34] The voting model was run for Latino and Asian citizens. Besides identity choice and perceptions of discrimination (and their interactions), control variables included age, education, strength of partisanship, political knowledge, generation, and language spoken at home.

might be more likely to promote participation than to detract from it, simply due to the fact that perceptions of discrimination are so common.

DISCUSSION

The goals of this chapter were to see if adopting a non-American identity reduces trust and obligation (as well as patriotism and voting) and if the psychological mechanisms detailed in group consciousness theory and social identity theory help us to understand the conditions under which identities become consequential. Table 6.5 summarizes the results with respect to the key independent variables for Latino, Asian, and black respondents. The first row of the table underscores that identity choices on their own (absent perceptions of discrimination) are rarely a problem when it comes to trust and obligation.[35] The concerns of immigration critics regarding this score are validated in only two cases: a panethnic identity can make Latinos and Asians (who do not perceive discrimination) less trusting of government and can make blacks less likely to say they have an obligation to serve in the military. Otherwise, whether a person sees herself primarily as American or as a member of a panethnic or national origin group appears to be inconsequential, but only if she does not perceive discrimination – a big "if."

The second row of the table shows that perceptions of discrimination cause a fair amount of alienation. Adopting a non-American identity can mitigate the effects of discrimination with respect to trust in government, and panethnic identities are more likely to exhibit this power than national origin identities (see third row). But they can also activate the alienating power of discrimination with respect to one's sense of obligation to the American people. In some cases, such as trust in law enforcement, one's self-identification does nothing at all.

In the end, group consciousness theory and social identity theory provide useful frameworks for understanding how identity choices affect trust in government, certain obligations to the national community, and voting. Politicized identities can provide an important psychological resource that mitigates the damaging effects of discrimination, yet they can also lead people to close ranks around the mistreated group and be less willing to make sacrifices for the national community. These theoretical approaches, however, provide less help when examining trust in law enforcement, the obligation to serve in the military, or pride in being American. When examining those factors, identities – and theories about identities – don't emerge as relevant. Regardless of one's group attachment or degree of politicization, discrimination is where all of the action is. Simply put, Table 6.5 shows that the ways national and ethnic

---

[35] Recall Chapter 5, in which I argued that it is more likely that perceptions of discrimination influence identity choices rather than the other way around. If identity choices on their own generated perceptions of discrimination, then they should also exhibit independent power in the analyses in this chapter. By and large, they do not.

TABLE 6.5. *Summary of Key Findings (blacks, Latinos, and Asians only)*

	Trust in Government	Trust in Law Enforcement	Obligation to Donate	Obligation to Volunteer	Obligation to Serve	Pride in being American
Impact of identity attachment on…	Less trust for Latinos and Asians (panethnic)	No impact	No impact	No impact	Less obligation for blacks (panethnic)	No impact
Impact of perception of discrimination on…	Less trust for blacks (individual level) and Latinos and Asians (panethnic level)	Less trust for blacks, Latinos, and Asians (individual level)	No impact	Greater obligation for blacks (individual level)	Less obligation for blacks (panethnic level)	Less obligation for Latinos and Asians (panethnic) Greater obligation for Latinos and Asians (national origin)
Impact of politicized identity on… (identity attachment plus perception of discrimination)	Panethnic ID + discrimination bolsters trust for all American ID + discrimination reduces trust	No impact	Panethnic ID + panethnic discrimination reduces obligation for Latinos and Asians	Panethnic ID + panethnic discrimination increases obligation for blacks National origin ID + national origin discrimination reduces obligation for Latinos and Asians	No impact	Panethnic ID + individual discrimination increases pride for blacks

attachments influence attitudinal engagement is complicated. Such attachments can be a blessing, a curse, or neither.

Individual-Level Discrimination vs. Group-Level Discrimination

One key question to examine at this point is whether individual-level or group-level mistreatment is more consequential. For black respondents, individual-level mistreatment seems to dominate, as it did in Chapter 5. It reduces their trust in government and law enforcement, and makes them less likely to say they have an obligation to serve in the military.

But for Latinos and Asians, group-level mistreatment matters more than individual-level mistreatment. The only exception is with trust in law enforcement. In all other cases in which perceptions of discrimination matter for Latinos and Asians, it is primarily the perception of panethnic discrimination (for trust in government, obligation to donate to charity, and patriotism) and, in one case (obligation to volunteer), the perception of discrimination against one's national origin group that produce the kind of alienation that immigration critics decry. In sum, findings from the past two chapters suggest that for Latinos and Asians in the United States, individual-level discrimination affects how people see themselves in relation to salient cultural groups, while perceptions of how those groups – the panethnic group in particular – are treated affect people's sense of connection to political institutions and the political community.

Panethnicity vs. National Origin Identity Prioritization

Another relevant question to examine at this point is whether it is panethnic or national origin attachments that can enhance trust and/or diminish obligation in the presence of discrimination. It turns out that there is no consistent pattern here. Sometimes it is a panethnic attachment that matters (trust in government, obligation to donate to charity). Other times it is a national origin attachment (obligation to volunteer). Together with Chapter 5, I am left to conclude that these two identity types are similar in their causes and their effects among nonwhites in the United States. There is still much to learn, however, about when it is the panethnic identity that matters and when it is the national origin identity because they both matter at different points in this analysis. At this point, it would be premature to simply study American identifiers versus non-American identifiers.

BEING AMERICAN VS. BEING CONNECTED

For both trust and obligation, the ideal advanced by immigration critics as well as by some democratic theorists and social psychologists – having all people in the United States identify primarily as American – is ideal only if people do not feel that they or their group is mistreated. Once perceptions of discrimination are added to the mix, the normative question of whether we should or should not want people to see themselves primarily as American becomes much more complicated. As Lisa García Bedolla warns, feeling stigmatized while lacking a positive attachment to the aggrieved group leads to disengagement, and "for members of stigmatized groups, establishing a positive attachment to their social group may be a necessary first step toward their attachment to the political community as a whole" (2005, 190). My research here suggests she is right with respect to trust but not with respect to obligation. In both cases, however, my findings underscore the need to focus our attention on perceptions of mistreatment more so than on identity choices, or rather, along with identity choices. Without appreciating the conditional nature of how identity attachments shape engagement with American society or how perceptions of threat activate the ability of identities to have political consequences, we run the risk of concentrating our attention on the wrong things. If we seek pathways to achieve a society in which people share attachments to a superordinate national identity and in which they trust political institutions and feel that they have obligations to the political community, we will never find them if we fail to look beyond simply whether people do or do not see themselves as American.

7

Immigrant Resentment

When the Work Ethic Backfires

Even though many nonwhite Americans, immigrant and native born alike, define the normative content of American identity the same as whites do (Chapter 3), think of themselves as American (Chapter 5), and differ minimally from whites in their sense of obligation, patriotism, and trust – with differences diminishing across each immigrant generation (Chapter 6), media coverage of immigration issues suggests that many white native-born Americans think otherwise. One is left with the impression that native-born whites believe that today's immigrants and their descendants reject American norms, a belief that generates a kind of resentment that I call "immigrant resentment." The purpose of this chapter is to examine such resentment.

The constitutive norms that define the meaning of one's national identity provide stereotypes that help people derive expectations about the behavior of their fellow citizens. Negative feelings toward particular subgroups in society often stem from perceptions that members of such groups violate particular national norms, and thus threaten the meaning of one's own identity. For instance, the perception that African Americans violate cherished liberal American norms such as individualism or the work ethic has been shown to be relatively widespread and enduring, and it has proved to be a potent force driving preferences on race-targeted policies such as affirmative action (Kinder and Sanders 1996). This particular perception of norm violation has multiple terms in the literature, including symbolic racism, modern racism, and racial resentment (Henry and Sears 2002). The view that blacks threaten a central element of the national value system holds up as a powerful predictor of attitudes even when more tangible threats are included in models of opinion formation.

When it comes to immigrants, perceptions of norm violation abound and have existed for some time. We hear that immigrants, like blacks, violate American liberalism by coming to the United States in order to take advantage of generous social welfare policies, a critique that has seen a resurgence as opponents of President Barack Obama's proposed health care reform contended that his policy would serve as a magnet for illegal immigrants searching for free medical care (King 2009; Malkin 2009); that immigrants violate civic republicanism by not wanting to think of themselves as American or by sending the money they earn back to their home countries rather than investing in their new communities; and that immigrants violate incorporationist norms by insisting that public institutions help them maintain their own cultural traditions at the expense of American traditions, such as learning English (Izumi 2001; Aijan 2007; Schlafly 2008). To date, the study of norm violation in the United States has tended to focus on racial resentment directed toward blacks or on whether immigrants, mainly Latinos and Asians, are likewise the target of such racial resentment versus whether more "realistic" concerns, such as sociotropic or pocketbook economic assessments, shape preferences. In this chapter, I argue that the framework developed by scholars of racial resentment provides a useful model for studying attitudes toward immigrants and immigration-related public policies, and I extend that model in appropriate ways in order to capitalize on its contributions. In particular, I use the notion of norm violation to develop and analyze immigrant resentment.

Immigrant resentment, like racial resentment, combines an adherence to traditional norms and values associated with American national identity with the belief that minority groups fail to live up to them. But the specific values in question are derived from civic republican and incorporationist notions of national identity, not liberal ones. Whereas racial resentment involves viewing minorities as violating the liberal norms of self-reliance and hard work, immigrant resentment involves viewing Latinos, Asians, and recent immigrants as not being concerned enough with the public good, placing too much of an emphasis on particularistic ethnic concerns, and rejecting the civic duty of assimilation. The idea that immigrant resentment exists as a distinct concept first occurred to me when I analyzed focus group discussions about American identity in earlier research (Schildkraut 2005a). I expected to find people harboring resentment toward immigrants, but I had expected it to be a form of racial resentment grounded in liberalism. I expected that people would feel that immigrants violate traditional liberal norms such as the work ethic. The image of immigrants as lazy freeloaders featured prominently in national debates about Proposition 187 in California and about national welfare reform just a few years earlier, fostering a climate that I thought would still be salient to focus group participants.[1]

Though some focus group participants did argue that immigrants are lazy and take advantage of American generosity, I found that a different kind of resentment appeared more regularly, one that focused on a different set of American norms. For example, a complaint that appeared in several focus groups was that immigrants use the United States to get a job in order make

---

[1] Proposition 187 was a ballot initiative passed by California voters in 1994 that made undocumented immigrants ineligible for a wide range of government services. The campaign for the proposition generated nationwide attention. Despite its passage, court challenges successfully prevented the proposition from ever being enacted.

money and then send that money to family members in the home country. Unlike racial resentment, which maintains that nonwhites do not work hard enough, this manifestation of resentment holds that immigrants work very hard and quite possibly work too hard. The norms being violated in this complaint are not liberal. Rather, they appeal to an alternative set of constitutive norms about American identity. In this example, immigrant resentment involves disparaging immigrants for taking advantage of economic opportunities in the United States while shirking the responsibilities of citizenship, a clear violation of civic republican principles. This complaint only makes sense when one appreciates the powerful hold that civic republican ideals have had in shaping how people define what being American means. Recall from Chapter 3 that volunteering in one's community and being informed about local and national politics were widely endorsed as constituting an "action-oriented" image of American identity. In the focus group discussions, it became clear that people felt that rather than invest one's attention and resources in their communities, immigrants violate this image and remain committed to a foreign land.

Other resentments stemmed from the concern that immigrants today have no interest in thinking of themselves as American or becoming a part of the community in which they now reside. Instead, they keep their attention focused on their own culture and on the happenings in their country of origin. Such focus, discussants claimed, transformed too easily into unfair desires and demands for local and national government to accommodate their distinct lifestyles.[2]

These complaints led me to wonder: Do similar resentments exist among Americans more generally? Are these resentments distinct from the kind of norm violation public opinion scholars have been studying? How can we measure these resentments in a more generalizable fashion? To what extent does immigrant resentment drive policy preferences? These questions motivate the analyses in this chapter. To date, we know little about the factors that determine the extent of immigrant resentment or about the role it plays in opinion formation on ethnicity-related policies because survey-based analyses of it have not existed.

I use the term *immigrant resentment* to underscore that this set of attitudes is a unique set of resentments directed toward today's immigrants, and that, like racial resentment, it is rooted in entrenched values that people associate with the very idea of America. The term also aids the juxtaposition with the racial resentment that is more familiar to students of public opinion in the United States. Likewise, I use the term *racial resentment* throughout my analysis when I refer to the perception that immigrants violate liberal American norms (i.e., I replace "black" with "immigrant" in racial resentment measures). Both resentments center on the violation of traditional national norms, yet the particular norms in question differ between the two concepts.

---

[2] See Paxton and Mughan (2006) for additional focus group analysis in which immigrants are chastised for their "self-imposed segregation."

In the following section, I discuss racial resentment in more detail and explain how it contributes to the study of attitudes about immigrants. Next I summarize the history of stereotypes about, and resentment of, immigrants in the United States. Then I develop measures of immigrant resentment and test their adequacy. I compare immigrant resentment to racial resentment and examine the social, contextual, and attitudinal factors that shape both sets of attitudes. I also compare them with antiimmigrant attitudes that stem from more "old-fashioned" ascriptivist understandings of American national identity, which I call "ethnocultural resentment." I show that immigrant resentment, racial resentment, and ethnocultural resentment all exist, yet that all are distinct concepts with both distinct and shared roots. Each one, for example, is exacerbated by the belief that whites have been discriminated against due to their race or ethnicity. At the same time, each one is rooted in particular understandings about the meaning of American national identity. Immigrant resentment, for example, is more prevalent among people that rely on particular civic republican norms when defining the meaning of American national identity more generally. Racial resentment is more prevalent among people who see the work ethic as a constitutive national norm. Ethnocultural resentment is more prevalent among people who adhere to ascriptive definitions of being American. Finally, I show how each of these forms of resentment shape attitudes toward immigration-related policies, such as whether immigrants should be eligible for government services.

RESENTMENT: BEHAVIOR, NOT BIOLOGY

Racial resentment is a phenomenon long recognized as an important factor shaping race-targeted policy preferences. It is the combination of believing in the traditional liberal values of individualism and the work ethic and feeling that African Americans violate these entrenched American norms (Kinder and Sanders 1996). People who harbor such resentment feel that structural barriers to equality in the United States have been removed, and that gaps between blacks and whites in achieving "the good life" must therefore be the fault of blacks (Henry and Sears 2002). Racial resentment is prevalent in American society and influences whites' opinions on a range of race-targeted policies even when views on whether one is personally threatened are controlled. As Mendelberg shows, racial resentment emerged from the unique history of race relations in the United States (2001). It has deep roots in justifications for slavery, which in part relied on portraying blacks as lazy. Their laziness, along with violent tendencies and sexual aggression, was viewed as an inherent trait. Viewing these negative traits as products of biology – and the resulting social acceptability of justifying inequality – persisted throughout the Jim Crow years and the era of eugenics and Social Darwinism.

Throughout the struggle for civil rights, a new egalitarian norm eventually replaced beliefs about – and hence explicit support for – inequality. This new norm became increasingly accepted among Americans of all backgrounds and at all levels of political power. The earlier justifications for slavery, and later, segregation, were increasingly discredited. Now, Mendelberg notes, "most whites know that they should treat blacks equally, and they are inclined to chastise those who do not" (2001, 114). Despite the rejection of inegalitarianism and the removal of formal barriers to equality, gaps between whites and blacks have persisted with regard to material measures of success. Such gaps, along with the rise of inner-city pathologies, have led to frustration and ambivalence, which Mendelberg notes paves the way for resentment to become mobilized for political gain. The history she recounts (and related analyses, e.g., Kinder and Sanders [1996] and Sears et al. [1997]) provides a compelling rebuke of the critique that racial resentment is not really any different from "old-fashioned" racism. The change in norms is real; the new egalitarian norms are deeply held.

People adhere to norms because they think it is the right thing to do as well as because they fear the social sanctions that violation might bring. Norms about how people in one's ingroup (such as one's fellow Americans) should behave (aka injunctive norms) – as opposed to how they do behave (aka descriptive norms) – are especially powerful (Christensen et al. 2004). As Gilens, Kuklinski, and Sniderman argue, some people are reluctant to express their opposition to affirmative action not only because they fear how others will interpret it, but also because they are uncomfortable with their own attitude (1998). They are torn between their adherence to egalitarianism, on the one hand, and their discomfort with certain race-based policies, on the other. In short, norms that people believe in are powerful and violation can have psychological consequences. These consequences are wrought by friends, neighbors, employers, the media, and by our own inner selves; it is not merely a case of avoiding legal sanction. Fazio and Hilden show that priming racial stereotypes among people who claim to reject such stereotypes produces shame, embarrassment, and guilt (2001). Experiencing one's own hypocrisy or ambivalence is distressing. As Mendelberg observes, "several strands of literature agree that [ambivalence about race] is widespread among whites" (2001, 117n).

Reconciling one's desire to adhere to egalitarian norms with one's attempts to understand continuing racial disparities fuels ambivalence and generates resentment. As Kinder and Sanders (1996) put it, "the core of this new resentment [is] not whether blacks possessed the inborn ability to succeed, but whether they would try" (105). Being seen as rejecting the work ethic, the bedrock of how many Americans define their national identity, has led to blacks remaining a target of hostility. I argue that the ambivalence that has characterized attitudes about racial policy exists with attitudes related to immigration as well. The internalized egalitarian norm conflicts with attributions for observations of concrete realities. The concrete reality in the case of immigration involves the extent to which native-born Americans encounter ethnic, linguistic, and religious diversity in comparison to the recent past. As Paxton and Mughan note, "assimilation is not automatic" (2006). The high immigration rates of the past few decades have increased the frequency with which people encounter difference. These frequent encounters generate the perception that assimilation to traditional American norms is not happening, despite social science evidence to the contrary (Alba and Nee 2003; Citrin et al. 2007). In the age of egalitarianism, the reason attributed to this failure to "become American" comes down to behavioral choices.

Several features of the racial resentment scholarship are useful when thinking about attitude formation toward immigrants and the growing nonwhite segments of American society that immigration yields. First, the way it distinguishes between symbolic threats and tangible or "real" ones is a useful way to think about attitudes toward immigrants because political debate often centers on the economic consequences of immigration. Concerns about the impact of immigration on American workers, for instance, have been a part of debates about immigration for well more than a century. Determining the extent to which immigration-related attitudes derive from attachments to national norms and values and more tangible concerns about economic well-being is an important task.

Second, its focus on resentment rather than on "old-fashioned" biologically based hostility is also useful because doing so more accurately captures the symbolic and normative roots of contemporary attitudes. Recent experimental work by Daniel Hopkins and colleagues confirms that the newly dominant egalitarian norm in the United States that renders the expression of antiblack rhetoric socially undesirable also renders the expression of antiimmigrant and anti-Latino rhetoric undesirable (2009). Their study also contains evidence that antiimmigrant activists carefully select their language so as to avoid being labeled as racist. Yes, there are still people who harbor beliefs about racial superiority. However, there are also many people who genuinely reject those views, but who still possess negative stereotypes about how members of immigrant outgroups behave. The sources of those stereotypes are beliefs about how people choose to act, not how they are biologically determined to act. Feeling that immigrants could become "good" Americans if they wanted to, but that they simply don't want to, is different from feeling that immigrants are inherently "non-assimilable," as FDR once wrote about the Japanese (Robinson 2001).

Third, the particular resentment involved in racial resentment – violation of the work ethic – provides some, but by no means all, of the fodder for contemporary immigrant resentment. The view that other nonwhite minority groups in the United States seek unfair advantages does exist. Yet the unique role immigration has played in American history and the resulting value placed on assimilation and active citizenship mean that attitudes about immigrants and immigration are more varied and complex than a simple importation of black/white models allows. Just as the history of race relations holds the key to racial resentment, the history of immigration holds the key to immigrant resentment. To be sure, there are important common roots here, the most important one being the development over the course of the twentieth century of the new norm that rejects arguments about biological hierarchies among different racial and ethnic groups. The genuine adherence to egalitarian views directs resentment to focus on behavior rather than on biology. Hence, seemingly voluntary norm violation becomes the locus of attention.

ATTITUDES ABOUT IMMIGRANTS OVER TIME

Contradictory stereotypes about immigrants have coexisted in the United States for some time. Immigrants are lazy, and they are hardworking. They seek new opportunities in the United States, and they take unfair advantage of those opportunities. They are the "new Americans," and they don't want to become Americans. As with racial attitudes, attitudes about immigrants in the United States have undergone some transformations while also retaining certain similarities across time. In particular, the rise of the norm of egalitarianism has rendered biological explanations of stereotypes essentially obsolete; the characteristics people lament are now largely attributed to behavior rather than biology. But simply taking this understanding, which derives from what we know about how whites form attitudes about blacks in the United States, and importing it to studying attitudes about immigrants is insufficient. The unique role of immigration in American history means that the set of behaviors in question is different from the behaviors that dominate opinion formation about African Americans and race-targeted policies. This section briefly summarizes the range of norms that immigrants have been said to violate and notes how attributions for those violations have changed over time. It focuses on immigration discourse from the late 1800s – the era in which the federal immigration bureaucracy began to solidify – to today, and it is admittedly sweeping; more detailed accounts can be found elsewhere (Higham 1963; King 2000; Tichenor 2002; King 2005).

Among the many stereotypes about immigrants that have evolved since the dawn of the industrial age is the view that immigrants are a drain on society because of laziness and biological limitations. As King (2000, 175) explains, restrictionists at the turn of the twentieth century argued that these limitations would lead immigrants to "degenerate" and "require institutional care." Far from being voiced just among a fringe element, President Rutherford B. Hayes described Chinese immigrants as belonging to a "weaker race" when advocating their exclusion (King 2005, 50). Biological deficiencies were attributed not only to immigrants from Asia but also to immigrants from southern and eastern Europe. The eugenics movement was influential in lending credibility to such charges (Gould 1996). The beliefs about biological hierarchies and natural abilities to succeed that justified racial segregation came to permeate elite discourse about immigration as well.

Yet in addition to being seen as "intellectually inferior" (King 2000, 61), immigrants were also criticized for being concentrated in ethnic enclaves and for primarily being employed in unskilled jobs, a set of factors that was said to hinder assimilation. As immigrants were being portrayed as a drain on national resources, they were simultaneously being portrayed as too hardworking. They were especially resented by labor unions in this regard. Chinese immigrants in

California, for example, were disparaged for accepting lower wages and poor working conditions, thus hurting the economic fortunes of American laborers. In these complaints, being hardworking was not a virtue despite the centrality of hard work to the American ideal. Their alleged ability and desire to work, like their alleged laziness, was invoked to support claims about the unlikelihood of assimilation.[3]

This stereotype of the excessively hardworking immigrant was not limited to Asians. Immigrants from southern and eastern Europe were also disparaged for flooding unskilled labor markets and for accepting working conditions that threatened American livelihoods. The Dillingham Commission, a congressional commission that produced recommendations on immigration policy in 1911, was particularly worried about "single, unskilled males immigrating from southern and eastern Europe, whom [it] judged both uninterested in assimilation and mostly unsuitable for naturalization" (King, 2000, 76). Members of the commission relied heavily on eugenics studies to support their concerns. Thus, in addition to being unfit for a life of hard work and self-sufficiency, it was argued that immigrants were unwilling and unable to become Americans in their hearts and minds, which therefore made them unworthy of being welcomed into the American political community (also see Johnson 1997).

During the turn of the last century, immigrants were placed in an untenable position. They were criticized for working too hard while also being criticized for lacking the ability to be self-sustaining. They were chastised for isolating themselves in ethnic enclaves that prevented assimilation while also being viewed as inherently unable to assimilate. Critiques of "hyphenated" Americans, as famously expressed by Theodore Roosevelt and Woodrow Wilson, were emblematic of the widespread view that immigrants shunned full immersion (Higham 1963). Yet becoming American was an opportunity that Asian immigrants in particular did not even have due to laws restricting naturalization to whites only. Being too concentrated in their own communities, uninterested in assimilation, and unable to assimilate even if they wanted to were concerns intimately connected to the phenomenon of immigration. They all stemmed from fears about whether people from faraway lands with foreign customs could adopt the American way of life. The consequences for failure in this regard were frightening, and that fear was powerful. Antiimmigrant forces had their greatest success in 1924 with the passage of the National Origins Act, which significantly reduced the number of immigrants allowed to enter the country and ensured that nearly all of those immigrants would be from northern and western Europe (Roberts 1997). These limits were in place until 1965.[4]

---

[3] Unions also charged that Chinese immigration was essentially involuntary and that it was a threat to free labor (Tichenor, 2002, ch. 4).

[4] Other prominent strains of antiimmigrant discourse at this time included anti-Catholicism and fear of anarchists (Higham 1963).

There were some voices at the time that offered a more charitable view of immigrants. The early 1900s saw the rise of exclusion but also of arguments that immigrants can assimilate. The metaphor of the melting pot emerged in the early twentieth century and came to signify the ability – as well as the desire – of immigrants to become Americans. This metaphor, with help from Emma Lazarus's poem "The New Colossus," gave rise to the archetypal "huddled masses" optimistically eyeing the Statue of Liberty as their boat reached American shores. But these views went against a more popular norm. The sympathetic voices achieved some success with the creation of Americanization programs (Miller 1998), but the victorious voices of the day maintained that Americanization efforts could only produce superficial changes; the only way to have immigrants become American was to make sure that only people of the "right" backgrounds were allowed to immigrate in the first place (Tichenor, 2002, 140). The idea that assimilation by people from all backgrounds was possible did not become more widely accepted until decades later.

The virtual moratorium on immigration led the issue largely to fade from national discourse. When immigration numbers began to rise again starting in the late 1960s, they did so under dramatically different domestic conditions. As he signed the bill that repealed the quotas, President Lyndon Johnson called the exclusionary regime "un-American" (King 2005, 129), a complete reversal of the justifications for earlier presidential support for quotas. Echoes of concerns from decades earlier eventually returned, but they had changed in the process due to the rejection of eugenics and to the newly ascendant norm of egalitarianism. Today, we still hear concerns that immigrants violate a wide range of American norms: they reject the work ethic, work too hard, focus on their own ethnic communities at the expense of their broader surroundings, and do not want to become American. The key difference is that just as stereotypes about blacks changed from thinking that they could not achieve success to thinking that they choose to act in ways that prohibit success, stereotypes about immigrants changed from thinking that they could not become American to thinking that they choose to avoid becoming American. Take, for example, Senator James Vardaman (D-MS), who stated during floor debate of the Immigration Act of 1917:

The natives of [Africa and Asia] should be excluded. I do not think the inhabitants of either are fit for citizenship in this Republic. And I say this not in the spirit of hostility to the black man, or the yellow man, but for the preservation of the purity of the white race in America and the conservation of the white man's civilization. (*Congressional Record* 1916, 157)

Senator James Reed (D-MO) concurred, saying, "I think the time has come when we ought to keep our country from being filled up with people who are not capable of becoming first-class citizens of the United States" (*Congressional Record* 1916, 157). Statements such as these were in no way unique at the time.

Even the most casual observer of contemporary American society would agree that such outright ascriptivism would hardly be accepted on the floor of the Senate today. Today, one is more likely to hear the charge that immigrants can assimilate, that they can become Americans, but that they do not. Politicians are understandably reluctant to point the finger at immigrants. Instead, they tend to blame government. It is not uncommon to hear arguments such as those put forward by Representative Joe Knollenberg (R-MI), who in 1996 argued in favor of making English the official language by stating:

For more than 200 years our Nation has been a melting pot of cultures and nationalities united by one common bond – our English language. When our ancestors came to America, they came to this country knowing they had to learn English to survive. Today, our melting pot has become a patchwork quilt of cultures, isolated because they cannot speak English. They aren't assimilating into our society like our ancestors did. Our current bilingual policies are shredding the common bond that has made our Nation great. (*Congressional Record* 1996, 9760)

Scholars and political commentators have also sounded alarms along these lines (Miller 1998; Schlesinger 1998; Huntington 2004). Such critics say American society now errs too much on the side of diversity and on preserving difference rather than on seeking common ground. It is argued that we have become too accepting of difference and, worse, too accommodating, which only serves to encourage and enable the violation of civic republican and incorporationist norms (also see Shuck 1998). Critics lament that the welfare state and the liberal elite teach new arrivals that they are victims and should not feel compelled to change themselves in any way once they arrive. The result is a generation of immigrants who do not assimilate and do not want to. Huntington blamed many actors, including leaders of ethnic organizations, the American political establishment, and immigrants (2004). He wrote, for example, that too many of today's immigrants choose to "eat their cake and have it too, combining the opportunity, wealth, and liberty of America with the culture, language, family ties, traditions, and social networks of their birth country" (192).

Just like one hundred years ago, Americans find themselves encountering an impressive amount of cultural diversity, and many Americans have seen their communities change quite dramatically in a relatively short time frame. So much difference emerging in such a short period of time creates the impression that assimilation does not happen. Because most of us now accept that biology does not prevent cultural change, the seeming stagnation must be a product of choice. John Miller, discussing activists at a political rally in California to protest Proposition 187 who waved the Mexican flag, wrote, "Their confrontational rally represented the emblematic rejection of American national identity. It signaled a profound violation of the assimilation ethic that has allowed the United States to become a nation of immigrants . . . [seeing Mexican flags at a political rally] forced a troubling conclusion into the minds of many Californians: The immigrants of today aren't like the immigrants of yesterday. *They don't want to be Americans*" (1998, 4–5, emphasis added). Similar concerns were voiced during marches for immigrant rights in the spring of 2006 when Mexican flags flew alongside American flags. As one observer warned the demonstrators, "When Latinos embrace their ancestral flag, it suggests . . . that maybe all they are interested in are the dollars they can send back to Mexico" (Badie 2006; also see Gorman 2006; Soto 2006).

It is important to point out that we still hear that immigrants are a drain on national resources. Current resentment is not entirely civic republican and incorporationist in nature. Though again, the charge now emphasizes behavior rather than biology. Such views drove much support for California's Proposition 187 in 1994, in which many people in California and across the nation felt that immigrants took too many public resources in the form of welfare and other social services (Muller 1997). Much of that debate focused on illegal immigrants, though what started in California as debate about illegal immigrants quickly turned into a national conversation about all immigrants and their eligibility for public services in general (Chavez 1997; Michelson 2001). This conversation influenced national welfare reform legislation passed in 1996, which rendered legal immigrants ineligible for various social services (Michelson 2001), though eligibility for many of those benefits was eventually restored.

Current public opinion data reveal the ambivalence and contradictions in contemporary assessments of immigrants. A 2004 survey by the Kaiser Family Foundation, National Public Radio, and the Kennedy School of Government found the following patterns among their nonimmigrant respondents: 41 percent (a plurality) said there is no difference in the extent to which new immigrants and other Americans love America; 59 percent think immigrants keep the right amount – not too much or too little – of their own culture and traditions; 42 percent said recent immigrants are more hardworking than most other Americans while 48 percent said there is no difference (with a meager 7% saying that immigrants are less hardworking than Americans). Sixty percent said immigrants send most of the money they earn in the United States back to their home country, and 62 percent agreed that most recent immigrants do not pay their fair share of taxes. Forty-two percent think immigrants "strengthen our country because of their hard work and talents" while 52 percent think immigrants "are a burden on our country because they take our jobs, housing, and health care."[5]

John Higham notes that nativism is concerned with neutralizing perceived threats to the American way of life, threats uniquely attributed to foreign elements (1963). Concerns that immigrants threaten the American way of life are nothing new. What has changed is whether those threats are seen as stemming from biology or behavior. In this section, I have sought to underscore that the racial resentment model is an appropriate one to adopt and to demonstrate how it needs to be expanded in order to account for the norms that are uniquely implicated in the phenomenon of immigration. Those norms include coming to see oneself as a member of the national community, being invested in the

[5] Survey details available at http://www.kff.org/kaiserpolls/pomr100604pkg.cfm (accessed July 22, 2005).

community, being and active and informed member of the community, and not simply using the United States as a place to make money while retaining an untransformed "old world" lifestyle. It is clear that the most egregious exclusionary norms of earlier eras have passed. People do not, for example, argue that immigrants from certain countries are too biologically inferior to become Americans. Rather, a more modern and socially acceptable form of immigrant resentment has developed over the years. In focus groups, this modern resentment emerged most clearly when participants described immigrants as violating civic republican and incorporationist principles. To date, this immigrant resentment has not been subject to rigorous empirical analysis (though see Paxton and Mughan [2006] for an important first step).

APPLYING NORM VIOLATION TO IMMIGRANTS

Survey-based research on attitudes toward immigrants has generally taken one of two approaches. In the first approach, studies focus on the causes and consequences of the perceived impact that increased numbers of Latinos and Asians will have on the local and national community, often pitting such concerns against more tangible or economic factors such as a person's income or whether respondents have children who attend public school. A classic article by Citrin and colleagues provides an excellent example of this approach (1990). The authors combine perceptions of tangible economic effects – such as the fear that immigrants will cause an increase in the unemployment and crime rates – with more symbolic effects – such as the view that immigrants will enrich our culture – to form a scale they call the Hispanic/Asian Impact Index. People with high scores on the authors' "Americanism" scale were more likely than people with low scores to think increased immigration from these groups would have a negative impact on California. The impact indices, in turn, affected immigration-related policy preferences. The authors write, "A major source of opposition to cultural minorities among the majority ethnic group in America is the perception that they fail to conform to cherished notions of Americanism" (1142). Here, then, we see early evidence of attitudes toward immigrants being driven by perceptions of norm violation. Yet as I have argued, more detailed measures of Americanism can yield more accurate insights in this regard. Citrin's "Americanism" scale provides little guidance about which norms in particular people think are being violated. The task at hand thus becomes to do more to understand which norms are most implicated in opinion formation and among which segments of the American public.

Other examples of research in this vein likewise find that individual-level economic indicators such as household income are not significant predictors of hostility aimed at immigrants, Latinos, or Asians (Hood and Morris 1997; Fetzer 2000). Hood and Morris do, however, find that having a pessimistic outlook regarding the national economy (aka sociotropic concerns) leads to more antiminority affect, whereas neither Fetzer nor Citrin find sociotropic effects. Fetzer, like Citrin, concludes that attitudes about immigrants seem to be shaped by perceived threats to "the traditionally dominant majority's cultural views" (2000, 107).

More recently, Sniderman and colleagues have found that cultural concerns drive immigration-related attitudes in the Netherlands more so than economic concerns (2004). Concerns about whether immigrants fit in culturally were more powerful than concerns about whether they fit in economically. Moreover, respondents who were primed to think of themselves in terms of their national identity were more hostile toward immigration than people who were primed to think of themselves as individuals. Though Sniderman's study did not examine how people define "what it means to be Dutch," it provides clear evidence that preserving "Dutchness" is a priority as well as further support for the notion that violating constitutive norms in the abstract shapes immigration-related attitudes.

In the second approach, studies do hone in on specific types of norm violation by taking traditional racial resentment measures and changing the target group from "black" to "immigrant" or "Hispanic" (Huddy and Sears 1995; Vidanage and Sears 1995). Huddy and Sears examine if opinions about bilingual education funding are affected by respondents' perceptions that Latinos fail to work hard and whether respondents attribute the economic hardship of Latinos to Latinos ("internal attributions") or to external factors such as the lack of good jobs. They find that internal attributions help to explain opposition to bilingual education, as does being ideologically conservative, having school-aged children, or simply harboring anti-Latino affect. They also find that adhering to the norm of hard work results in a person being more likely to think that Hispanics violate that norm, whereas the respondent's income has no impact (1995).

Vidanage and Sears show that Hispanic and Asian resentment, measured by asking respondents if Hispanics and Asians are too demanding of government, are too demanding in pushing for equal rights, and should work their way up like other minority groups, is a strong predictor of support for a variety of restrictive preferences, including denying citizenship to children born to illegal immigrants and decreasing overall levels of immigration (1995). They also find that such resentment is a powerful predictor of whether respondents think Hispanic and Asian immigration will have negative consequences (analogous to Citrin's "impact index").

Paxton and Mughan, using a small undergraduate sample, provide the only analysis to date that delves more fully into the roots of resentment toward immigrants in the United States by tapping into norms that are uniquely related to immigration debates, such as language use and naturalization (2006). Using focus group analysis to guide their survey design, they develop measures that ask people if immigrants violate the American norms of citizenship, language, and productivity. They posit that a perceived failure to assimilate drives immigration attitudes and show the utility of measures tailored to these specific aspects of American culture.

Studies that examine what people think the social and economic impact of immigration will be and whether immigrants are the targets of racial resentment have produced valuable results. Except for Paxton and Mughan's recent study, we have yet to conduct empirical analyses that examine the kinds of resentments that were voiced regularly in my focus group discussions and have evolved from antiimmigrant views that prevailed in earlier decades. My aim, then, is not to argue that previous studies such as the ones described here are wrong, but rather to show that they only tell part of the story and to provide the tools needed to take the story further.

MEASURING IMMIGRANT RESENTMENT

As discussed in detail in Chapter 3, the Twenty-First-Century Americanism Survey (21-CAS) asked respondents to assess the extent to which they feel that particular characteristics should be important in determining whether someone is a "true" American. These questions evoke the normative content of American identity and were designed to tap into four clusters of norms: liberalism, ethnoculturalism, civic republicanism, and incorporationism. The analysis in Chapter 3 shows that the norms associated with these four concepts are, to varying degrees, widely endorsed among Americans of all racial and ethnic backgrounds. Together, they prescribe a set of norms regarding how group members are expected to look, sound, and act. For the present purposes, the relevant norms are the liberal demand to work hard and be self-sustaining, the civic republican demand to be an informed and active member of the community who values and prioritizes one's community membership, the incorporationist demand to try and find the right balance between cultural assimilation and maintenance, and the ethnocultural demand to be a white Protestant. In this chapter, the "true American" questions serve as independent variables, with liberalism and incorporationism measured by single survey questions and civic republicanism and ethnoculturalism measured by scales created from multiple questions (see Chapter 3 for details on scale construction).

The 21-CAS also asked respondents the extent to which they agree or disagree with certain statements about immigrants in the United States. These statements were designed to gauge the three kinds of resentment that people might feel toward immigrants: immigrant resentment, racial resentment, and ethnocultural resentment. Immigrant resentment combines civic republican and incorporationist norms. Though civic republicanism and incorporationism are distinct elements of American national identity, focus group participants consistently linked the two when voicing concerns about norm violation. Distinct political principles are often blended in practice at the elite level (Smith 1988, 1997); it should not be surprising to see that ordinary citizens likewise combine complementary elements of each when expressing their political preferences (Schildkraut 2005a). In this case, the civic republican demand for the centrality of community membership blends easily with the incorporationist demand for people to find the right balance between their immigrant history and their new membership in the American political community. The five questions used to measure immigrant resentment were designed to capture this blend by asking if immigrants are too focused on pursuing jobs and opportunity at the expense of both assimilation and meeting the demands that good citizenship in the United States requires. They were derived directly from themes that emerged in focus group discussions and, in some cases, adopt the exact words used by discussants. The wording of these items and the percentage of white respondents that agreed strongly or somewhat are presented in the top third of Table 7.1.[6] Note that percentages omit "don't know" responses (which constituted roughly 3% in each case). The distribution of white opinions shows that there is a fair amount of agreement that immigrants today violate such norms. Respondents were especially likely to think that immigrants do not want to be informed about "what's going on in the United States" and that they do not try hard enough to "fit in."

The second kind of resentment explored here is racial resentment. Many questions have been asked over the years to measure this kind of resentment; the four questions used in the 21-CAS were adopted from the Symbolic Racism 2000 scale (Henry and Sears 2002). I simply changed the target group in these racial resentment questions from "blacks" to "immigrants." The wording and distribution of responses appears in the middle third of Table 7.1. The results show that the perception of liberal norm violation is clearly not restricted to how whites feel about blacks. Many respondents agree that immigrants need to try hard if they want to "work their way up" and be "just as well off" as the native born. The American Dream is alive and well; formal barriers to success do not exist, and immigrants can have their piece of the pie, it is believed, if only they work hard enough.

Finally, ethnocultural resentment is explored. This kind of resentment explicitly laments the nonwhite and non-Christian backgrounds of many of today's immigrants. That such views are widely understood to be "politically incorrect" speaks to the true change in norms that we have seen during the course of the twentieth century. But such change does not mean that the views have disappeared or are without relevance. The 1990s nativist surge certainly included some ethnoculturalist voices, such as Pat Buchanan and Peter Brimelow. Brimelow, for example, warned, in his best seller, *Alien Nation*, that current immigration trends are dangerous because "the American nation has always had a specific ethnic core. And that core has been white" (1995). I call this type of resentment "ethnocultural resentment" because it stems from concerns that immigrants no longer meet the restrictive demands that ethnoculturalism places on membership in the American community. Though I heard very little resentment of this nature among focus group participants, it was expressed among a small segment. Moreover, the sense among proimmigrant groups and observers is that such "old-fashioned" antiimmigrant sentiment is still widespread

[6] The analyses here examine the views of whites only due to the historically powerful role of whites in dictating national sentiment and policy regarding immigrants.

TABLE 7.1. *Immigrant Resentment, Racial Resentment, and Ethnocultural Resentment*

	% Strongly Agree	% Somewhat Agree	N
Immigrant resentment			
Immigrants today take advantage of jobs and opportunities here without doing enough to give back to the community	17	27	1525
Immigrants today come to think of themselves as Americans just as much as immigrants from earlier eras did*	9	21	1519
Immigrants should really know what's going on in the United States if they want to stay here, but a lot of them just don't want to be bothered	33	29	1525
Blending into the larger society while maintaining cultural traditions is difficult, but a lot of immigrants today seem to do a good job of it*	3	10	1570
If immigrants only tried harder to fit in, then more Americans would accept their cultural differences	20	33	1573
Racial resentment			
Irish, Italians, and Jews overcame prejudice and worked their way up. Today's immigrants should do the same	49	31	1554
Years of discrimination have created conditions that make it difficult for immigrants to work their way out of the lower class*	27	26	1601
If immigrants would only try harder, they could be just as well off as people born in America	22	27	1587
Over the last few years, immigrants have gotten less than they deserve*	37	36	1480
Ethnocultural resentment			
The country would be better off if more of our immigrants were from Europe instead of from Asia and Latin America	3	8	1551
Immigrants who are Muslim just won't ever seem American to me	7	13	1547
The idea of an America where most people are not white bothers me	5	11	1604

Note: Whites only, "don't know" excluded. * = reverse coded (strongly disagree and somewhat presented in cells).

Source: Twenty-First-Century Americanism Survey, 2004.

(Perea 1997; Gonzalez 2001), especially after the terrorist attacks of 9/11. Yet surveys have generally not explored such ascriptive beliefs explicitly. The wording and distribution of responses of the ethnocultural resentment items appear in the bottom third of Table 7.1. As we would expect, few respondents express the view that immigrants who are Muslim, Asian, or Latino are problematic, yet enough respondents agreed with these items to justify analyzing ethnocultural resentment further.

IMMIGRANT RESENTMENT, RACIAL RESENTMENT, AND ETHNOCULTURAL RESENTMENT

Before moving on to examining the causes of the attitudes expressed in Table 7.1, it is first useful to examine whether scales for the three concepts of immigrant resentment, racial resentment, and ethnocultural resentment can reasonably be constructed from these items. A combination of analytic tools, including Cronbach's α and factor analysis, were used (for white respondents only) to assess the quality of the three resentment scales. The results (see Appendix E) led me to create an immigrant resentment scale that has three of the five immigrant resentment questions from Table 7.1. Two measures – whether immigrants come to think of themselves as Americans and whether immigrants do a good job of finding the balance between assimilation and maintaining difference – were dropped, resulting in a scale that asks if people agree that immigrants take advantage of jobs and opportunities without doing enough to give back to the community, don't want to be bothered to know what's going on in the United States, and don't try hard enough to fit into mainstream American life ($\alpha = 0.73$). The results also led to the creation of a racial resentment scale that consists of all four racial resentment questions ($\alpha = 0.65$). Likewise, I created an ethnocultural resentment scale that consists of all three measures listed at the bottom of Table 7.1 ($\alpha = 0.62$).[7] Running the factor analysis after the two immigrant resentment measures were dropped produced a scree plot that supports the retention of the three scales described

---

[7] The highest α for immigrant resentment (and the best fit according to the factor analysis) would have entailed adding the racial resentment item about whether immigrants could be just as well off as the native born if only they tried harder ($\alpha = 0.76$). But because the analysis here is a test of the theoretical concept as much as it is an exploration of which items cohere best, I chose to keep each of the items with their most appropriate theoretical construct. As DeVellis notes, in addition to looking at factor loadings and α coefficients when constructing scales, one must also consider whether the items make theoretical and logical sense (2003). Given the lineage of the "trying hard" item in racial resentment scholarship, I chose to keep that item with the other racial resentment measures. The α scores presented here compare well to scores from studies of distinct forms of racism (see Sears et al. 1997). Note that all remaining analyses were also run with the "trying hard" item included in the immigrant resentment scale. Doing so failed to change any of the substantive conclusions. Paxton and Mughan (2006) suggest that people might view economic productivity as a necessary precursor to cultural assimilation. Additionally, the "trying hard" item might have multiple interpretations; respondents may think that immigrants should try hard to fit in and not just to achieve economic success.

here. The average inter-item correlations for each scale do not exceed 0.15, as is recommended (Clark and Watson 1995), but bivariate correlations among all items (see Appendix E) show that items correlate within scales more than across them, suggesting construct validity (Paxton and Mughan 2006). Moreover, across the three scales, item-rest correlations range from 0.34 to 0.58.

Each scale was created by adding together responses to each item and then dividing by the total number of questions on the scale that the respondent answered. Then I constrained each scale to run from 0 to 1, in which 1 means the respondent gave the most resentful response to all items on the scale and 0 means the respondent gave the least resentful response to all items. The means (and standard deviations) for whites for each scale are immigrant resentment = 0.53 (s.d. = 0.28); racial resentment = 0.61 (s.d. = 0.24); and ethnocultural resentment = 0.21 (s.d. = 0.22). These means show that racial resentment is still a relevant concept to explore when examining attitudes toward immigrants; its mean score is well over the midpoint on the scale. At the same time, Americans are also likely to think that immigrants concentrate too much time and energy on individual pursuits and on cultural maintenance and not enough on immersing themselves in their new environs. Immigrant resentment is correlated with racial resentment (r = 0.48) and with ethnocultural resentment (r = 0.42).[8] That these resentments are correlated underscores that many Americans individually hold ambivalent and even contradictory assessments of today's immigrants; they simultaneously agree, for example, that immigrants focus too much on jobs while not working as hard as native-born Americans.

PREDICTING RESENTMENT

The next step in understanding the nature of these resentments is to examine their antecedents. Which factors make a person likely to think that immigrants violate civic republican or liberal norms? Are the determinants of one kind of resentment the same determinants of other kinds of resentment? To what extent does the way in which a person defines what being American means determine whether he or she perceives particular kinds of norm violation? Or is resentment driven by feeling one's own family is losing ground?

For the analysis that follows, I examine each kind of resentment in turn. I used ordinary least squares (OLS) to examine the impact of three sets of independent variables on each kind of resentment. The first set of independent variables includes standard demographic and political measures: age, education, partisan identification, ideological orientation, household income, assessment of the national economy (getting worse, staying the same, or getting better), and the percentage of people living in the respondent's Zip Code that are Hispanic or Asian (as determined by the 2000 Census). The first of these (from age to ideology) have long been understood to shape attitudes regarding an

---

[8] Racial resentment and ethnocultural resentment have a correlation of 0.27. These correlations parallel correlations among related yet distinct forms of racism (Sears et al. 1997).

array of political and social matters.[9] Household income and the perception of the national economy are included to capture individual-level material interest and sociotropic concerns, respectively.[10] As studies discussed earlier have shown, the influence of such economic measures on attitudes toward immigrants generally pales in comparison to the influence of more abstract and symbolic sentiments – if they have any influence at all (see Appendix A for question wording not described here).

Whether diverse contexts leads to more or less animosity toward outgroups has been a hotly debated question for some time. How best to measure context and uncover the causal mechanism are also questions analysts struggle to answer. In previous studies, contextual measures were shown to have an inconsistent influence on immigration-related attitudes. Using county-level data, for example, Hood and Morris find that "Anglos living in more heavily Hispanic and Asian areas generally have a more positive outlook on the potential contributions that these two groups can make to society" (1997) and that a more diverse context can lead to more liberal views on immigration. Other research, however, fails to confirm such relationships (Citrin, Reingold, and Green 1990; Frendreis and Tatalovich 1997). Stein, Post, and Rinden, who also use county-level data, argue that positive assessments of Hispanics are conditional on a diverse context plus actual behavioral contact (2000). Living in a diverse context but lacking actual interaction leads to negative attitudes toward Hispanics. I include Zip Code–level measures here in order to provide another test of the relationship between context and attitudes. The Zip Code level is generally more local and compact than the county-level measure used in other studies, though the present data set lacks measures of personal contact and interaction.[11]

The second set of independent variables contains measures that capture the extent to which the respondent defines the content of American identity in ethnocultural, liberal, civic republican, or incorporationist terms. The measures are the ones developed in Chapter 3. To remind the reader, I measure ethnoculturalism with a scale that captures whether respondents think true Americans should be Christian, be white, have European ancestors, and be born in the United States. I capture civic republican understandings of the meaning of American identity through two measures. The measure labeled

---

[9] Other potentially relevant individual characteristics, such as citizenship status, nativity, and language spoken at home were not included because nearly all whites in the sample are U.S. citizens, were born in the United States, and speak only English at home.

[10] Including household income in the models leads the overall N to drop by about 150 cases, because many respondents refused to answer that question. Omitting income increases the N, but does not change the main substantive results reported in this section.

[11] Respondents were also asked if they think their neighborhood is "mostly white, mostly black, mostly Latino, mostly Asian, or multi-ethnic." Two dummy variables were included in earlier tests to account for respondents who think their neighborhood is mostly Latino or mostly Asian, but these measures never achieved statistical significance and were thus dropped from the analysis.

civic republicanism ("action") asks whether respondents think it is important for true Americans to be informed about and involved in public life and to volunteer in their local communities. The measure labeled *civic republicanism ("identity")* asks whether respondents think it is important for true Americans to think of themselves as American, feel American, and have American citizenship. I measure liberalism by asking whether respondents think true Americans should pursue economic success through hard work. Finally, I measure incorporationism by asking if true Americans should blend into the larger society and preserve elements of their particular cultural traditions.

Here again I am using studies of racial resentment as a guide. Such studies have found that people who value hard work or individualism in general are more likely to think that blacks violate this cherished American norm. Likewise, people who value hard work are also more likely to think that Latinos do not work hard enough (Huddy and Sears 1995). It is generally assumed that peoples' most deeply held values tend to be salient to them and thus shape how they interpret their surroundings. As Sears and colleagues write, abstract values are influential "because [they] reflect [people's] moral codes about how society should be organized" (1997). Norms should shape the form that resentment will take. In practical terms for the analysis at hand, this means, for example, that respondents who score highly on the identity-oriented civic republicanism scale should exhibit more immigrant resentment than other respondents.

The third and final set of independent variables contains measures that capture whether the respondent thinks that whites as a group have been discriminated against in American society and whether the respondent thinks he or she has been discriminated against due to his or her race or ethnicity (see Chapter 5 for a discussion of these measures). These variables are included to control for another set of quasirealistic threats. Perceptions of group standing have been shown to affect candidate evaluation (Mutz and Mondak 1997), and perceptions of group position can be an important influence over race-related policy attitudes (Bobo 2000). Moreover, public discourse about immigration is replete with anecdotes about whites losing jobs to their newer, often bilingual, neighbors (see *Sun Sentinel* story from Chapters 2 and 5). The 21-CAS offers a rare opportunity to examine whether perceptions of mistreatment among whites fuel resentment.

All independent and dependent variables are coded to range from 0 to 1, which means that all coefficients can be interpreted as the change in the relevant resentment scale when the independent variable in question goes from its lowest to its highest value. The results appear in Table 7.2.

Immigrant Resentment

The results show that Republicans, people with lower household incomes, and people with lower levels of education are more likely to harbor immigrant resentment than their counterparts with higher incomes and educational levels or who are Democrats. Sociotropic economic concerns are insignificant, as

TABLE 7.2. *Determinants of Immigrant Resentment, Racial Resentment, and Ethnocultural Resentment*

Independent Variable	Immigrant Resentment	Racial Resentment	Ethnocultural Resentment
Age	0.05	0.07**	0.13***
	(0.03)	(0.03)	(0.03)
Education	−0.08***	−0.09***	0.01
	(0.03)	(0.02)	(0.02)
Republican	0.08***	0.09***	0.02
	(0.02)	(0.02)	(0.02)
Conservative	−0.01	0.05**	0.02
	(0.02)	(0.02)	(0.02)
Household income	−0.05*	0.04	0.04*
	(0.03)	(0.03)	(0.02)
National economy getting worse	0.03	−0.03*	−0.01
	(0.02)	(0.02)	(0.01)
% Hispanic in Zip Code	0.09***	0.05	−0.07**
	(0.04)	(0.04)	(0.03)
% Asian in Zip Code	0.13	0.10	0.01
	(0.08)	(0.08)	(0.07)
Ethnoculturalism	0.30***	−0.01	0.40***
	(0.04)	(0.03)	(0.03)
Civic republicanism ("action")	0.02	−0.06*	−0.08**
	(0.04)	(0.03)	(0.03)
Civic republicanism ("identity")	0.29***	0.34***	0.04
	(0.04)	(0.42)	(0.04)
True Americans should pursue economic success through hard work	0.05	0.12***	0.04*
	(0.03)	(0.03)	(0.02)
True Americans should blend into the larger society	0.07***	0.08***	0.01
	(0.02)	(0.02)	(0.02)
True Americans should carry on the cultural traditions of their ancestors	−0.07***	−0.08***	−0.06***
	(0.02)	(0.02)	(0.02)
Perceives group-level discrimination	0.24***	0.13***	0.10***
	(0.03)	(0.02)	(0.02)
Perceives individual-level discrimination	−0.08**	−0.0004	0.04
	(0.04)	(0.03)	(0.04)
Constant	0.04	0.14	−0.002
N	1123	1128	1126
R-squared	0.38	0.34	0.32
F	48.05	44.81	33.34

Note: * $p < 0.1$; ** $p < 0.05$; *** $p < 0.01$; robust standard errors in parentheses. Dependent variables range from 0 to 1, in which 1 = highest level of resentment; whites only.
Source: Twenty-First-Century Americanism Survey, 2004.

is the percentage of Asian residents in the respondent's Zip Code. As the percentage of Hispanic residents increases so does immigrant resentment. This finding fits well with the notion that immigrant resentment is driven by the increasing encounters whites have with ethnic and linguistic diversity and their attempts to attribute causes for the apparent lack of "Americanization" that such encounters render salient. Overall, however, demographic variables have weak effects; none has a significant coefficient that exceeds +/-0.1.

Action-oriented civic republicanism fails to affect levels of immigrant resentment. Contrary to expectations, valuing active citizenship does not lead to heightened sensitivity to this norm when it comes to evaluating immigrants. Thinking that active citizenship is a hallmark of being a good American does not make a person more likely to think that immigrants fail to do their part. However, placing a priority on *thinking of oneself* as part of the community does make a person more likely to perceive norm violation in this regard on the part of immigrants. Going from 0 to 1 on identity-oriented civic republicanism moves a person up the immigrant resentment scale by an impressive 0.29 points.

Incorporationist norms are an important component of immigrant resentment and like identity-oriented civic republicanism, measures of incorporationism influence respondents' scores on the immigrant resentment scale. Americans who place a priority on assimilation are more likely to exhibit such resentment while Americans who place a priority on cultural preservation are less likely. It is important to note, however, that both incorporationist measures are weak relative to identity-oriented civic republicanism.

Ethnoculturalism rivals identity-oriented civic republicanism in driving immigrant resentment, with a coefficient of 0.30. Old-fashioned ascriptivism still characterizes how a nontrivial segment of the population defines American identity, and it makes people more likely to think that immigrants violate civic republican and incorporationist norms. It is not just a heightened sensitivity to civic republican and incorporationist norms that drives the perception that such norms are violated. Defining American identity in narrowly ascriptive terms also drives such perceptions.[12] Yet it is important to note that civic republicanism is much more widely endorsed as a central component of American identity than ethnoculturalism. Among whites, the mean civic republicanism "identity" score is 0.87 while the mean ethnoculturalism score is 0.27. Thus, in terms of real-world magnitude, the civic republican demand for seeing one's identity and well-being as intricately tied to the identity and well-being of the community has a greater societal impact on the prevalence of immigrant resentment.

Finally, it is important to note that perceptions of group-level mistreatment are powerful predictors of immigrant resentment as well. Thinking that discrimination against whites in American society is a problem increases one's

---

[12] Note that Sears et al. (1997) find that old-fashioned racism likewise plays a role in explaining levels of racial resentment.

immigrant resentment score by 0.24 points. Perceptions of individual-level mistreatment seem to make such resentment less likely, though the size of the coefficient is small.

Racial Resentment

Turning next to racial resentment, we again see that Republican respondents and respondents with lower levels of education are more likely to exhibit racial resentment than their Democratic counterparts and people with higher levels of education. Here we also see that age and ideology matter, with older and more conservative respondents more likely to think that immigrants violate the liberal norm of hard work than younger and politically liberal respondents. Neither measure of community context predicts this kind of resentment nor does household income. Assessment of the national economy is barely significant, and not in the direction that intuition would dictate. As with immigrant resentment, these demographic variables generally have weak effects, with no significant coefficient exceeding +/−0.1.

In terms of conceptions of American identity, ethnoculturalism is insignificant, a stark contrast from its powerful role in immigrant resentment. In addition, valuing active citizenship makes a person less likely to exhibit racial resentment. People who define American identity through an informed and involved citizenry are less likely to think that immigrants are lazy.

In line with years of research on racial resentment directed toward blacks, valuing the role of the work ethic in American society is a relatively strong predictor of racial resentment aimed at immigrants. Its magnitude outweighs that of any of the significant demographic measures. The strongest predictor of racial resentment, however, is whether the respondent defines being American in terms of the identity demands of civic republicanism.

With respect to incorporationism, Americans who place a priority on assimilation are more likely to think that today's immigrants violate the work ethic while Americans who place a priority on cultural preservation are less likely to exhibit such resentment, though both incorporationist measures are weak relative to the civic republican and liberal assessments of the meaning of American identity.

As with immigrant resentment, the perception that whites as a group have suffered from discrimination in the United States makes racial resentment more likely while the perception of personal discrimination has no impact.

Ethnocultural Resentment

Turning finally to ethnocultural resentment, Table 7.2 shows that older respondents are more likely than their younger counterparts to resent immigrants for being nonwhite and non-Christian. The coefficient on age is the only demographic coefficient in the entire table to exceed +/−0.1, providing evidence to support the claim that a generational shift on ascriptivism has occurred.

Education, partisanship, and ideology are all insignificant, as is the percentage of Asians living in the Zip Code. A higher household income generates more ethnocultural resentment, though the coefficient is small and of marginal significance. Notably, a higher percentage of Hispanics in one's Zip Code leads respondents to harbor less ethnocultural resentment, the opposite direction of how such context affects immigrant resentment. People who encounter Hispanics more frequently avoid blaming ancestry for their concerns and instead blame behavior.

The ethnoculturalism scale is a very potent predictor of ethnocultural resentment, with the largest coefficient in all of Table 7.2. Moving from 0 to 1 on that scale moves respondents up the ethnocultural resentment scale by 0.40. The impacts of all other determinants pale in comparison. Civic republican concerns about whether people see themselves as American, which was a powerful determinant of immigrant resentment and racial resentment has no impact whatsoever on whether people harbor ethnocultural resentment. People who define America in terms of cultural diversity do not harbor ethnocultural resentment. Likewise, defining America in terms of assimilation has no impact, in contrast to its role in the previous models. Assimilationist and identity-oriented civic republican views affect the extent to which people think immigrants choose to shun assimilation and their new American communities; they do not make them old-fashioned nativists. These differences across the models underscore that although immigrant resentment and ethnocultural resentment are related, they each represent distinct sentiments about the relationship between the meaning of American identity and how immigrants are evaluated.

Finally, the perception that whites are mistreated in American society makes ethnocultural resentment more likely, though its impact is not as strong as its impact on immigrant resentment.

Discussion

There are important differences between attitudes toward immigrants and attitudes toward blacks that are overlooked when we focus primarily on the violation of the work ethic. The unique history of immigration in the United States and the evolution of attitudes toward immigrants make it important to focus on additional national norms and cherished values. These norms are not liberal in nature but rather derive from our civic republican and incorporationist traditions. In addition to perceiving that immigrants violate the work ethic, people also perceive that immigrants violate norms and behaviors associated with these other cherished components of American society. The analysis thus far tells us about where such perceptions of norm violation come from. First, traditional partisan, ideological, and demographic divides matter. Republicans and conservatives were more likely to harbor immigrant and racial resentment than Democrats and liberals. Older respondents and those with lower levels of education also tended to be more resentful than younger respondents and those with higher levels of education. As with previous studies, economic self-interest and national economic conditions yield inconsistent and unimpressive results. Economic pessimism generates more immigrant resentment, and having a lower income generates immigrant resentment and ethnocultural resentment, yet these effects are small.

Abstract ideas about the norms and behaviors that shape what people think being American means clearly affect resentment more than the concrete factors of income, how the national economy is doing, and whether one lives in a diverse community. In that sense, the findings here are in line with previous work. What we have gained is a more detailed account of what it is exactly that people resent about immigrants and which specific aspects of American culture drive their resentment. Instead of concluding that general ideas of Americanism dominate general antiimmigrant affect, we can say that of the many American traditions people value, the civic republican call to be a proud member of the community whose identity is only complete when it is connected to the nation is especially relevant when people assess immigrants, and that it increases the likelihood that people will disparage immigrants for seeming to shun this norm. People do not just view immigrants as lazy. They also recognize that many immigrants work quite hard; but rather than celebrate such effort, many Americans see it as yet another kind of threat. Immigrant resentment is prevalent in American society and stems in large part from the enduring power of civic republican traditions. Ethnocultural traditions also promote immigrant resentment, yet this tradition is not nearly as widely endorsed as civic republicanism.

Combined with findings from Chapter 4, which show that identity-oriented civic republicanism is also a powerful predictor of support for restrictive language policies and of whether Arab immigrants and citizens should be interned in the wake of another terrorist attack, the findings here raise some troubling questions about this aspect of American identity. The notion that Americans should think and feel that they are American seems almost obvious. As noted throughout this book, many prominent political theorists would score highly on this civic republican scale, and for noble reasons. But are the alleged gains that this version of civic republicanism brings (such as a greater trust in one's fellow Americans, willingness to compromise and sacrifice, and a greater commitment to redistribution) worth the hostility and resentment uncovered here? As with the findings in Chapters 4 and 6, my findings here highlight just how complex any empirical and/or normative approach to national identities really is. As more and more scholars uncover empirically the contradictions that attachments to national identities yield (see, e.g., Theiss-Morse 2009), the normative question – not to mention the practical challenges faced by national leaders – of whether to cultivate or repress the view that Americans should see themselves first and foremost as American will present even more of a dilemma.

The resentments explored here are related, but they constitute distinct feelings that merit separate investigations. One says immigrants are lazy, another says they work hard at the expense of other demands, and still another says they should be white, Christian, and European. That the resentments are correlated and share certain demographic roots suggest that ambivalence and contradiction exist within individuals and not just at a societal level. This ambivalence may lead some readers to question whether immigrant resentment is simply a more politically correct way to express concerns about the racial and religious backgrounds of today's immigrants. Could it be that many Americans really do wish that today's immigrants were white Christians, but that they succumb to social norms that prohibit the expression of such views and instead opt to say that immigrants today simply don't work hard enough to become a part of their new communities? It is clear that societal norms have changed. It is no longer acceptable to claim that certain backgrounds are superior to others. Those norms do not come from nowhere. People in society have to subscribe to them in order for them to take root and develop such power (Mendelberg 2001). It is also clear that many people are torn between their adherence to new norms of egalitarianism and lingering discomfort with immigrants. People become emotionally disturbed when they find themselves acting in ways that go against norms of racial egalitarianism not only because they fear how other people might react, but also because they are upset by their ambivalence. As Gilens and colleagues write with respect to affirmative action, "presentational pressures exist to disguise not only those attitudes that would be deemed deplorable by wider society, but those that would present respondents in a light that *they themselves* would find unflattering (1998, emphasis in original). As discussed earlier, people then look to behavior as a source of their resentment in order to help relieve their internal conflicts. In short, immigrant resentment exists because of the rejection of ethnocultural sentiments.

Even if some respondents are inclined to agree with the ethnocultural resentment items but feel uncomfortable with their agreement, the important point for my purposes is that egalitarianism has created such a predicament for them in the first place. They genuinely subscribe to egalitarian norms, yet may find themselves uncomfortable with today's immigrants. How might one reconcile this conflict? By turning to thoughts about the freely chosen behaviors of immigrants. "If only they behaved more in line with particular American values," such a person thinks, "then I would be totally fine with them, even if they are Mexican/Muslim/Asian/etc." The important theoretical and analytical contribution of this analysis is to document how the behaviors in question that ambivalent Americans rely on in such reconciliation are often intimately connected to the immigration experience and thus derive from the nation's civic republican and incorporationist traditions in addition to its liberal tradition.

Finally, it is important to note the real possibility that the ethnocultural resentment items are not as "politically incorrect" as questions about old-fashioned antiblack attitudes are, despite recent evidence suggesting that it is (Hopkins, Tran, and Williamson 2009). Especially after the terrorist attacks on 9/11, the social sanctions for claiming a preference for white Christian immigrants are likely to be weaker than the social sanctions for saying that whites should be able to keep blacks out of their neighborhoods. To the extent that this is true, the concern that immigrant resentment is a cover for ethnocultural resentment is further diffused.

Discrimination and Context

A word on the role of perceptions of discrimination and context is in order. The analysis in Chapter 5 showed that the perception that whites as a group have been discriminated against in the workplace, in schools, and when it comes to achieving success in the United States has the potential to increase nationalistic sentiment. Here we see that it shapes attitudes toward immigrants. White respondents who think that discrimination against whites is a problem are significantly more likely to harbor all three types of resentment, and it is an especially potent predictor of immigrant resentment. It makes sense that perceptions of group-level discrimination should be more powerful over immigrant resentment relative to the other two forms of resentment because the perception and the resentment relate to the notion of immigrants being primarily concerned about jobs and taking jobs that might otherwise go to a native-born American. Together with the findings in Chapter 6, these findings suggest that perceptions of mistreatment, regardless of one's race, are an overlooked factor in attitude formation that merit further scrutiny in political science.

Finally, the percentage of Asians and Hispanics living in a respondent's Zip Code had little effect on resentment. The percentage of Asians was insignificant in all three models. The percentage of Hispanics was significant in two, leading to more immigrant resentment and less ethnocultural resentment. The meager effects overall are in line with recent findings about support for ethnicity-related ballot initiatives in California, where the county-level size of the Hispanic population only slightly increased the likelihood of voting for Proposition 187 (Campbell, Wong, and Citrin 2006).

IMMIGRANT RESENTMENT AND IMMIGRATION POLICY

The goals of the analyses in this chapter thus far were to develop measures that account for immigrant resentment, see how widespread it is, examine its relationship to other forms of resentment, and confirm that it is driven by how the content of American identity is defined. Having accomplished these tasks, I can now investigate the extent to which these resentments shape preferences toward immigration policy. The expectation is that immigrant resentment will lead people to prefer more restrictive policies, though this portion of the analysis is admittedly more exploratory, especially with regard to whether immigrant resentment will be more or less influential than the other forms of resentment. The dependent variables are whether overall levels of legal immigration should be decreased and whether legal and/or illegal immigrants should be eligible for social services.

To gauge attitudes toward overall levels of immigration, respondents were asked, "Do you think the number of immigrants from foreign countries who are permitted to come to the United States to live should be increased, decreased or left the same as it is now?" This is the same wording used by the National Election Study (NES) and is also quite similar to the wording used in other surveys such as Gallup and the General Social Survey (GSS). In the 21-CAS, 39 percent of whites thought immigration levels should be decreased, 50 percent thought they should be kept the same, and 11 percent thought they should be increased. In other surveys conducted around this time (including the NES, the GSS, and surveys by CBS, NBC, and Gallup), the percentage wanting immigration decreased was slightly higher. For instance, 47 percent of respondents in the 2004 NES said they want the immigration level decreased.

To measure attitudes about immigrant eligibility for benefits, respondents were asked, "Do you think that people who immigrated legally should be allowed to benefit from government assistance programs like Medicaid and food stamps?" Then they were asked, "What about people who immigrated illegally?" They could answer with yes or no, and they could volunteer "it depends." The survey asked about legal and illegal immigrants separately in order to remove ambiguity about the referents. Estimates at the time of the 21-CAS suggested that illegal immigrants constituted 26 percent of all foreign-born residents in the United States (Passel, Capps, and Fix 2004). Despite this fact, most Americans think that most immigrants are illegal, as indicated in a 2007 survey by CBS News and the *New York Times* in which 75 percent thought that "most of the people who have moved to the United States in the last few years are here illegally."[13] It is quite likely, therefore, that respondents will think of illegal immigrants if asked whether "immigrants" should be eligible for benefits. Asking about legal and illegal immigrants separately ensures a more accurate recording of preferences.

In 21-CAS, 75 percent of whites thought that legal immigrants should be allowed to benefit from government assistance programs, 14 percent thought they should not, and 11 percent volunteered "it depends." In strong contrast, 81 percent of white respondents thought illegal immigrants should not be allowed to benefit from government assistance programs, 10 percent thought they should, and 9 percent volunteered "it depends." When given a chance, people clearly distinguish between legal and illegal immigrants. Questions like these were not asked in other national surveys around the time of the 21-CAS but were asked in selected states during the early months of the 2008 presidential primary campaigns and often in the mid-1990s. Similar to the 21-CAS respondents, in late 2007, 85 percent of registered voters in Ohio and 86 percent of registered voters in Pennsylvania said they opposed "providing illegal immigrants with social services, such as welfare, food stamps, and housing assistance."[14] Compared to the mid-1990s, the patterns in the 21-CAS appear

[13] Survey information available at Polling the Nations, http://poll.orspub.com.ezproxy.library .tufts.edu/ (accessed May 27, 2008).
[14] Polls conducted by Quinnipiac University. Survey information available at Polling the Nations, http://poll.orspub.com.ezproxy.library.tufts.edu/ (accessed June 3, 2008).

to be less restrictive when it comes to legal immigrants but more restrictive when it comes to illegal immigrants. For instance, a 1996 survey by CBS News and the *New York Times* asked if people "favor or oppose allowing *legal* immigrants who are not American citizens to receive welfare benefits" (emphasis added). Only 27 percent said they were in favor.[15] Two years earlier, a *Times Mirror* survey found that 69 percent were in favor of having illegal immigrants ineligible for "welfare, Medicaid, and other government benefits."[16]

The issue of whether immigrants should be eligible for social services garnered much national attention in the mid-1990s. In 1994, the nation watched as Californians debated whether to bar illegal immigrants from social services, including public school and nonemergency health care, with Proposition 187 (Martin 1995). Two years later, President Clinton enacted national welfare reform with the Personal Responsibility and Work Opportunity Reconciliation Act (PRWORA). PRWORA significantly altered legal immigrant eligibility for public assistance. Importantly, legal immigrants who arrived after the enactment of PRWORA incurred a five-year ban on eligibility for most means-tested programs, including food stamps, cash assistance through Temporary Assistance to Needy Families, and Medicaid. Additionally, states were given freedom to decide whether to provide assistance to those who were both ineligible and eligible under federal law (Haider et al. 2004). Illegal immigrants remain ineligible for means-tested programs (National Conference of State Legislatures 2008).

Debates about cash assistance are not as prominent as they were in the 1990s, but debates about immigrants and benefits are still very much in the headlines. One state-level benefit receiving particular attention as of this writing is whether to allow illegal immigrants to receive in-state tuition at public universities. Four state-level surveys show wide variation in levels of support for in-state tuition, with a low of 19 percent in Nevada and a high of 49 percent in North Carolina (and 30% in Massachusetts and 46% in New Jersey).[17] At the federal level, the DREAM Act, if passed, would allow states to grant in-state tuition to illegal immigrant residents and allow illegal immigrant children to become eligible for legalized status and for federal education grants (Migration Policy

---

[15] Survey information available at Polling the Nations, http://poll.orspub.com.ezproxy.library
.tufts.edu/ (accessed May 28, 2008). It should be noted that most existing survey questions regarding immigrants and benefits ask only about illegal immigrants. I found few questions that ask specifically about legal immigrants. Thus, I recognize that comparisons between the 21-CAS results and the CBS News/*New York Times* question are imperfect. The CBS News/*New York Times* question explicitly notes that the beneficiaries, while legal residents, are not citizens, whereas the 21-CAS question only implies that the beneficiaries are not citizens. It is possible that at least some respondents had naturalized citizens in mind when answering this question.

[16] Survey information available at Polling the Nations, http://poll.orspub.com.ezproxy.library
.tufts.edu/ (accessed May 28, 2008).

[17] Nevada survey of registered voters by the *Las Vegas Review-Journal* (April 2006); North Carolina survey by Elon University (April 2005); Massachusetts survey by the University of New Hampshire and the *Boston Globe* (September 2006); New Jersey survey by Monmouth University Polling Institute (July 2007). Survey information available at Polling the Nations, http://poll.orspub.com.ezproxy.library.tufts.edu/ (accessed June 3, 2008).

Institute 2006). As of this writing, Californians are once again gearing up for a Proposition 187–type battle, with activists gathering signatures for a ballot initiative that would deny welfare benefits to the U.S.-born children of illegal immigrants (Rutten 2009).

Analysis

Still using studies of racial resentment as a guide, I use the immigrant resentment scale as an independent variable to compare the power of immigrant resentment to the power of more traditional influences, including racial resentment, ethnocultural resentment, and measures of economic self-interest in predicting attitudes on the policy questions described previously. Racial resentment has been shown to influence attitudes toward affirmative action, school desegregation programs, the confederate flag, the death penalty, and welfare (to name a few), even when controlling for more tangible factors such as having a child involved in a busing program (McConahay 1982; Jacobson 1985; Kinder and Sanders 1996; Virtanen and Huddy 1998; Mendelberg 2001; Henry and Sears 2002; Orey 2004). Other than the research cited earlier, there is little work that looks at how resentment shapes immigration policy preferences, though studies found that racial resentment toward blacks makes whites more likely to favor reduced levels of immigration (Kinder and Sanders 1996) and favor denying benefits to immigrants (Citrin et al. 2001). The expectation here is that immigrant resentment will be a powerful predictor over attitudes not only after controlling for tangible factors but also after controlling for racial resentment and ethnocultural resentment.

All three dependent variables are coded from 0 to 1, in which 1 means that immigration should be decreased or that immigrants should not be eligible for benefits ("it depends" is coded as 0.5 for the benefits analyses). I used ordered probit models to estimate the impact of resentment on the three dependent variables described. In addition to the resentment scales, the other independent variables are age, education, partisan identification, political ideology, perceptions of the national economy, and the percentage of people living in the respondent's Zip Code that are Hispanic or Asian. As before, all independent variables are coded to range from 0 to 1.[18]

The results appear in Table 7.3. They show that immigrant resentment is a consistent and powerful predictor of restrictive immigration preferences, even after controlling for other forms of resentment. It appears to be more powerful than "old-fashioned" ethnocultural resentment in two of the three models. Racial resentment is likewise significant in all three models, and ethnocultural resentment is significant in two (overall level of immigration and benefits for legal immigrants). The impact of immigrant resentment outweighs the impact of other variables in the models, notably perceptions of the national economy.

---

[18] All three models were run with respondent's income included as an independent variable. Including income resulted in a loss of approximately 150 observations in each case, and income was insignificant in every model.

TABLE 7.3. *Determinants of Immigration Policy Preferences*

Independent Variable	Overall Level of Immigration Decreased	Oppose Benefits for Legal Immigrants	Oppose Benefits for Illegal Immigrants
Immigrant resentment	1.23**	0.78**	1.19**
	(0.16)	(0.19)	(0.20)
Racial resentment	0.72**	0.98**	1.31**
	(0.18)	(0.23)	(0.23)
Ethnocultural resentment	1.14**	0.97**	0.38
	(0.18)	(0.19)	(0.26)
Age	−0.29*	0.08	−0.18
	(0.16)	(0.18)	(0.23)
Education	−0.51**	−0.44**	−0.40**
	(0.12)	(0.14)	(0.16)
Republican	0.03	0.18	0.40**
	(0.12)	(0.14)	(0.15)
Conservative	0.23**	0.003	0.42**
	(0.12)	(0.13)	(0.15)
National economy getting worse	0.10	0.17	−0.20*
	(0.10)	(0.11)	(0.12)
% Hispanic in Zip Code	−0.07	0.02	−0.46*
	(0.22)	(0.28)	(0.28)
% Asian in Zip Code	−0.20	−1.06*	0.78
	(0.43)	(0.55)	(0.53)
Cutpoint 1	−0.39	1.94	−0.13
	(0.18)	(0.22)	(0.21)
Cutpoint 2	1.49	2.41	0.42
	(0.19)	(0.23)	(0.21)
Chi-square	283.75	174.95	248.00
N	1230	1316	1312

Note: * $p < 0.1$; ** $p < 0.05$; *** $p < 0.01$; robust standard errors in parentheses. Dependent variables range from 0 to 1, in which 1 = highest level of resentment; whites only. Cell entries are ordered probit coefficients.

Source: Twenty-First-Century Americanism Survey, 2004.

Having more education consistently reduces the likelihood of restrictionist views, and being politically conservative increases the likelihood of such views. Context matters somewhat, and it does so in an immigrant-friendly way: living in a Zip Code with a higher percentage of Hispanic residents reduces opposition to giving benefits to illegal immigrants, and living in a Zip Code with a higher percentage of Asian residents reduces opposition to giving benefits to legal immigrants.

To assess the actual magnitude of the impact of immigrant resentment and compare it to other forms of resentment, it is useful to examine predicted probabilities in addition to probit coefficients. Figures 7.1, 7.2, and 7.3 display the predicted probabilities of saying that immigration should be decreased and

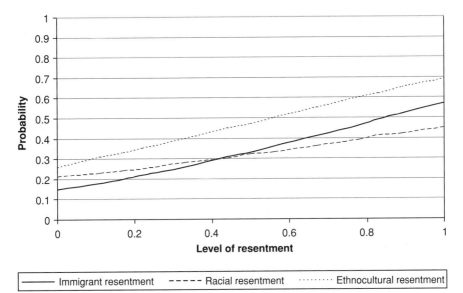

FIGURE 7.1. The probability of saying immigration should be decreased, as resentment varies. *Source:* Twenty-First-Century Americanism Survey, 2004.

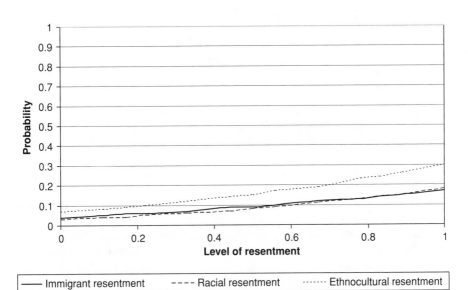

FIGURE 7.2. The probability of saying legal immigrants should not receive benefits, as resentment varies. *Source:* Twenty-First-Century Americanism Survey, 2004.

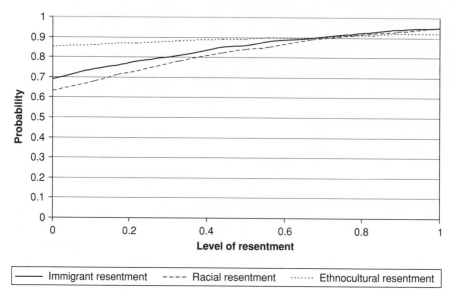

FIGURE 7.3. The probability of saying illegal immigrants should not receive benefits, as resentment varies. *Source:* Twenty-First-Century Americanism Survey, 2004.

that legal or illegal immigrants should be eligible for social services, as each level of resentment varies across its range and as all other independent variables are held constant at their means. In Figure 7.1, for instance, the solid line shows the predicted probability of saying that immigration levels should be decreased as immigrant resentment changes from 0 to 1 while all other variables, including racial resentment and ethnocultural resentment, are held constant at their means. Figure 7.1 shows that immigrant resentment and ethnocultural resentment each produce an impressive 42 percentage point increase in the likelihood of saying that immigration levels should decrease. A person who scores a 0 on the immigrant resentment scale has only a 15 percent chance of saying "decrease," while a person who scores a 1 has a 57 percent chance. Although racial resentment also has an impact, it never leads the probability of saying "decrease" to cross the 50 percent mark. Immigrant resentment and ethnocultural resentment change the average respondent's predicted preference as they move from 0 to 1 while racial resentment does not.

Figure 7.2 shows that immigrant resentment and racial resentment have a nearly identical influence over whether people think that legal immigrants should be eligible for benefits. Both increase the predicted probability of opposing such eligibility by about 15 percentage points. Ethnocultural resentment increases it by 23 percentage points. It should be noted, however, that even a person with a high degree of this more old-fashioned resentment still only has a 30 percent chance of opposing having legal immigrants be eligible for benefits.

Figure 7.3 shows that even the least resentful people are uncomfortable with the idea of providing benefits to illegal immigrants. That said, immigrant resentment and racial resentment increase opposition substantially. A person who scores a 0 on the immigrant resentment scale has a 69 percent chance of opposing eligibility while a person who scores a 1 has a 95 percent chance, an increase of 26 percentage points. A person who scores a 0 on the racial resentment scale has a 63 percent chance of opposing eligibility while a person who scores a 1 has a 95 percent chance, an increase of 32 percentage points. The impact of ethnocultural resentment is statistically insignificant.

All three forms of resentment are clearly important to immigration policy attitudes. Perhaps it is not surprising that racial resentment would dominate when discussing benefits for illegal immigrants. After all, such resentment is grounded in beliefs about self-reliance and hard work. But more important for my purposes is that this analysis has added evidence that racial resentment and old-fashioned nativism are not the only types of antiimmigrant sentiment that shape policy views. Feeling that today's immigrants choose to violate civic republican and incorporationist norms is not only prevalent in American society, but it is also consequential. In two of the three models, it increases restrictionist sentiment by substantively significant margins. Its influence in the third model (benefits for legal immigrants) is weaker but still notable. In all three models, it is more important than many other traditional explanatory variables.

CONCLUSION

Racial resentment scholars are quick to acknowledge that the change in national norms that led to the demise of biological racism should be celebrated. But their mission is to point out that we still need to acknowledge the emergence of resentment, that resentment is based on inaccurate stereotypes, and that it possesses an enduring and powerful hold over white racial attitudes and policy preferences. The same can be said of immigrant resentment. Although it is important to celebrate the progress of egalitarianism, it is equally important to recognize and understand continuing aversions. Immigrant resentment is a modern set of beliefs that has evolved as national norms have evolved. It is based on inaccurate assessments of norm violation on the part of immigrants and has a powerful hold over white attitudes toward immigrants and immigration. Moreover, it forces us to question whether valuing an attachment to being American is misguided, if not harmful. Although many people genuinely believe that immigrants can assimilate and become "good" Americans, they also believe that today's immigrants choose not to. In doing so, immigrants are seen to threaten the very idea of American identity. We may have come a long way since the days of the National Origins Act, but negative views of immigrants continue to be a source of tension and conflict. My goal, therefore, has not been to absolve Americans of nativist views but rather to show that what it means to be nativist today is more complex than what it meant to be nativist before the current "egalitarian era." Immigrant resentment is a modern antiimmigrant sentiment that exists alongside the view that immigrants violate the work ethic and the enduring belief that the United States would simply be better off if most immigrants were white European Christians. These views have similar effects on immigration policy preferences, but they are not the same.

In *The Unmaking of Americans*, Miller writes, "Could today's immigrants, coming from seemingly exotic locales, really subvert American national unity? The only way is if they do not become Americans, if they remain permanently apart from the American national identity as outsiders, people who might eventually break the country to pieces because they have no sense of belonging to it" (1998). Believing that the scenario Miller describes characterizes the current reality, perhaps not surprisingly, fosters resentment. But this resentment is not the same as racial resentment. The symbolic images it invokes relate to the context of immigration and the set of traditional American values that we expect immigrants to revere and strive to meet. Those values include the duty to value the common good over personal private gain and possess the desire to see oneself first and foremost as an American rather than primarily as a member of an ethnic group or loyalist to some other national identity.

When Americans think about what being American means, they draw upon a broad range of norms and values. Some are liberal in nature, but others are more civic republican and incorporationist. They think that Americans should see themselves as American and be informed about and involved in public life. Moreover, they recognize that most American families came from somewhere else, and they define America as a place where people can form a core identity while still maintaining the immigration-related diversity that makes the United States so unique among nations. Yet people sense that today's immigrants violate these civic republican and incorporationist principles, and they resent them for it. This resentment exists to the extent that people do draw upon such principles to arrive at a particular understanding of what being American means. The irony, however, is that this resentment can cause the rejection of American society on the part of immigrants and minorities, which then gives it even more fuel.

8

The Politics of American Identity

The question of what it means to be American has preoccupied Americans, not to mention foreign visitors such as Alexis de Tocqueville and James Bryce, since the founding of the country. Debating that question means debating the legal, territorial, and conceptual boundaries of membership. For much of American history, legal and conceptual boundaries have been determined in part by physical characteristics. In 1790, Congress passed the country's first naturalization law, which restricted naturalization to free whites. This restriction remained in place until 1952 (Pickus 2005). Today, legal boundaries are determined by beliefs and behaviors. Once the requisite five-year waiting period has passed, a person can naturalize if he or she is willing to take an oath of allegiance to the Constitution, can pass a civics test that shows an understanding of American history and political institutions (and basic knowledge of English), and is "of good moral character." In short, if you understand us, believe in us, and obey the law, then you can become one of us. The beliefs and sympathies of potential new members were a concern at the founding as well, but that concern existed alongside powerful racial restrictions. Conceptual boundaries have evolved much the way legal boundaries have, although there is still a portion of the American public that overtly delineates American identity in ascriptive terms. Even among people who reject ascriptivism, there can still be an overlearned tendency to assume that people who are not white or who have an accent are foreigners.

Regardless of whether the boundaries in question have been ascriptive or normative, being concerned about the nature of American identity inevitably means being concerned about immigration. Even the most politically apathetic American probably knows that the country's demographic makeup has diversified substantially over the past several decades. Today, the foreign born comprise roughly 13 percent of the population, compared to 6 percent in 1980. The United States has not experienced such high levels of immigration, proportionally, for one hundred years.[1] These changes are not just being felt in border states. Interior states such as Iowa, Nebraska, and Kansas are also seeing notable increases in their immigrant populations. It is also essential to note that most of today's immigrants are coming from Latin America and Asia. In 2000, 52 percent of the foreign born were from Latin America, compared to only 9 percent in 1960. Comparable numbers for Asians are 26 percent in 2000 and 5 percent in 1960.[2] Consequently, contending with immigration also means contending with new languages and traditions to which many Americans are not accustomed.

It would be foolish if we did not wonder about the impact these changes will have on a variety of cultural and political factors, including the conceptual boundaries of American identity. It is not outlandish to think that such rapid change might eventually bring about disastrous consequences if not managed properly. After all, world history, even modern history, is replete with examples of violent conflicts over territory, culture, and power when groups of people from different backgrounds encounter one another. In just the past decade, England and France have experienced violent riots among alienated immigrant populations. Far-right parties have gained success in several European countries recently in large part because of their hard-line stance on immigration. Even putting aside a violent doomsday scenario, it is not inconceivable that the notion of what being American means might change substantially in the wake of rapid ethnic diversification. If it does, what does that mean for the ability of the country to remain intact?

But it is also foolish to rely on the occasional anecdote to conclude that American culture, society, and government are in demise due to our experiments with immigration over the past few decades. What is even more foolish is to espouse those conclusions with heated rhetoric, for doing so only serves to make the very consequences being decried more likely to occur. That rhetoric, as is often the case, rarely relies on careful analyses to see whether the alleged negative outcomes are occurring. The main goal of this book has been to provide systematic examinations of some of the common claims that we hear today. My focus has been strictly on the side of public opinion about American identity rather than on policy analysis. I examine native-born whites, first-generation immigrants, their Latino and Asian descendants, and African Americans. I have examined not only what their views about American identity are, but I also have explored the causes of those views and the influence of those views on policy preferences. I have sought to uncover lines of conflict and consensus and advance our understanding of the conditions under which identities are deeply held versus instrumental, and politically consequential versus benign.

---

[1] Data on demographics were found at the Migration Policy Institute, http://www .migrationinformation.org/datahub/charts/final.fb.shtml (accessed June 19, 2008).

[2] Data found at the Migration Policy Institute, http://www.migrationinformation.org/datahub/ charts/fb.2.shtml (accessed June 19, 2008).

NORMATIVE CONTENT AT THE DAWN OF THE
TWENTY-FIRST CENTURY

Recent scholarship on the social nature of national identities highlights the importance of studying the boundaries people use when conceptualizing the nature of the national group. Additionally, the question of whether we should aspire to have conationals share a common understanding of what those boundaries are has preoccupied political theorizing for some time. With respect to how American identity is defined, I found diversity and commonality, consensus and divergence. Diversity exists not so much across individuals but within them. The notion of "Americanism" cannot be reduced to a single dimension with ascriptive ethnoculturalism on one end and classical liberalism on the other. Civic republican and incorporationist norms also have been and continue to be key constitutive American norms. Commonality exists in that this broad range of constitutive norms is similarly adopted across Americans of all stripes. We cannot say that Americans can be divided into "liberals," "civic republicans," and "incorporationists." Most Americans accept tenets of all three of these traditions and agree that they are at the core of what it means to be American. To the extent that democratic theorists are right that it is important for members of a democratic society to agree on what it is that make them a "we," these findings are encouraging.

There are, however, trends we should monitor. First, although it is true that a majority of Americans think that assimilating to American society and maintaining the traditions of one's ancestors need not be mutually exclusive, Latinos are among the people most likely to think that is the case. They do not prioritize the maintenance of traditions over assimilation, but rather they value both and see both as defining elements of what being American means. As Latinos will continue to make up a larger and larger share of the American population, it is possible that true incorporationism will solidify in the American mind. I do not, however, find evidence that incorporationism will supplant the traditions of liberalism or civic republicanism.

Second, conservatives and Republicans are more likely to promote the norm of assimilation while liberals and Democrats are more likely to promote the norm of preserving cultural traditions. This divergence is worth watching for its own sake, but also because it can shape the nature of policy debates and, ultimately, policy implementation. As I showed in Chapter 4, people who see assimilation as a central American norm are driven to different preferences regarding language policy and ethnic profiling than people who see the maintenance of cultural traditions as a central American norm. The divergence I found in this regard is small now, but it might not stay that way.

There are two other findings in my analysis that suggest that all is not rosy when it comes to the content of American identity. The first is that the conceptual boundaries people place around being American provide the fodder for resentment toward today's immigrants. This resentment has a great deal to do with the particular American norms that people value and very little to do with the facts on the ground. The charitable view of this resentment is that people are seeing lots of diversity due to high immigration rates, which creates the impression that immigrants choose to avoid learning English, thinking of themselves as American, and becoming informed and involved members of their communities. Despite the fact that the charitable view likely has some validity, it is still troubling that the resentment exists to the degree that it does, and that it so clearly affects policy preferences on immigration. Arguably, such sentiment has played a role in subverting congressional efforts at comprehensive immigration reform as well as hindering state and local efforts to address immigration-related issues within their jurisdictions.

The second finding of concern is that the allegedly beneficial set of beliefs that I labeled "identity-oriented" civic republicanism turns out to be a strong predictor of immigrant resentment and restrictive policy preferences that range from the relatively benign (requiring signs in stores to have some English) to the severe (interning Arab Americans). Many political theorists argue that think-ing and feeling of oneself as part of the national community brings a range of benefits that enhance group harmony and democratic stability. Results pre-sented here suggest that when Americans profess that people need to have such attachments in order to be a "true" American, they can be sowing the seeds of resentment and promoting the very alienation among the nation's newest members that they decry. A less pessimistic interpretation of these findings is to note that identity-oriented civic republicanism is distinct from ethnocul-turalism or nativism. That is, Americans are perhaps not as xenophobic as a mere examination of their policy preferences might suggest. They desire unity and a sense of fellowship, not uniformity. Nonetheless, the question of how to mitigate the negative consequences of this set of constitutive norms remains. One possibility, noted in Chapter 4, is to render other widely endorsed Ameri-can norms, such as liberalism and "action-oriented" civic republicanism, more salient when the topic of immigration arises such that the impact of identity-oriented civic republicanism can be counterbalanced. Other scholars who study the double-edged nature of national identities have made similar suggestions (Theiss-Morse 2009).

THE CAUSES AND CONSEQUENCES OF THINKING OF ONESELF AS AMERICAN

Immigrant resentment involves thinking that today's immigrants are different from immigrants of earlier generations. It is argued that the huddled masses that arrived at Ellis Island were eager to become American and participate wholeheartedly in their new American communities, whereas today's immi-grants want to take advantage of opportunities in the United States without becoming a part of it. Just as the myths about the Ellis Island immigrants are overblown, so are the myths about today's immigrants. Just as the sky is not falling with respect to how people of different backgrounds define the content of American identity, the sky is not falling with respect to identity attachment either.

For Latinos and Asians, non-American identities were not the most common nor were they particularly consequential with respect to trust in institutions, obligations, or patriotism. To be sure, the likelihood that a person will say she thinks of herself as American most of the time depends on her racial background, generational status, and primary language. But first-generation immigrants and people who do not speak English were the only groups of people in which a plurality prioritized a non-American identity. Again, the perception of the rejection of an American identity is driven by the fact that there are simply so many first-generation immigrants in the country today. There are a lot of people in the United States who do not see themselves first and foremost as Americans. It should not surprise us nor trouble us that a recent arrival from China thinks of herself as Chinese more often than she thinks of herself as American. What might be troubling is if her children and grandchildren also feel that way, for that might signal actual rejection, yet I do not find this to be the case. Once we get past the first generation, not only is English acquired but so is the idea that one is American more so than the idea that one is primarily attached to a panethnic or national origin group.

Even when a non-American identity is prioritized in the second generation or beyond, such prioritization can actually be beneficial with respect to trust and participation. I find that all things being equal, identifying as American "most of the time" can be beneficial when it comes to trust, obligation, and voting. But all things are not equal. A nonwhite American who prioritizes his American identity will suffer with regard to political engagement if he perceives discrimination, and as I show in Chapter 5, it is quite likely that any nonwhite American perceives discrimination in some form. Therefore, encouraging the prioritization of an American identity – as many pundits as well as scholars contend we should – can come at a cost. Conversely, being attached to the aggrieved group "most of the time" can bolster participation and trust in government, or can at least neutralize the damage done by discrimination in the absence of this attachment. The particular matrix of identity type (panethnic vs. national origin) and type of discrimination (panethnic vs. national origin vs. personal) needed to bring about such a result varies, as I show in Chapter 6. But the important point is that promoting an American identity is not always the best or obvious option. If we care about American identity for instrumental purposes – that is, if we care about it because, as many argue, we think it will bolster trust, participation, and active citizenship – then we might want to promote a panethnic mentality (or perhaps a hyphenated mentality) rather than an American one given how widespread perceptions of panethnic discrimination are.

As if that weren't complicated enough, I also found that in some cases, promoting a panethnic identity can backfire when it comes to the instrumental goals of trust, obligation, and group harmony more broadly. I found in

Chapter 6 that a panethnic identity can, absent discrimination, diminish trust in government among Latinos and Asians. When perceptions of discrimination are present, a panethnic identity can diminish the sense that one has an obligation to donate to charity while a national origin identity can diminish the sense that one has an obligation to volunteer in one's community. Those are the only findings in the entire book that support the charges of immigration critics and the arguments of those theorists and psychologists who warn of the destabilizing effects that subgroup identities can have on the national community. Yet given how widespread perceptions of mistreatment are, this finding of withdrawal is troubling and should give pause to those who dismiss the concerns of immigration critics as the ramblings of reactionary nativists.

Finally, when I started this project, I expected to find systematic differences between panethnic and national origin attachments. I did find some, but I also found interesting similarities. Both diminish with acculturation, though this is particularly true of national origin identities. Both can increase with perceptions of individual discrimination, though this is particularly true of panethnic identities. One key difference is that panethnic identities are generally more effective at helping people overcome the negative effects of discrimination. Panethnicity thus emerges as more politically potent than national origin identities, as we might expect. We still have much to learn here, and we would do well to continue measuring these identities separately in our surveys.

In sum, this book has findings that people on all sides of immigration debates can point to in support of their claims. But picking and choosing which finding to latch onto would be a mistake, for it would miss the larger messages that I put forward. The first message is that the role of national and subgroup identities in shaping group interactions and democratic stability is far more complicated than is often portrayed. Sometimes these identities are quite powerful – in ways that we should welcome and in ways that should concern us. Still other times, however, their power is actually quite limited. In short, the notion of American identity is a predisposition that the government has good reason to cultivate but also has good reason to approach with caution. The second message is that perceptions of discrimination are a key reason why the role of these types of identities is so complicated. If such perceptions were less common, our assessments of how identities influence the outcomes studied here would be far more straightforward. More importantly, if such perceptions were less common, then we would have good reason to be much less preoccupied with the politics of identity prioritization and attachment in the first place.

"FED UP AND FRUSTRATED"

Just as we should be wary when people critical of immigration argue with anecdotes instead of data, so too should we be wary of those who portray whites as irrational nativists without substantiating their claims. Underlying the presumption of nativism is the belief that native-born white Americans feel "under siege" in the face of increasing ethnic diversity. One straightforward way to assess this sentiment is to ask whites directly if they feel that whites are mistreated due to their race. Unfortunately, when surveys include questions about perceptions of discrimination, they generally skip over their white respondents. I think that has been a mistake. By asking whites such questions in the Twenty-First-Century Americanism Survey (21-CAS), I found that perceptions of discrimination among whites are, not surprisingly, not nearly as common as they are for nonwhites. Most whites do not feel that whites are disadvantaged and are even less likely to think that they have suffered mistreatment. That said, the mean score on the panethnic discrimination scale for whites was 0.29, with 20 percent of whites scoring at the midpoint of the scale and an additional 13 percent scoring even higher. Moreover, for those that do think that whites suffer from discrimination, there are some troubling implications. Thinking that whites are mistreated leads to a greater attachment to Americanness, higher levels of patriotism, a greater sense of obligation to serve in the military, and dramatically higher levels of immigrant resentment. Although having an attachment to America, being patriotic, and feeling obligated to serve in the military are not in and of themselves problematic, it is concerning if those sentiments are driven by racially charged reactions to contemporary politics.

As the flow of immigrants continues and as the American population becomes less white, will such attitudes become more common? Will whites increasingly draw the boundaries of American identity in ascriptive terms? Or will the next generation of native-born whites be more accustomed to diversity and less likely to feel that they are losing out? In order to answer these questions, it is important that we continue asking whites about their feelings in this regard. It is quite possible that the perception of mistreatment among whites is becoming more widespread. The Southern Poverty Law Center reports a 48 percent rise in the number of hate groups in America from 2000 to 2007, an increase they attribute to debates about immigration. They also note that the number of hate crimes against Latinos rose 35 percent from 2003 to 2006, and that "experts believe that such crimes are typically carried out by people who think they are attacking immigrants" (Holthouse and Potok 2008). As the nation continues to diversify, it is imperative that we continue to track how whites feel about their own place in American society.

IDENTITY INFORMS POLICY

We should investigate the dynamics of public opinion about American identity for their own sake, and because they play an instrumental role in shaping people's relationship with their communities and American political institutions. Yet we should also study these opinions because of their influence over attitudes about contentious policy matters. Policies such as the ones investigated here are not going away anytime soon. Although overall immigration policy is a federal concern, many of these issues are decided more locally and have noticeable consequences on the day-to-day lives of Americans in cities and towns across the country, such as policies on signs, bilingual education, and the role of local law enforcement in combating illegal immigration. These are issues that people are thinking about more and more. When they think about them, they tap into their thoughts about American identity in order to help them sort through the arguments on both sides. The concept of American identity is central here precisely because such policies so explicitly relate to the legal and conceptual boundaries of membership in the American community. Thus, how content is defined matters greatly, though exactly which aspects of American identity matter when can vary considerably from issue to issue.

First the good news. I found that Americans are sometimes quite sensible in how they form opinions. In the aggregate, they make reasonable distinctions among different policies in the same domain. For instance, support for official-English is quite high, yet support for English-only election ballots is low. Some may see this difference as a sign of inconsistency or nonattitudes, but I argue that it reveals a discerning public motivated by unity on the one hand and a compassionate leniency on the other (especially because identity-oriented civic republicanism dominates attitudes on official-English, while action-oriented civic republicanism is a strong influence on attitudes about ballots). Likewise, I found that there is broad support for allowing legal immigrants to be eligible for social services, yet little support for allowing illegal immigrants to have such eligibility. As we have seen in countless examples, when people are provided with clarity and specificity, their assessments of the political world respond accordingly (Kinder and Herzog 1993). So too with immigrant policy and when we ask people to make distinctions between these two classes of immigrants. People are not random, and whites are not all narrow-minded nativists. Some of that exists, but the desire to have unity amid diversity is stronger than the desire to eliminate diversity. Not only is the public lenient in the aggregate, but also those attitudes are driven by widely endorsed constitutive norms in sensible ways.

Yet all is not well. Yes, people make meaningful distinctions among the policies studied here, and on concrete matters such as election ballots and education, they prefer a moderate approach in lieu of strict and unforgiving "sink-or-swim." But when asked about where they would draw the line in response to a terrorist attack, many respondents would seemingly not draw any line at all. More than two-thirds would allow people to be stopped by police simply based on their appearance, and about one-third would allow people to be interned until their innocence could be determined, even if the internees were American citizens. These numbers are troubling, and so is the fact that America's widely celebrated long-standing norm of political freedom does not do more to diminish this sentiment.

What do these findings say about how to move forward? Are there ways to craft policies that will satisfy broad segments of the American population while still preserving the rights and opportunities of all citizens and residents? On profiling, the only way to preserve rights is simply to find ways to diminish support for the policy altogether. My findings suggest that an important way to do that is to reduce adherence to ethnoculturalism, because that is a key driving force on attitude formation. Luckily, ethnoculturalism is the least supported of the constitutive American norms studied here. We have made great gains over the past few decades, and such gains will likely continue with the "browning of America." But we should not just sit back, cross our fingers, and wait for that to happen. "Browning," after all, might just create more backlash among whites, especially in the short term. Decades of research on the contact hypothesis, which is the proposition that group conflict will diminish in the presence of increased interethnic contact, have shown us that contact can sometimes just provide more opportunities for conflict. Rather, contact has to be managed and involve genuine interaction (Forbes 1997). Managing contact among adults is a tall order, but it is much easier to do with children in the context of schooling. Calling for an end to the increasing segregation of public school districts (Orfield and Lee 2007) is all well and good, though unlikely to happen anytime soon. Even if it did, mere desegregation is not enough to improve group relations. But rather than watch our immigration experiment inexorably unfold, educators should, whenever possible, take the lessons of social psychologists on best practices for managing contact and introduce them into their curricula with explicit attention to the immigration situations in their local communities.[3]

Beyond the issue of managing contact, it is important for public discourse to render alternative conceptions of American identity salient, such as political liberalism and incorporationism. In Chapter 4, these traditions did not completely undo the effect of ethnoculturalism in shaping attitudes on profiling, but they helped. After 9/11, the media – particularly newspaper editorial boards – did a surprisingly good job of reminding readers about the benefits of diversity and of the importance of preserving civil liberties as we combat terrorism, especially when compared to media commentary after Pearl Harbor (Schildkraut 2002). Because ideas that are at the "top of the head" dominate opinion formation (Zaller 1992; Zaller and Feldman 1992), and because liberalism and incorporationism are already widely supported, continuing to enhance the accessibility of these traditions in people's minds is an important way to protect against support for profiling.

But not all seemingly restrictive policy views are driven primarily by ethnoculturalism. A desire for people to have unity – not uniformity – gets translated into support for official-English and other restrictive language policies. Official-English policies will not encourage people to learn English, especially because

---

[3] In 2009, I participated in a workshop for K–12 educators in New England about immigration in the United States and in Massachusetts. The organization that sponsored this workshop, Primary Source, partners with local school districts to offer programs on diversity and globalization that enrich the training and curricular activities that teachers bring to the classroom. Although such workshops often concentrate on history, they provide an excellent opportunity to discuss how teachers can productively manage contact in their classrooms among native-born and foreign-born students. See http://primarysource.org for more information on some of the types of programs available in New England (accessed July 1, 2009).

the incentives to learn English are quite strong even without an official language. But that does not mean we should dismiss the concerns people have about whether we can maintain a sense of common purpose in the face of rapid ethnic and linguistic change. The English language is seen as the glue that keeps us together despite our cultural diversity, and it is not necessarily nativist to prefer that all Americans and potential American citizens know it. Perhaps another important way to prevent backlash among whites is actually to take some of their concerns seriously and enact policy change that helps bring about the desired ends. Thus, rather than make English official, it is important that all levels of government take steps that genuinely help people learn English, especially the newest immigrants and their children, because subsequent generations already acquire English at a reasonable rate (Citrin et al. 2007).[4] People's concerns are arguably driven by their encounters with the first generation, so it is essential to provide newcomers with better opportunities to learn English.

Recent systematic studies have documented just how difficult it can be for immigrants to participate in English classes. In 2006, the National Association of Latino Elected and Appointed Officials (NALEO) Education Fund published a report called *The ESL Logjam*. Its findings paint a bleak picture. More than half of the adult ESL programs they studied have waitlists, and many more do not even bother maintaining waitlists because the demand is just too large (Tucker 2006). For one nonprofit program run by nuns outside Chicago, for instance, it can take a year for the immigrant women served by the program to get into an evening class (Noel 2007). Even those immigrants who are lucky enough to get into an ESL program find that they can only learn rudimentary English due to a lack of intermediate and advanced courses.

Despite this clear and overwhelming demand among immigrants to learn English, some ESL providers report that they have actually had to reduce their existing offerings due to resource shortages (most adult ESL classes are free for the students). Moreover, resource shortages often result in the use of teachers who are insufficiently trained (Tucker 2006). The federal government and the states provide grant money for adult ESL programs, but it is clearly not enough. Federal funds in 2003/2004 amounted to roughly $560 million, and states provided around $700 million. Those funds helped serve an estimated 1.2 million students that year (Tucker 2006; McHugh, Gelatt, and Fix 2007). Yet according to the Migration Policy Institute, about 5.8 million legal permanent residents need language instruction. In their 2007 report on adult English instruction, McHugh, Gelatt, and Fix argue that the need for English instruction "dwarfs the scale and abilities of the current service system" (2007). Their report concludes that an additional $200 million per year is needed – based on the needs of legal residents only.

---

[4] Of the 137 respondents who answered the 21-CAS in Spanish, 133 (or 97%) were first-generation immigrants. The other 4 were second generation. Similarly, of the 426 respondents who said they primarily speak a language other than English at home, 357 (or 84%) were first-generation immigrants. Another 42 (or 10%) were second generation.

Some private businesses have tried to help their employees learn English by providing instruction on site, but even those opportunities face more demand than supply can meet. In Massachusetts, for example, companies like Legal Sea Foods, Harpoon Brewery, and Boston Marriott offer free classes to employees with some instruction even occurring on company time. As of 2007, such Boston-area programs had a waitlist more than three thousand names long (Sacchetti 2007). McDonald's has a pilot program called English Under the Arches that it hopes to take nationwide. It is paid for by franchise owners, incorporates instructors from local community colleges, and allows employees to participate while on the clock. Early results indicate that the program has been successful in teaching job-related English skills to its participants (Jaschik 2009). To encourage more businesses to consider similar programs, Representative Mike Honda (D-CA) introduced legislation in 2009 that would provide tax credits to employers that offered English-language instruction.[5]

Finally, let me once again address the fact that "identity-oriented" civic republicanism was the most powerful influence shaping preferences for restrictive language policies and, through immigrant resentment, was also a powerful influence shaping restrictive immigration policies. It also influenced support for interment. People want their fellow Americans to think of themselves primarily as American and prioritize that aspect of their identity. This desire motivates the policy preferences studied here. As such, another implication of my findings is the need to educate Americans about the fact that many of their perceptions about immigrants – such as that they prioritize a panethnic or national origin identity or do not share dominant views about the meaning of American identity – are actually *mis*perceptions. Given the tone of much rhetoric surrounding immigration in the United States today, it will prove difficult to get that message across. Unfortunately, the "punditocracy" doesn't lend itself to subtlety, complexity, or moderate data analysis (Berry and Sobieraj 2008). Even if the message is made more available, misperceptions are notoriously difficult to change (Kuklinski et al. 2000), and policy attitudes can be resistant to factual information (Sides and Citrin 2007).

LOOKING AHEAD

The 21-CAS has provided a unique opportunity to study these important contemporary issues among people from a wide variety of backgrounds. But it represents just one snapshot at one point in time. The issues studied here are not going away anytime soon. As more and more immigrants come to the United States, as many become citizens, and as they produce the next generation of Americans, it is crucial that we continue to track attitudes about national identity and perceptions of mistreatment over time. My findings regarding

---

[5] Information on the bill (H.R. 3249) is available at "Strengthening Communities through Education and Integration," http://honda.house.gov/index.php?option=com_content&view=article&id=91&Itemid=77 (accessed May 21, 2010).

today's second and third generation won't necessarily characterize tomorrow's second and third generation. The 21-CAS provides a valuable baseline, but it is just the beginning. In recent years, national surveys of nonwhite populations in the United States have become more common; examples include the Pilot National Asian American Political Survey (PNAAPS) (2000–1), the Latino National Survey (2006), and periodic surveys by the Kaiser Family Foundation and its partners. I fully suspect this trend will continue, thanks to technological developments that make large-N surveys of nonwhites more feasible than in the past. The notion that national identities are a kind of social identity, in which attachments to the group and definitions of what the group stands for are central features that shape subsequent attitudes and behaviors, dictates that measures of identity content and attachment need to play a central role in our ongoing inquiries. As such, the types of questions included in the 21-CAS should be included in future data-collection efforts. Additionally, the same questions should also be asked of whites. I hope I have convinced readers to agree that we cannot, for example, assume that questions about discrimination are only relevant to nonwhites.

The particular policy issues at the center of debates related to immigration and ethnic diversity will evolve over time. The study of immigration attitudes has for years been focused on the basic question of whether overall levels of immigration should be increased, decreased, or kept the same. Yet a wide variety of specific approaches to immigration policy and immigrant policy has been getting increasing attention, and we still know little about how the public feels about these possibilities. Since 2006, the policy debate about immigration has become more complex. Attitudes about comprehensive immigration reform, including earned legalization for undocumented immigrants, guest-worker programs, and building a wall along the border, are still poorly understood. But these types of questions will characterize the debate for the foreseeable future, and any data-gathering effort in regard to this issue should attempt to measure attitudes about them reliably, so we can track how they evolve, examine whether they solidify, and investigate the factors that shape these processes. We also should be more vigilant in tracking and studying attitudes about racial and ethnic profiling. No studies beyond this one have looked at the fact that one-third of Americans would be willing to intern Muslim Americans in the wake of another terrorist attack. That statistic is troubling. The war on terror has become known as "the long war," signifying that our efforts to uncover terrorist plots in the making will be a political reality for the foreseeable future; we simply need to continue learning more about opinions on counterterrorism profiling.[6]

---

[6] The Pentagon's Quadrennial Defense Review Report in 2006 was called, "Fighting the Long War," though the phrase was in use since at least 2004. In 2007, however, Admiral William J. Fallon, the new head of Central Command, decided to cease using the phrase (Widmer 2007).

Finally, identities are not static, as social identity scholarship has long documented. Although cross-sectional surveys can uncover conditional relationships through interaction terms and by controlling for certain variables, there are other valuable ways to study the various causes of identity prioritization and the conditions under which our identities are more or less politically consequential. The growing corpus of scholarship on American national identity would be well served by studies that implement other methodologies, such as interviews, focus groups, case studies, and experiments – as well as alternative methods of measuring one's primary identity than those employed here – in order to help further advance our understanding of the kinds of conditional relationships examined in this book.

THE POLITICS OF AMERICAN IDENTITY

Stories of how places throughout the United States are dealing with diversity seem to become more common by the day. Each one rightly challenges us to wonder what they signify about the future of American identity. For example, in the small farming town of Mattawa, Washington (population 3,200), where the majority of the year-round residents primarily speaks Spanish, police used to rely on bystanders to help translate at crime scenes. But in 2008, the U.S. Justice Department developed a language plan with the city that now "requires Mattawa to employ at least one bilingual employee during regular business hours,... to make vital information available in Spanish as well as English,... [and] requires the police to have qualified interpreters on call at all times" (Glascock 2008). After hearing about a place like Mattawa, many questions come to mind. How will the English-speaking whites in Mattawa react when they hear of this situation? What about people who don't live there but just read about it in their newspaper (or in this book) or hear about it on a cable news talk show? Will they get angry at the federal government for intervening in this way? Will they resent the immigrants for seemingly requiring that their new community adapt to them rather than the other way around? Will Mattawa's Spanish-speaking population develop stronger ties to its local political institutions and begin to feel that they truly belong there, or will the availability of Spanish prevent them from thinking of themselves as American? Or will it be the white backlash that does that? Is Mattawa unique? Or can other places expect the Justice Department to come to town as well? More broadly, what do the answers to these questions say about how Americans think about the meaning of American national identity and about where it is, and is not, acceptable to draw boundaries around membership in the national community? The findings throughout this book provide answers to some of these questions, but the questions will continue to be asked. Our efforts to answer them should not abate.

National symbols and norms loom large in these debates, and they play a strong role in shaping public opinion, along with the perception that cherished

American norms are being violated. The findings throughout this book are
generated by the norms that people use to define the content of American
identity more so than by economic measures, measures of one's community
makeup, and one's background in terms of age, education, and other factors.
People's preferences are driven by desires to protect their view of what being
American means, but the salience of particular American norms varies across
policy debates. Moreover, content evolves, albeit glacially. As it does, so too
will the way in which ideas about "what it means to be an American" shape
answers to the types of questions listed here. Only future systematic inquiries
will help us answer them.

In the meantime, we will continue to see and hear heated debates about
the meaning of American identity and how it is implicated in immigration and
related policies. The findings throughout this book do not always provide clear-
cut answers to those pundits, scholars, and ordinary Americans who wonder
if the status quo is "good" or "bad" for the future of American identity. There
is a lot of nuance and many conditional relationships. I cannot, for example,
argue that people should or should not think of themselves as American. The
answer to that question depends on who is doing the thinking and in what
context.

In June 2008, the conservative Bradley Foundation released a report on
American identity. The first sentence declares, "America is facing an identity
crisis." The authors state that their efforts are motivated by their belief that "a
sense of national identity is necessary to enable individuals to transcend self-
absorption and commit to the public good" (Bradley Foundation 2008). This
belief echoes the arguments of the many eminent democratic theorists described
in earlier chapters. In putting together the report, the foundation consulted a
broad range of academics and commissioned its own survey conducted by the
respected Harris Interactive. The report does not portray immigrants as lazy
or as people who only want to make a buck and return home. But without
providing any supporting evidence, it states, "With a single-minded emphasis
on our differences, every group is encouraged to retain its separate identity.
The United States is no longer 'we the people,' but 'we the peoples.' To this way
of thinking, loyalty to one's native land is as important as loyalty to America,
and the rewards of being in this country need not be repaid in undivided
allegiance" (Bradley Foundation 2008). Not only have I been unable to find
evidence of a "single-minded" emphasis on separate identities, but I have also
shown that reports such as these, even if not inflammatory, promote stereotypes
that are simply not borne out by the evidence. Yet when such stereotypes are
promoted, they have the potential to bring about alienation and a diminished
sense of commitment, especially among the very people that already think of
themselves primarily as American. If we want fewer people to feel like Paloma,
the young woman I interviewed who said she didn't think of herself as American
(despite her U.S. citizenship) because she felt American society did not accept
her, then we need fewer people who act like Joey Vento, the owner of the

cheesesteak shop who generated a cult following with his incendiary discourse. As with the authors of the Bradley Foundation report, I too care deeply about the future of American identity and recognize the importance of being able to sustain unity amid diversity. This book represents my attempt to provide some much needed careful scrutiny to the issues at stake. I hope it is just one of many that will help us navigate our age of immigration with the sanity and compassion that the topic deserves.

Appendix A

21-CAS Survey Questions

1. Are you a citizen of the United States?

   1. Yes
   2. No

2. Were you born in the United States?

   1. Yes
   2. No

3. How long have you been living in the United States? (Only asked of respondents who said no to question 2)
   (*Note*: Interviewers were instructed to round to the closest number of years, with less than 6 months coded as zero.)

4. In what country were you born? [open-ended response]

5. Were your parents born in the United States?

   1. Yes, both parents born in United States
   2. One parent born in United States
   3. No, neither parent born in United States

6. Thinking about all four of your grandparents, how many of them were born in the United States?

   1. Yes, all 4 grandparents born in United States
   2. Some grandparents born in United States
   3. No, no grandparent born in United States

"Don't know" and "no answer" were allowed as volunteered responses for all questions. Numbering of questions in this appendix is sequential for purposes of presentation. Numbering of questions in data file is different due to editing of the survey instrument, including question order, after numbers were assigned to questions.

7. What countries did your ancestors come from? [open-ended response] (*Note*: Respondents were allowed up to 3 responses.)

8. Which of those countries do you identify with most? [Skipped if respondent said "don't know" or refused to answer question 7.]

   1. First mention from question 7
   2. Second mention from question 7
   3. Third mention from question 7
   4. None/Neither/Can't Choose

9. Are you of Hispanic or Latin origin or descent?

   1. Yes
   2. No

10. What is the primary language spoken in your home?

    1. English
    2. Spanish
    3. Japanese
    4. Chinese
    5. Other [open-ended response]

11. What race do you consider yourself to be?

    1. White/Caucasian
    2. Black/African American
    3. Asian
    4. Native American
    5. Some other race [open-ended response]
    6. Hispanic/Latino
    7. Mixed (Please specify multirace) [open-ended response]

People use different terms to describe themselves. I'm going to read you a few examples based on what you have already said.

12. Do you describe yourself as (*country of origin selected in question 8*)? [Skipped if respondent said "don't know" or refused to answer question 7.]

    1. Yes
    2. No

13. Do you describe yourself as (*race/ethnicity from question 11*)? [Skipped if respondent said "don't know" or refused to answer question 11.]

    1. Yes
    2. No

14. Do you describe yourself as an American?

    1. Yes
    2. No

15. Which one of these best describes how you think of yourself most of the time?

   1. (Country of origin selected in question 8)
   2. (Race/ethnicity from question 11)
   3. American

16. How important is being (*answer from question 15*) to you, is it very important, somewhat important, somewhat unimportant, or very unimportant? (Skipped if R said "don't know or refused to answer question 15.)

   1. Very important
   2. Somewhat important
   3. Somewhat unimportant
   4. Very unimportant

17. Now I have some questions about immigration policy in the United States. Do you think the number of immigrants from foreign countries who are permitted to come to the United States to live should be increased, decreased, or left the same as it is now?

   1. Increased
   2. Decreased
   3. Left the same

18. Do you think that people who immigrated legally should be allowed to benefit from government assistance programs like Medicaid and food stamps?

   1. Yes, allowed
   2. No, not allowed
   3. Depends

19. What about people who immigrated illegally?

   1. Yes, allowed
   2. No, not allowed
   3. Depends

I'm going to read a list of things that some people say are important in making someone a true American. The first one is . . .

(*Note*: Half of the following series was asked now [determined randomly within each identity type, i.e., two ethnocultural items now, two ethnocultural items later]. The other half was asked in questions 52 to 69. Within each half, the order was rotated randomly.)

20. Being born in America
21. Being a Christian
22. Having European ancestors
23. Being white

24. Pursuing economic success through hard work
25. Respecting America's institutions and laws
26. Having American citizenship
27. Letting other people say what they want, no matter how much other people disagree with them
28. Doing volunteer work in one's community
29. Thinking of oneself as American
30. Being informed about local and national politics
31. Being involved in local and national politics
32. Carrying on the cultural traditions of one's ancestors, such as the language and food
33. Respecting other people's cultural differences
34. Blending into the larger society
35. Seeing people of all backgrounds as American
36. Being able to speak English
37. Feeling American

    1. Very important
    2. Somewhat important
    3. Somewhat unimportant
    4. Very unimportant

For the next set of questions, please tell me if you strongly agree, somewhat agree, somewhat disagree, or strongly disagree.

(*Note:* Questions 38–44 were rotated randomly and were asked of citizens only.)

38. When I think of the American people, I think of people who are a lot like me.
39. Being an American is important to the way I think of myself as a person.
40. I would feel good if I were described as a typical American.
41. When someone criticizes America, it doesn't bother me at all.
42. I am proud to be an American.
43. I feel strong ties to the American people.
44. In many respects, I am different from most Americans.

    1. Strongly agree
    2. Somewhat agree
    3. Somewhat disagree
    4. Strongly disagree

45. Now I have some questions about the government. How much of the time do you think you can trust the government in Washington to do what is right...just about always, most of the time, some of the time, or never?

    1. Just about always
    2. Most of the time

3. Some of the time
4. Never

46. How much of the time do you think you can trust the police and law enforcement to do what is right . . . just about always, most of the time, some of the time, or never?

    1. Just about always
    2. Most of the time
    3. Some of the time
    4. Never

47. Now I have some questions about language policy in the United States. Do you favor or oppose a law making English the official language of the United States, meaning most government business would be conducted in English only?

    1. Favor
    2. Oppose
    3. Neither favor nor oppose

48. Do you believe that election ballots should be printed only in English, or should they also be printed in other languages in places where lots of people don't speak English?

    1. In English only
    2. In other languages

49. You may have noticed that in some neighborhoods, the sign on the front of a store or a business will be in a language other than English. Over the past several years, some cities and towns have adopted policies that require a certain percentage of the words on such signs be in English. Do you think you would favor or oppose such a policy?

    1. Favor
    2. Oppose

50. People have different ideas about how to teach non-English-speaking children when they enter public schools. I am going to read a few of them. Please tell me which one comes closest to your view.

    1. First, all classes should be conducted only in English.
    2. Second, children should be able to take some classes in their native language, just for a year or two.
    3. Third, children should be able to take classes in their native language all the way through high school.
    4. All classes should be bilingual (volunteered).

51. People have different ideas about what the main goal of bilingual education should be. I am going to read a few of them. Please tell me which one comes closest to your view.

1. First, teach English to nonnative children as quickly as possible.
2. Second, teach English to nonnative children while making sure they do not fall behind in other subjects.
3. Third, teach English to nonnative children while making sure they remain fluent in their first language.

(*Note*: The remaining half of American identity battery was asked here, in questions 52–69.)

I am going to read some statements that have been used to describe immigration and immigrants today. For each one, please tell me whether you strongly agree, somewhat agree, somewhat disagree, or strongly disagree.

(*Note*: Questions 70–74 were rotated randomly)

70. Immigrants today take advantage of jobs and opportunities here without doing enough to give back to the community.
71. Immigrants today come to think of themselves as Americans just as much as immigrants from earlier eras did.
72. Immigrants should really know what's going on in the United States if they want to stay here, but a lot of them just don't want to be bothered.
73. Blending into the larger society while still maintaining cultural traditions is difficult, but a lot of immigrants today seem to do a good job of it.
74. If immigrants only tried harder to fit in, then more Americans would accept their cultural differences.

   1. Strongly agree
   2. Somewhat agree
   3. Somewhat disagree
   4. Strongly disagree

75. This next set of questions focuses on the government. Many people do not know the answers to these questions. If there are some you don't know, please just say so. What are the first 10 amendments to the Constitution called?
   (*Note*: For each political knowledge question, interviewers were instructed to encourage respondents to make their best guess if they initially said "don't know.")

   1. The Bill of Rights
   2. Wrong answer

76. What position is held by William Rehnquist?

   1. Correctly identifies Rehnquist as Chief Justice of the Supreme Court
   2. Identification is incomplete or wrong

77. Which political party has the most members in the House of Representatives: the Democrats or the Republicans?

   1. Republican Party

2. Wrong answer (Democratic Party)
3. Other [open-ended response]

78. How many years is the term of a United States Senator?

    1. Six years
    2. Wrong answer

Next I am going to read a list of possible obligations. For each one, please tell me if you think this is an obligation you owe to other Americans.
    (*Note*: Questions 79–83 were rotated randomly.)

79. Serving in the military
80. Giving money to charities
81. Paying taxes
82. Helping when there is a crisis or disaster in the nation
83. Volunteering in your local community

    1. Yes, an obligation
    2. No, not an obligation
    3. Depends (volunteered)

Now I am going to read you some more statements about immigrants in the United States. For each one, please tell me if you strongly agree, somewhat agree, somewhat disagree, or strongly disagree.
    (*Note*: Questions 84–90 were rotated randomly.)

84. Irish, Italians, and Jews overcame prejudice and worked their way up. Today's immigrants should do the same.
85. Years of discrimination have created conditions that make it difficult for immigrants to work their way out of the lower class.
86. It's really just a matter of some people not trying hard enough. If immigrants would only try harder, they could be just as well off as people born in America.
87. Over the last few years, immigrants have gotten less than they deserve.
88. The country would be better off if more of our immigrants were from Europe instead of from Asia and Latin America.
89. Immigrants who are Muslim just won't ever seem American to me.
90. The idea of an America where most people are not white bothers me.

    1. Strongly agree
    2. Somewhat agree
    3. Somewhat disagree
    4. Strongly disagree

Now I have some more questions about your opinions on policies and current events.

91. Generally speaking, would you say that most people can be trusted, or that you can't be too careful in dealing with people?

    1. Most people can be trusted
    2. Or, you can't be too careful

92. It has been reported that some police officers stop motorists of certain racial or ethnic groups because the officers believe that these groups are more likely than others to commit certain types of crime. This practice is known as racial profiling. Do you approve or disapprove of the use of racial profiling by police?
    (*Note*: Question 92 only asked of respondents randomly assigned to "form 1.")

    1. Approve
    2. Disapprove

93. Since September 11th, some law enforcement agencies have stopped and searched people who are Arab or of Middle Eastern descent to see if they may be involved in potential terrorist activities. Do you approve or disapprove of this kind of profiling?
    (*Note*: Question 93 only asked of respondents randomly assigned to "form 2.")

    1. Approve
    2. Disapprove

94. If there were another terrorist attack in the United States with Arab or Middle-Eastern suspects, would you support or oppose allowing the government to hold Arabs who are U.S. citizens in camps until it can be determined whether they have links to terrorist organizations?
    (*Note*: Question 94 only asked of respondents randomly assigned to "form 1.")

    1. Support
    2. Oppose

95. If there were another terrorist attack in the United States with Arab or Middle-Eastern suspects, would you support or oppose allowing the government to hold Arab immigrants in camps until it can be determined whether they have links to terrorist organizations?
    (*Note*: Question 95 only asked of respondents randomly assigned to "form 2.")

    1. Support
    2. Oppose

96. How worried are you about the possibility that there will be more major terrorist attacks in the United States in the near future... are you very worried, somewhat worried, not worried at all?

    1. Very worried
    2. Somewhat worried
    3. Not worried at all

97. How worried are you that you or a close relative or friend might be the victim of a terrorist attack in the United States... are you very worried, somewhat worried, or not worried at all?

    1. Very worried
    2. Somewhat worried
    3. Not worried at all

98. In general, do you think discrimination against (*race/ethnicity from question 11*) is a major problem, a minor problem, or not a problem in schools?

    1. Major problem
    2. Minor problem
    3. Not a problem

99. What about in the workplace?

    1. Major problem
    2. Minor problem
    3. Not a problem

100. What about in preventing (*race/ethnicity from question 11*) in general from succeeding in America? Do you think that is a major problem, a minor problem, or not a problem?

    1. Major problem
    2. Minor problem
    3. Not a problem

101. In general, do you think discrimination against (*country of origin selected in question 8*) is a major problem, a minor problem, or not a problem in schools?

    1. Major problem
    2. Minor problem
    3. Not a problem

102. What about in the workplace?

    1. Major problem
    2. Minor problem
    3. Not a problem

103. What about in preventing (*country of origin selected in question 8*) in general from succeeding in America? Do you think that is a major problem, a minor problem, or not a problem?

    1. Major problem
    2. Minor problem
    3. Not a problem

104. Do you think you have ever been denied a job or a promotion because of your racial or ethnic background?

    1. Yes
    2. No

105. Do you think you generally receive worse service than other people at restaurants or stores because of your racial or ethnic background?

    1. Yes
    2. No

106. Do you think your racial or ethnic background has made it difficult for you to succeed in America?

    1. Yes
    2. No

107. Would you say that in the past year the national economy has gotten better, stayed the same, or gotten worse?

    1. Better
    2. Same
    3. Worse

108. As you know, people can belong to various organizations or associations such as labor unions, professional associations, fraternal groups such as Lions or Elks, hobby clubs or sports teams, groups working on political issues, community groups, and school groups. Of course, there are lots of other types of organizations, too. Not counting membership in a local church, synagogue, or mosque, are you a member of any of these kinds of organizations?

    1. Yes
    2. No

109. About how many?

    [open-ended response]

110. As you know, there are many ways people can be active members of their organizations. I am going to read a few of those ways. Please tell me

which one comes closest to describing your activity in the organization or association you have been most active in during the past year.

1. Paying membership dues only
2. Paying dues and reading newsletters
3. Attending meetings occasionally
4. Attending meetings often
5. Serving in an official leadership position

111. My final set of questions asks you a little bit more about yourself. These questions are for statistical purposes only. What is your age?

[open-ended response]

112. What is the highest grade of school or year of college you have completed?

1. Less than high school diploma
2. High school grad
3. Trade/vocational school
4. Some college (no degree or associate's degree)
5. Bachelor's degree (BA or BS)
6. Some graduate school (no degree)
7. Graduate-level degree

113. Generally speaking, do you consider yourself a Republican, an independent, a Democrat, or something else?

1. Republican
2. Independent
3. Democrat
4. Other (please specify) [open-ended response]

114. Would you call yourself a strong Republican/Democrat or a not very strong Republican/Democrat? (Only asked of Republicans and Democrats.)

1. Strong
2. Not very strong

115. Do you think of yourself as closer to the Republican or Democratic Party? (Only asked of Independents.)

1. Closer to Republican Party
2. Closer to Democratic Party
3. True Independent

116. What, if any, is your religious preference?

1. Agnostic
2. Atheist

3. Baptist/Southern Baptist
4. Buddhist
5. Catholic
6. Christian
7. Episcopalian
8. Jehovah's Witness
9. Jewish
10. Lutheran
11. Methodist/United Methodist
12. Mormon/Church of Latter Day Saints
13. Muslim
14. Presbyterian
15. Protestant
16. Quaker
17. Seventh Day Adventist
18. Other [open-ended response]

117. What is your current status of employment?
(*Note*: Multiple responses were allowed.)

1. Full time
2. Part time
3. Unemployed
4. Homemaker
5. Student
6. Retired
7. Disabled

118. Please tell me if the total amount of income, before taxes, received by all of the members in your household during 2003 was above or below $45,000.

1. Above or equal to $45,000
2. Below $45,000

119. Please tell me which income category best describes the total amount of income, before taxes, received by all of the members in your household during 2003. Please stop me when I reach the correct income category. Would you say . . . (Only asked of respondents who had an income below $45,000.)

1. Less than $10,000
2. $10,000 up to $15,000
3. $15,000 up to $20,000
4. $20,000 up to $25,000
5. $25,000 up to $30,000
6. $30,000 up to $35,000

7. $35,000 up to $40,000
8. $40,000 up to $45,000

120. Please tell me which income category best describes the total amount of income, before taxes, received by all of the members in your household during 2003. Please stop me when I reach the correct income category. Would you say . . . (Only asked of respondents who had an income at or above $45,000)

1. $45,000 up to $50,000
2. $50,000 up to $60,000
3. $60,000 up to $75,000
4. $75,000 up to $100,000
5. $100,000 up to $125,000
6. $125,000 up to $150,000
7. $150,000 up to $200,000
8. $200,000 or more

121. Generally speaking, do you think of yourself as conservative, moderate, or liberal?

1. Conservative
2. Moderate
3. Liberal
4. Other [open responses]

122. Are you registered to vote?

1. Yes
2. No

123. Did you vote in the 2000 presidential election? (Only asked of respondents registered to vote.)

1. Yes
2. No
3. Was not eligible to vote in 2000 (volunteered)

124. Do you intend to vote in the 2004 presidential election?

1. Yes
2. No

125. Which candidate do you intend to vote for? (Only asked of people who answered yes to question 124).

1. George W. Bush
2. John Kerry
3. Ralph Nader
4. Other [open-ended response]

126. What is your Zip Code?

    [Zip Code range from 00000 to 99999]

127. In general, would you say that your neighborhood is . . .

    1. Mostly white
    2. Mostly black
    3. Mostly Latino
    4. Mostly Asian
    5. Or multiethnic

128. For survey purposes, I need to ask are you male or female?

    1. Male
    2. Female

Appendix B

Supplementary Tables from Chapter 3

TABLE B.1. *Bivariate Correlations among American Identity Items*

	Born in America	Being a Christian	Having European Ancestors	Being White	Respecting America's Political Institutions and Laws	Having American Citizenship	Pursuing Economic Success through Hard Work	Letting Other People Say What They Want	Doing Volunteer Work in One's Community	Thinking of Oneself as American	Feeling American	Being Informed about Local and National Politics	Being Involved in Local and National Politics	Carrying on the Cultural Traditions of One's Ancestors	Respecting Other People's Cultural Differences	Blending into the Larger Society	Seeing People of All Backgrounds as American	Being Able to Speak English
Born in America	1.00																	
Being a Christian	0.42	1.00																
Having European ancestors	0.36	0.44	1.00															
Being white	0.32	0.41	0.52	1.00														
Respecting America's political institutions and laws	0.09	0.13	0.06	0.04	1.00													
Having American citizenship	0.24	0.22	0.16	0.12	0.22	1.00												
Pursuing economic success through hard work	0.21	0.26	0.17	0.12	0.20	0.24	1.00											
Letting other people say what they want	-0.04	-0.12	-0.05	-0.04	-0.01	-0.02	-0.01	1.00										
Doing volunteer work in one's community	0.15	0.23	0.18	0.14	0.17	0.15	0.30	0.00	1.00									
Thinking of oneself as American	0.14	0.15	0.11	0.07	0.26	0.29	0.25	0.04	0.17	1.00								
Feeling American	0.19	0.20	0.14	0.10	0.24	0.27	0.27	0.00	0.21	0.50	1.00							
Being informed about local and national politics	0.11	0.13	0.09	0.06	0.20	0.19	0.27	0.06	0.31	0.20	0.21	1.00						
Being involved in local and national politics	0.09	0.16	0.11	0.08	0.17	0.12	0.19	0.08	0.33	0.19	0.19	0.44	1.00					
Carrying on the cultural traditions of one's ancestors	0.12	0.18	0.19	0.15	0.04	0.04	0.19	0.01	0.34	0.06	0.10	0.19	0.22	1.00				
Respecting other people's cultural differences	-0.07	-0.06	-0.02	-0.05	0.08	-0.01	0.08	0.11	0.17	0.05	0.02	0.17	0.10	0.24	1.00			
Blending into the larger society	0.19	0.22	0.22	0.18	0.22	0.20	0.27	0.01	0.25	0.23	0.28	0.26	0.23	0.16	0.06	1.00		
Seeing people of all backgrounds as American	-0.15	-0.08	-0.07	-0.09	0.04	0.01	0.04	0.15	0.09	0.14	0.09	0.14	0.12	0.11	0.18	0.07	1.00	
Being able to speak English	0.29	0.28	0.21	0.17	0.22	0.34	0.32	-0.05	0.23	0.23	0.23	0.22	0.15	0.14	0.00	0.34	-0.04	1

TABLE B.2. *Rotated Factor Matrix (varimax rotation)*

	Factor 1	Factor 2	Factor 3
Born in America	0.16	−0.51	0.04
Being a Christian	0.15	−0.61	0.12
Having European ancestors	0.07	−0.67	0.09
Being white	0.03	−0.64	0.03
Respecting America's political institutions and laws	0.37	−0.03	0.18
Pursuing economic success through hard work	0.31	−0.20	0.32
Letting other people say what they want	0.06	0.11	0.11
Doing volunteer work in one's community	0.15	−0.20	0.53
Thinking of oneself as American	0.63	−0.07	0.12
Feeling American	0.60	−0.14	0.13
Being informed about local and national politics	0.24	−0.04	0.53
Being involved in local and national politics	0.17	−0.08	0.51
Carrying on the cultural traditions of one's ancestors	−0.01	−0.22	0.45
Respecting other people's cultural differences	0.02	−0.09	0.36
Blending into the larger society	0.32	−0.23	0.30
Seeing people of all backgrounds as American	0.17	0.17	0.23
Being able to speak English	0.32	−0.26	0.21
Having American citizenship	0.40	−0.18	0.09
Eigenvalue	3.24	1.24	0.71

Source: Twenty-First-Century Americanism Survey, 2004.

Appendix C

Supplementary Tables from Chapter 5

TABLE C.1. *Rotated Factor Loadings for Perceptions of Discrimination (varimax rotation)*

	Factor 1	Factor 2	Factor 3
Panethnic discrimination in school	0.33	0.73	0.09
Panethnic discrimination at work	0.36	0.73	0.16
Panethnic discrimination prohibits success	0.43	0.53	0.14
National origin discrimination at school	0.85	0.29	0.12
National origin discrimination at work	0.87	0.26	0.15
National origin discrimination prohibits success	0.75	0.24	0.15
Individual-level discrimination in hiring/promotion	0.27	0.25	0.43
Individual-level discrimination in service	0.30	0.19	0.48
Individual-level discrimination prohibits success	0.29	0.19	0.52
Eigenvalue	4.23	0.56	0.43

Source: Twenty-First-Century Americanism Survey, 2004.

TABLE C.2. *Determinants of Identity Prioritization, Full Sample, Multinomial Logit*

Independent Variable	Country of Origin		Panethnic	
	b	s.e.	b	s.e.
Education	0.10	0.30	−0.48*	0.26
Age	−1.98**	0.49	−2.51**	0.37
Male	−0.39**	0.18	−0.51**	0.15
Black	0.81**	0.36	1.57**	0.22
Asian	0.71**	0.29	0.27	0.33
Latino	0.57**	0.28	0.01	0.24
Generation (1st to 4th+)	−2.48**	0.31	−0.50**	0.26
Speaks primarily English at home	−1.03**	0.23	−1.12**	0.28
Perception of panethnic discrimination	−0.54	0.38	−0.37	0.33
Perception of national origin discrimination	0.70**	0.35	0.47	0.30
Perception of individual-level discrimination	0.84**	0.30	0.87**	0.27
Constant	0.48	0.49	0.53	0.33
N	1993		1993	
Chi-squared	592.58		592.58	

Note: ** p < 0.05; * p < 0.1. All nondummy variables coded 0 to 1. Data weighted with weights provided by SESRC. The base category is American.
Source: Twenty-First-Century Americanism Survey, 2004.

TABLE C.3. *Determinants of Perceptions of Discrimination, Full Sample, OLS*

Independent Variable	Against Panethnic Group		Against National Origin Group		Against Self Personally	
	b	s.e.	b	s.e.	b	s.e.
Education	−0.11**	0.02	−0.13**	0.02	−0.001	0.02
Age	0.05*	0.03	0.03	0.03	−0.002	0.02
Male	0.01	0.01	−0.02	0.01	0.04**	0.01
Black	0.44**	0.02	0.48**	0.02	0.37**	0.02
Asian	0.16**	0.03	0.28**	0.03	0.12**	0.02
Latino	0.25**	0.02	0.32**	0.02	0.15**	0.02
Generation (1st to 4th+)	0.01	0.02	0.001	0.02	0.01	0.02
Speaks primarily English at home	−0.07**	0.03	−0.07**	0.02	−0.05**	0.02
Unemployed	0.002	0.02	0.03	0.02	0.02	0.02
National economy gotten worse	0.02*	0.01	0.03**	0.01	0.05**	0.01
Constant	0.36**	0.03	0.23**	0.03	0.07**	0.03
N	2495		2036		2506	
F	89.98		132.50		76.74	
R-squared	0.27		0.40		0.24	

Note: ** $p < 0.05$; * $p < 0.1$. All nondummy variables coded 0 to 1.
Source: Twenty-First-Century Americanism Survey, 2004.

Appendix D

Supplementary Tables from Chapter 6

TABLE D.1. *Overall Levels of Trust and Obligation*

	Trust in:		Obligation to:			
	Government	Law	Donate	Volunteer	Serve in Military	n (raw)
Panethnic identity	0.42	0.55	56	69	33	384
National origin identity	0.46	0.59	52	69	44	295
American identity	0.42	0.63	57	74	48	2,007
Panethnic discrimination (bottom third)	0.46	0.65	57	71	45	1,429
Panethnic discrimination (middle third)	0.46	0.61	57	74	51	819
Panethnic discrimination (top third)	0.40	0.52	54	73	41	552
National origin discrimination (bottom)	0.46	0.64	57	73	47	1,489
National origin discrimination (middle)	0.44	0.59	55	76	46	495
National origin discrimination (top)	0.42	0.57	54	69	44	816
Personal discrimination (bottom)	0.47	0.63	56	72	46	2,415

(continued)

	Trust in:		Obligation to:			
	Government	Law	Donate	Volunteer	Serve in Military	n (raw)
Personal discrimination (middle)	0.39	0.49	60	73	42	234
Personal discrimination (top)	0.41	0.49	54	78	43	151
White	0.46	0.65	56	72	46	1,589
Black	0.35	0.45	65	78	39	281
Asian	0.45	0.59	54	75	45	276
Latino	0.51	0.61	49	68	48	422
U.S. citizen	0.44	0.61	57	73	45	2,435
Not a U.S. citizen	0.55	0.66	51	65	47	249
1st generation	0.50	0.63	54	71	52	530
2nd generation	0.42	0.58	56	72	45	166
3rd generation	0.44	0.61	56	71	48	175
4th generation or more	0.44	0.58	57	73	43	1,765
Speaks primarily English at home	0.44	0.61	57	73	44	2,281
Speaks another language at home	0.51	0.63	54	71	50	404

Note: n = unweighted. Cell entries for trust = mean (0–1), cell entries for obligation = % saying yes.

Source: Twenty-First-Century Americanism Survey, 2004.

TABLE D.2. *Pride in Being American*

	Mean Level of Pride (0–1)	n (raw)
Panethnic identity	0.87	149
National origin identity	0.88	319
American identity	0.95	1,959
Panethnic discrimination (bottom third)	0.93	1,139
Panethnic discrimination (middle third)	0.95	723
Panethnic discrimination (top third)	0.93	464
National origin discrimination (bottom)	0.94	1,376
National origin discrimination (middle)	0.93	441
National origin discrimination (top)	0.92	739
Personal discrimination (bottom)	0.93	2,223
Personal discrimination (middle)	0.90	186
Personal discrimination (top)	0.93	117
White	0.94	1,604
Black	0.93	287
Asian	0.88	212
Latino	0.93	298
1st generation	0.92	308
2nd generation	0.91	173
3rd generation	0.91	184
4th generation or more	0.94	1,804
Speaks primarily English at home	0.93	2,309
Speaks another language at home	0.90	215

Note: n = unweighted.

Source: Twenty-First-Century Americanism Survey, 2004.

TABLE D.3. *Obligation to Give Money to Charities, by Race, Ordered Probit*

Independent Variable	White		Black		Asian and Latino	
	b	s.e.	b	s.e.	b	s.e.
Education	0.31**	0.13	0.10	0.27	0.26	0.18
Age	0.54**	0.17	0.15	0.38	0.67**	0.27
Male	−0.18**	0.07	0.04	0.17	−0.11	0.10
Generation (1st to 4th+)	−0.26*	0.15	−0.30	0.33	0.38**	0.16
Speaks primarily English at home	–	–	–	–	−0.34**	0.15
Civic republican American identity	1.75**	0.21	1.54**	0.45	0.79**	0.30
Latino	–	–	–	–	−0.17	0.13
National origin self-identification	−0.16	0.23	–	–	0.02	0.20
Panethnic self-identification	−0.02	0.19	0.38	0.48	0.41	0.31
National origin discrimination	0.04	0.19	–	–	−0.05	0.24
Panethnic discrimination	−0.14	0.15	0.17	0.45	0.02	0.24
Individual-level discrimination	−0.07	0.23	0.22	0.30	0.05	0.27
National origin × national origin discrimination	0.57	1.06	–	–	0.07	0.36
National origin × individual discrimination	0.19	1.10	–	–	−0.32	0.35
Panethnic × panethnic discrimination	−0.20	0.47	−0.25	0.72	−0.86*	0.47
Panethnic × individual discrimination	2.10**	0.91	−0.09	0.53	0.58	0.43
Cutpoint 1	0.92	0.25	0.80	0.61	0.38	0.32
Cutpoint 2	1.20	0.25	0.99	0.61	0.69	0.32
Chi-square	116.40		15.01		35.23	
N	1168		271		604	

Note: ** p < 0.05; * p < 0.1. All nondummy variables coded 0 to 1. Unweighted data.
Source: Twenty-First-Century Americanism Survey, 2004.

TABLE D.4. *Obligation to Volunteer, by Race, Ordered Probit*

Independent Variable	White b	White s.e.	Black b	Black s.e.	Asian and Latino b	Asian and Latino s.e.
Education	−0.02	0.15	−0.43	0.32	0.23	0.20
Age	−0.001	0.19	0.34	0.51	0.41	0.31
Male	−0.21**	0.08	−0.32*	0.19	0.004	0.11
Generation (1st to 4th+)	0.01	0.16	−0.22	0.39	0.21	0.18
Speaks primarily English at home	–	–	–	–	−0.13	0.15
Civic republican American identity	2.51**	0.22	2.29**	0.53	1.51**	0.32
Latino	–	–	–	–	−0.19	0.14
National origin self-identification	−0.24	0.27	–	–	0.27	0.24
Panethnic self-identification	−0.55**	0.21	−0.60	0.52	−0.06	0.33
National origin discrimination	0.18	0.23	–	–	−0.16	0.27
Panethnic discrimination	0.03	0.17	−0.41	0.46	0.14	0.27
Individual-level discrimination	−0.05	0.27	0.90**	0.37	0.26	0.28
National origin × national origin discrimination	−0.11	0.99	–	–	−0.80**	0.4
National origin × individual discrimination	0.79	1.06	–	–	−0.11	0.38
Panethnic × panethnic discrimination	1.05**	0.54	1.24*	0.77	0.17	0.53
Panethnic × individual discrimination	−0.41	0.94	−0.71	0.57	0.39	0.47
Cutpoint 1	0.85	0.26	0.55	0.69	0.48	0.35
Cutpoint 2	1.12	0.26	0.66	0.69	0.66	0.35
Chi-square	157.69		29.83		46.75	
N	1167		272		605	

Note: ** $p < 0.05$; * $p < 0.1$. All nondummy variables coded 0 to 1. Unweighted data.
Source: Twenty-First-Century Americanism Survey, 2004.

TABLE D.5. *Obligation to Serve in the Military, by Race, Ordered Probit*

Independent Variable	White		Black		Asian and Latino	
	b	s.e.	b	s.e.	b	s.e.
Education	−0.71**	0.14	−0.50*	0.30	−0.54**	0.19
Age	1.81**	0.18	2.62**	0.41	1.43**	0.29
Male	0.26**	0.08	0.78**	0.17	0.15	0.10
Generation (1st to 4th+)	−0.33**	0.15	−0.11	0.28	−0.44**	0.17
Speaks primarily English at home	–	–	–	–	0.02	0.14
Civic republican American identity	1.11**	0.21	1.53**	0.44	1.51**	0.31
Latino	–	–	–	–	−0.07	0.13
National origin self-identification	−0.22	0.25	–	–	−0.03	0.21
Panethnic self-identification	−0.26	0.19	−0.77*	0.50	0.06	0.36
National origin discrimination	−0.07	0.19	–	–	0.09	0.24
Panethnic discrimination	0.25*	0.15	−0.95**	0.45	−0.22	0.24
Individual-level discrimination	−0.10	0.23	−0.14	0.31	0.07	0.27
National origin × national origin discrimination	0.63	0.93	–	–	−0.35	0.37
National origin × individual discrimination	−0.21	1.05	–	–	0.01	0.38
Panethnic × panethnic discrimination	0.20	0.49	0.39	0.73	−0.13	0.54
Panethnic × individual discrimination	0.48	0.76	−0.26	0.52	0.11	0.47
Cutpoint 1	0.84	0.25	1.01	0.60	0.86	0.33
Cutpoint 2	1.18	0.25	1.31	0.60	1.14	0.34
Chi-square	218.39		91.28		95.70	
N	1157		268		598	

Note: ** p < 0.05; * p < 0.1. All nondummy variables coded 0 to 1. Unweighted data.
Source: Twenty-First-Century Americanism Survey, 2004.

Appendix E

Supplementary Tables from Chapter 7

TABLE E.1. *Rotated Factor Matrix (varimax rotation)*

	Factor 1	Factor 2	Factor 3
Immigrants today take advantage of jobs and opportunities here without doing enough to give back to the community.	0.67	0.18	0.19
Immigrants today come to think of themselves as Americans just as much as immigrants from earlier eras did.	0.18	0.27	0.20
Immigrants should really know what's going on in the United States if they want to stay here, but a lot of them just don't want to be bothered.	0.62	0.11	0.15
Blending into the larger society while maintaining cultural traditions is difficult, but a lot of immigrants today seem to do a good job of it.	0.11	0.26	0.10
If immigrants only tried harder to fit in, then more Americans would accept their cultural differences.	0.60	0.13	0.18
Irish, Italians, and Jews overcame prejudice and worked their way up. Today's immigrants should do the same.	0.36	0.24	0.14
Years of discrimination have created conditions that make it difficult for immigrants to work their way out of the lower class.	0.16	0.61	-0.01
If immigrants would only try harder, they could be just as well off as people born in America.	0.51	0.32	0.18
Over the last few years, immigrants have gotten less than they deserve.	0.20	0.60	0.08
The country would be better off if more of our immigrants were from Europe instead of from Asia and Latin America.	0.29	0.01	0.51
Immigrants who are Muslim just won't ever seem American to me.	0.34	0.08	0.51
The idea of an America where most people are not white bothers me.	0.21	0.08	0.46
Eigenvalue	2.97	0.69	0.35

Note: Whites only, "don't know" excluded.
Source: Twenty-First-Century Americanism Survey, 2004.

TABLE E.2. *Bivariate Correlations among Resentment Items*

	Take Jobs	Should Know	Try to Fit in	Work Way Up	Discrimination	Try Harder	Deserve More	Favor Europe	Muslim	White America
Take jobs	1.00									
Should know	0.53	1.00								
Try to fit in	0.49	0.42	1.00							
Work way up	0.28	0.27	0.32	1.00						
Discrimination	0.20	0.17	0.17	0.24	1.00					
Try harder	0.43	0.40	0.38	0.37	0.31	1.00				
Deserve more	0.29	0.22	0.21	0.23	0.51	0.30	1.00			
Favor Europe	0.28	0.27	0.25	0.17	0.07	0.26	0.10	1.00		
Muslim	0.34	0.28	0.30	0.20	0.10	0.30	0.17	0.42	1.00	
White America	0.24	0.20	0.22	0.19	0.06	0.19	0.16	0.34	0.34	1.00

Note: Whites only, "don't know" excluded.
Source: Twenty-First-Century Americanism Survey, 2004.

References

Abdelal, Rawi, Yoshiko M. Herrera, Alastair Iain Johnston, and Rose McDermott. 2006. "Identity as a Variable." *Perspectives on Politics* 4(4): 695–711.

Abizadeh, Arash. 2002. "Does Liberal Democracy Presuppose a Cultural Nation? Four Arguments." *American Political Science Review* 96(3): 495–509.

Abramson, Paul R., Brian D. Silver, and Barbara A. Anderson. 1987. "The Effects of Question Order in Attitude Surveys: The Case of the SRC/CPS Citizen Duty Items." *American Journal of Political Science* 31(4): 900–8.

Aijan, George. 2007. "Modern Technology vs. Old Fashioned Assimilation – Is a Melting Pot Even Possible Anymore?" http://www.vdare.com/misc/070801_ajjan .htm (accessed April 22, 2008).

Alba, Richard D. 1990. *Ethnic Identity: The Transformation of White America*. New Haven, CT: Yale University Press.

Alba, Richard D., and Victor Nee. 2003. *Remaking the American Mainstream: Assimilation and Contemporary Immigration*. Cambridge, MA: Harvard University Press.

Alesina, Alberto, and Eliana La Ferrara. 2002. "Who Trusts Others?" *Journal of Public Economics* 85(2): 207–34.

Alesina, Alberto, Reza Baqir, and William Easterly. 1999. "Public Goods and Ethnic Divisions." *Quarterly Journal of Economics* 114(4): 1243–84.

American Civil Liberties Union. 2004. *Sanctioned Bias: Racial Profiling since 9/11*. New York: American Civil Liberties Union.

Anderson, Benedict. 1983. *Imagined Communities: Reflections on the Origin and Spread of Nationalism*. London: Verso.

Badie, Rick. 2006. "Protesters' Flags Send Mixed Signals." *Atlanta Journal-Constitution*, April 2, sec. J.

Banning, Lance. 1986. "Jeffersonian Ideology Revisited: Liberal and Classical Ideas in the New American Republic." *William and Mary Quarterly* 43(1): 3–19.

Bauer, Gary. 2006. "E Pluribus Pluribus?" *USA Today*, June 15, sec. A.

Berry, Jeffrey, and Sarah Sobieraj. 2008. "The Outrage Industry." Paper prepared for the Going to Extremes: The Fate of the Political Center in American Politics conference, Rockefeller Center for Public Policy and the Social Sciences, Dartmouth College, Hanover, NH.

Bobo, Lawrence. 2001. "Race, Interests, and Beliefs about Affirmative Action: Unanswered Questions and New Directions." In *Color Lines: Affirmative Action, Immigration, and Civil Rights Options for America*, ed. John Skretny, 191–213. Chicago: University of Chicago Press.

———. 2000. "Race and Beliefs about Affirmative Action." In *Racialized Politics: The Debate about Racism in America*, ed. David Sears, Jim Sidanius, and Lawrence Bobo, 137–64. Chicago: University of Chicago Press.

Braber, Liam. 2002. "Korematsu's Ghost: A Post-September 11th Analysis of Race and National Security." *Villanova Law Review* 47(2): 451–90.

Bradley Foundation. 2008. *E Pluribus Unum: The Bradley Project on America's National Identity*. Milwaukee, WI: The Bradley Foundation.

Brambor, Thomas, William Roberts Clark, and Matt Golder. 2006. "Understanding Interaction Models: Improving Empirical Analyses." *Political Analysis* 14: 63–82.

Branscombe, Nyla R., Michael T. Schmitt, and Richard D. Harvey. 1999. "Perceiving Pervasive Discrimination among African Americans: Implications for Group Identification and Well-being." *Journal of Personality and Social Psychology* 77(1): 135–49.

Branscombe, Nyla R., Naomi Ellemers, Russell Spears, and Bertjan Doosje. 1999. "The Context and Content of Social Identity Threat." In *Social Identity*, ed. Naomi Ellemers, Russell Spears, and Bertjan Doosje, 35–58. Oxford: Blackwell.

Brehm, John, and Wendy Rahn. 1997. "Individual-Level Evidence for the Causes and Consequences of Social Capital." *American Journal of Political Science* 41(3): 999–1023.

Brimelow, Peter. 1995. *Alien Nation: Common Sense about America's Immigration Disaster*. New York: Random House.

Brodie, Mollyann, Annie Steffenson, Jaime Valdez, and Rebecca Levin. 2002. *2002 National Survey of Latinos: Summary of Findings*. Washington, DC: Pew Hispanic Center.

Brubaker, Rogers, and Frederick Cooper. 2000. "Beyond 'Identity.'" *Theory and Society* 29(1): 1–47.

Buchanan, Patrick J. 2006. *State of Emergency: The Third World Invasion and Conquest of America*. 1st ed. New York: Thomas Dunne Books/St. Martin's Press.

Campbell, Andrea Louise, Cara Wong, and Jack Citrin. 2006. "'Racial Threat.' Partisan Climate, and Direct Democracy: Contextual Effects in Three California Initiatives." *Political Behavior* 28(2): 129–50.

Campbell, Angus, Phillip Converse, Warren Miller, and Donald Stokes. 1960. *The American Voter*. Chicago: University of Chicago Press.

Carroll, Susan. 2009. "Rivera Warns of Debate's Effects." *Houston Chronicle*, June 30, http://www.chron.com/disp/story.mpl/6505752.html (accessed July 7, 2009).

Chavez, Leo. 2008. *The Latino Threat: Constructing Immigrants, Citizens, and the Nation*. Stanford, CA: Stanford University Press.

———. 1997. "Immigration Reform and Nativism: The Nationalist Response to the Transnationalist Challenge." In *Immigrants Out! The New Nativism and the Anti-Immigrant Impulse in the United States*, ed. Juan Perea, 61–77. New York: New York University Press.

Cheryan, Sapna, and Benoit Monin. 2005. "'Where Are You Really From?': Asian Americans and Identity Denial." *Journal of Personality and Social Psychology* 89(5): 717–30.

Chong, Dennis, and James N. Druckman. 2007. "Framing Theory." *Annual Review of Political Science* 10(1): 103–26.

Chong, Dennis, and Dukhong Kim. 2006. "The Experiences and Effects of Economic Status among Racial and Ethnic Minorities." *American Political Science Review* 100(3): 335–51.

Chong, Dennis, and Reuel Rogers. 2005. "Racial Solidarity and Political Participation." *Political Behavior* 27(4): 347–74.

Christensen, P. Niels, Hank Rothgerber, Wendy Wood, and David C. Matz. 2004. "Social Norms and Identity Relevance: A Motivational Approach to Normative Behavior." *Personality and Social Psychology Bulletin* 30(10): 1295–1309.

Citrin, Jack. 2001. "The End of American Identity?" In *One America? Political Leadership, National Identity, and the Dilemmas of Diversity*, ed. Stanley Renshon, 285–307. Washington, DC: Georgetown University Press.

Citrin, Jack, and Samantha Luks. 2001. "Political Trust Revisited: Déjà Vu All Over Again?" In *What Is It About Government that Americans Dislike?* ed. John Hibbing and Elizabeth Theiss-Morse, 9–27. Cambridge: Cambridge University Press.

Citrin, Jack, Beth Reingold, and Donald P. Green. 1990. "American Identity and the Politics of Ethnic Change." *Journal of Politics* 52(4): 1124–54.

Citrin, Jack, Cara Wong, and Brian Duff. 2001. "The Meaning of American National Identity." In *Social Identity, Intergroup Conflict, and Conflict Resolution*, ed. Richard Ashmore, Lee Jussim, and David Wilder, 71–100. New York: Oxford University Press.

Citrin, Jack, Donald P. Green, Christopher Muste, and Cara Wong. 1997. "Public Opinion toward Immigration Reform: The Role of Economic Motivations." *Journal of Politics* 59(3): 858–81.

Citrin, Jack, Ernst B. Haas, Christopher Muste, and Beth Reingold. 1994. "Is American Nationalism Changing? Implications for Foreign Policy." *International Studies Quarterly* 38(1): 1–31.

Citrin, Jack, Amy Lerman, Michael Murakami, and Kathryn Pearson. 2007. "Testing Huntington: Is Hispanic Immigration a Threat to American Identity?" *Perspectives on Politics* 5(1): 31–48.

Citrin, Jack, David O. Sears, Christopher Muste, and Cara Wong. 2001. "Multiculturalism in American Public Opinion." *British Journal of Political Science* 31(2): 247–75.

Claassen, Ryan L. 2004. "Political Opinion and Distinctiveness: The Case of Hispanic Ethnicity." *Political Research Quarterly* 57(4): 609–20.

Clark, Lee Anna, and David Watson. 1995. "Constructing Validity: Basic Issues in Objective Scale Development." *Psychological Assessment* 7(3): 309–19.

Collins, Scott. 2008. "A Ratings Downer for Fox News." *Los Angeles Times*, May 8, http://articles.latimes.com/2006/may/08/entertainment/et-channel8 (accessed March 3, 2009).

Conover, Pamela Johnston. 1988. "Feminists and the Gender Gap." *Journal of Politics* 50(4): 985–1010.

Conover, Pamela Johnston, and Virginia Sapiro. 1993. "Gender, Feminist Consciousness, and War." *American Journal of Political Science* 37(4): 1079–99.

Conover, Pamela Johnston, Ivor M. Crewe, and Donald D. Searing. 1991. "The Nature of Citizenship in the United States and Great Britain: Empirical Comments on Theoretical Themes." *Journal of Politics* 53(3): 800–32.

Conover, Pamela Johnston, Donald D. Searing, and Ivor Crewe. 2004. "The Elusive Ideal of Equal Citizenship: Political Theory and Political Psychology in the United States and Great Britain." *Journal of Politics* 66(4): 1036–68.

Converse, Philip. 1964. "The Nature of Belief Systems in Mass Publics." In *Ideology and Discontent*, ed. David Apter, 206–61. London: Free Press.

Cortina, Jose M. 1993. "What Is Coefficient Alpha? An Examination of Theory and Applications." *Journal of Applied Psychology* 78(1): 98–104.

Crosby, Faye. 1984. "The Denial of Personal Discrimination." *American Behavioral Scientist* 27(3): 371–86.

Curtin, Richard, Stanley Presser, and Eleanor Singer. 2000. "The Effects of Response Rate Changes on the Index of Consumer Sentiment." *Public Opinion Quarterly* 64(4): 413–28.

Dagger, Richard. 1997. *Civic Virtues: Rights, Citizenship, and Republican Liberalism*. New York: Oxford University Press.

Dahl, Robert. 1998. *On Democracy*. New Haven, CT: Yale University Press.

———. 1991. *Democracy and its Critics*. New Haven, CT: Yale University Press.

Dale, Maryclaire. 2007. "Giuliani Campaigning at Speak English Cheesesteak Stand." The Associated Press State and Local Wire, October 2.

Davis, Darren. 2007. *Negative Liberty: Public Opinion and the Terrorist Attacks on America*. New York: Russell Sage Foundation.

Davis, Darren W., and Brian D. Silver. 2004. "Civil Liberties vs. Security: Public Opinion in the Context of the Terrorist Attacks on America." *American Journal of Political Science* 48(1): 28–46.

Davis, F. James. 2001. *Who Is Black? One Nation's Definition*. 10th anniversary ed. University Park: Pennsylvania State University Press.

Dawson, Michael C. 2000. "Slowly Coming to Grips with the Effects of the American Racial Order on American Policy Preferences." In *Racialized Politics: The Debate about Racism in America*, ed. David Sears, Jim Sidanius, and Lawrence Bobo, 344–57. Chicago: University of Chicago Press.

———. 1994. *Behind the Mule: Race and Class in African-American Politics*. Princeton, NJ: Princeton University Press.

Deaton, Joyce. 2008. *Charlotte: A Welcome Denied*. Washington, DC: Woodrow Wilson International Center for Scholars.

de Figueiredo, Rui, Jr., and Zachary Elkins. 2003. "Are Patriots Bigots? An Inquiry into the Vices of In-Group Pride." *American Journal of Political Science* 47(1): 171–88.

de la Garza, Rodolfo O., Angelo Falcon, and F. Chris Garcia. 1996. "Will the Real Americans Please Stand Up: Anglo and Mexican-American Support of Core American Political Values." *American Journal of Political Science* 40(2): 335–51.

DeSipio, Louis. 2006. "Transnational Politics and Civic Engagement: Do Home-Country Political Ties Limit Latino Immigrant Pursuit of U.S. Civic Engagement and Citizenship?" In *Transforming Politics, Transforming America: The Political and Civic Incorporation of Immigrants in the United States*, ed. Taeku Lee, S. Karthick Ramakrishnan, and Ricardo Ramirez, 106–26. Charlottesville: University of Virginia Press.

———. 2002. "Immigrant Organizing, Civic Outcomes: Civic Engagement, Political Activity, National Attachment, and Identity in Latino Immigrant Communities." Center for the Study of Democracy, paper #02–08, http://repositories.cdlib.org.ezproxy.library.tufts.edu/csd/02–08 (accessed February 10, 2004).

DeVellis, Robert. 2003. *Scale Development: Theory and Application*. 2nd ed. Thousand Oaks, CA: Sage Publications.

Devos, Thierry, and Mahzarin R. Banaji. 2005. "American = White?" *Journal of Personality and Social Psychology* 88(3): 447–66.

DeYoung, Karen. 2007. "Distrust Hinders FBI Outreach to Muslims." *Washington Post*, February 8, sec. A.

Dovidio, John, and William Morris. 1975. "Effects of Stress and Commonality of Fate on Helping Behavior." *Journal of Personality and Social Psychology* 31(1): 145–9.

Druckman, Daniel. 1994. "Nationalism, Patriotism and Group Loyalty: A Social Psychological Perspective." *International Studies Quarterly* 38(1): 43–68.

Eckstein, Susan. 2001. "Community as Gift-Giving: Collectivistic Roots of Volunteerism." *American Sociological Review* 66(6): 829–51.

Edwards, James. 2006. *Two Sides of the Same Coin: The Connection between Legal and Illegal Immigration*. Washington, DC: Center for Immigration Studies.

Elder, C. E., and Roger Cobb. 1983. *The Political Uses of Symbols*. New York: Longman.

Ellemers, Naomi, and Manuela Barreto. 2001. "The Impact of Relative Group Status: Affective, Perceptual, and Behavioral Consequences." In *Blackwell Handbook of Social Psychology: Intergroup Processes*, ed. Rupert Brown and Samuel Gaertner, 324–43. Malden, MA: Blackwell.

Ellemers, Naomi, Russell Spears, and Bertjan Doosje. 1999. *Social Identity*. Oxford: Blackwell.

Elliott, Andrea. 2006. "After 9/11, Arab-Americans Fear Police Acts, Study Finds." *New York Times*, June 12, sec. A.

Ellis, Richard. 2002. *Democratic Delusions: The Initiative Process in America*. Lawrence: University Press of Kansas.

El Nasser, Haya. 2000. "New Ways to Count Multiracial People; Despite Rules Change, Minority Groups Still Worry that Their Numbers Will Be Diluted." *USA Today*, March 13, sec. A.

Epstein, David. 1984. *The Political Theory of "The Federalist."* Chicago: University of Chicago Press.

Espiritu, Yen Le. 1992. *Asian American Panethnicity: Bridging Institutions and Identities*. Asian American History and Culture Series. Philadelphia: Temple University Press.

Facchini, Giovanni, Anna Maria Mayda, and Riccardo Puglisi. 2009. "Illegal Immigration and Media Exposure: Evidence from the United States." Paper prepared for the Dynamics of Public Opinion on Immigration in the U.S. and the West conference, University of Texas at Austin.

Farmer, John. 2006. "The Nation's Melting Pot Is Showing Huge Cracks." In *Star-Ledger* (Newark), http://www.nj.com/columns/ledger/farmer/index.ssf?/base/columns-0/1146590708102300.xml&coll=1 (accessed May 24, 2006).

Fazio, Russell, and Laura Hilden. 2001. "Emotional Reactions to a Seemingly Prejudiced Response: The Role of Automatically Activated Racial Attitudes and Motivation to Control Prejudiced Reactions." *Personality and Social Psychology Bulletin* 27(5): 538–49.

Federico, Christopher M. 2006. "Race, Education, and Individualism Revisited." *Journal of Politics* 68(3): 600–10.

Feldman, Stanley. 1988. "Structure and Consistency in Public Opinion: The Role of Core Beliefs and Values." *American Journal of Political Science* 32(2): 416–40.

Feldman, Stanley, and John Zaller. 1992. "The Political Culture of Ambivalence: Ideological Responses to the Welfare State." *American Journal of Political Science* 36(1): 268–307.

Fetzer, Joel S. 2000. *Public Attitudes toward Immigration in the United States, France, and Germany.* Cambridge and New York: Cambridge University Press.

Flippen, Annette R., Harvey A. Hornstein, William E. Siegal, and Eben A. Weitzman. 1996. "A Comparison of Similarity and Interdependence as Triggers for In-Group Formation." *Personality and Social Psychology Bulletin* 22(9): 882–93.

Floyd, Frank J., and Keith F. Widaman. 1995. "Factor Analysis in the Development and Refinement of Clinical Assessment Instruments." *Psychological Assessment* 7(3): 286–99.

Forbes, H. D. 1997. *Ethnic Conflict: Commerce, Culture, and the Contact Hypothesis.* New Haven, CT: Yale University Press.

Ford, C. Benjamin, and Sebastian Montes. 2007. "Police Worry about Growing Mistrust among Immigrants." *Maryland Gazette* (Gaithersburg), March 21, http://www.gazette.net/stories/032107/montnew222019_32321.shtml (accessed July 11, 2007).

Fox, Geoffrey. 1996. *Hispanic Nation: Culture, Politics, and the Constructing of Identity.* Tucson: University of Arizona Press.

Frendreis, John, and Raymond Tatalovich. 1997. "Who Supports English-Only Language Laws? Evidence from the 1992 National Election Study." *Social Science Quarterly* 78(2): 354–68.

Friess, Steve. 2007. "English Mandate Repealed." *New York Times*, February 15, sec. A.
———. 2006. "Stars and Strife: Flag Rule Splits Town." *New York Times*, December 18, sec. A.

Fuegen, Kathleen, and Monica Biernat. 2000. "Defining Discrimination in the Personal/Group Discrimination Discrepancy." *Sex Roles* 43(5): 285–310.

Furia, Pete. 2002. "Patriotism, Nationalism, and International Politics." Paper presented at the annual meeting of the American Political Science Association, Boston.

Gaertner, Samuel, and John Dovidio. 2000. *Reducing Intergroup Bias: The Common Ingroup Identity Model.* Philadelphia: Psychology Press.

Galston, William. 2003. "Can Civic Knowledge Motivate the Next Generation?" In *United We Serve: National Service and the Future of Citizenship,* ed. E. J. Dionne, K. Meltzer Drogosz, and R. Litan, 175–81. Washington, DC: Brookings Institution.

García, John A. 2003. *Latino Politics in America: Community, Culture, and Interests.* The Spectrum Series. Lanham, MD: Rowman and Littlefield.

García Bedolla, Lisa. 2005. *Fluid Borders: Latino Power, Identity, and Politics in Los Angeles.* Berkeley: University of California Press.

Geller, Adam. 1997. "Signs of Change; Fearful of Legal Lashing, Towns Back Off English-also Ordinances." *The Record* (Bergen County, NJ), July 10, sec. L.

Geohegan, Thomas. 2007. "Make 'em Vote: The Case for Requiring New Citizens to Register to Vote." In *The American Prospect,* http://prospect.org/cs/articles?article=make_em_vote (accessed June 7, 2007).

Gerstle, Gary. 2001. *American Crucible: Race and Nation in the Twentieth Century.* Princeton, NJ: Princeton University Press.

Gibson, James L., and Amanda Gouws. 2003. *Overcoming Intolerance in South Africa: Experiments in Democratic Persuasion.* Cambridge Studies in Political Psychology and Public Opinion. New York: Cambridge University Press.

Gilens, Martin, Paul Sniderman, and James Kuklinski. 1998. "Affirmative Action and the Politics of Realignment." *British Journal of Political Science* 28(1): 159–83.

Gingrich, Newt, and John Fonte. 2007. "Vote for English Ballots." *Chicago Sun-Times,* April 15, http://www.suntimes.com/news/otherviews/341036,CST-EDT-REF15.article (accessed July 6, 2007).

Glascock, Stuart. 2008. "A Town Confronts Its Language Barrier; with Federal Help – and Prodding – Mattawa, Wash., Tries to Accommodate the 90% of Residents Who Speak Spanish." *Los Angeles Times*, May 25, sec. A.

Glazer, Nathan. 1997. *We Are All Multiculturalists Now*. Cambridge, MA: Harvard University Press.

Gonzalez, Roseann, ed. 2001. *Language Ideologies: Critical Perspectives on the Official English Movement*. Vol. 2. Mahwah, NJ: Lawrence Erlbaum Associates.

Gorman, Anna. 2006. "Flag's Meaning Is in the Eye of the Beholder." *Los Angeles Times*, March 29, sec. A.

Gould, Stephen J. 1996. *The Mismeasure of Man*. New York: W.W. Norton and Company.

Greenberg, Cheryl. 1995. "Black and Jewish Responses to Japanese Internment." *Journal of American Ethnic History* 14(2): 3–37.

Grieco, Elizabeth, and Rachel Cassidy. 2001. *Overview of Race and Hispanic Origin*, Washington, DC: U.S. Census Bureau, Census Brief C2KBR/01-1, http://www.census.gov/prod/2001pubs/cenbr01-1.pdf (accessed June 8, 2007).

Groves, Robert, Stanley Presser, and Sarah Dipko. 2004. "The Role of Topic Interest in Survey Participation Decisions." *Public Opinion Quarterly* 68(1): 2–31.

Gutmann, Amy. 2003. *Identity in Democracy*. Princeton, NJ: Princeton University Press.

Hackney, Sheldon. 1997. *One America, Indivisible: A National Conversation on American Pluralism and Identity*. Washington, DC: National Endowment for the Humanities.

Hagen, Dirk. 2009. *2009 Immigration-Related Bills and Resolutions in the States*. National Conference of State Legislatures, http://www.ncsl.org/documents/immig/2009ImmigFinalApril222009.pdf (accessed June 10, 2009).

Haider, Steven J., Robert F. Schoeni, Yuhua Bao, and Caroline Danielson. 2004. "Immigrants, Welfare Reform, and the Economy." *Journal of Policy Analysis and Management* 23(4): 745–64.

Harris, David A. 2003. *Profiles in Injustice: Why Racial Profiling Cannot Work*. New York: New Press.

Harrison, Lawrence. 2009. "What Will America Stand for in 2050?" *Christian Science Monitor*, May 28, http://www.csmonitor.com/2009/0528/p09s01-coop.html (accessed June 3, 2009).

Hartz, Louis. 1955. *The Liberal Tradition in America: An Interpretation of American Political Thought since the Revolution*. 1st ed. New York: Harcourt, Brace.

Hayden, Shelly, Thomas Jackson, and J. Guydish. 1984. "Helping Behavior of Females: Effects of Stress and Commonality of Fate." *Journal of Psychology* 117(2): 233–7.

Held, David. 1996. *Models of Democracy*. 2nd ed. Stanford, CA: Stanford University Press.

Henderson, Nicole, Christopher Ortiz, Naomi Sugie, and Joel Miller. 2006. *Law Enforcement and Arab American Community Relations after September 11, 2001: Technical Report*. New York: Vera Institute of Justice.

Henry, P. J., and David O. Sears. 2002. "The Symbolic Racism 2000 Scale." *Political Psychology* 23(2): 253–83.

Hero, Rodney E. 1998. *Faces of Inequality: Social Diversity in American Politics*. New York: Oxford University Press.

Hetherington, Marc J. 2005. *Why Trust Matters: Declining Political Trust and the Demise of American Liberalism*. Princeton, NJ: Princeton University Press.

Hibbing, John, and Elizabeth Theiss-Morse. 2001. "The Means Is the End." In *What Is It about Government that Americans Dislike?* ed. John Hibbing and Elizabeth Theiss-Morse, 243–50. Cambridge: Cambridge University Press.

Hibbing, John R., and Elizabeth Theiss-Morse. 2002. *Stealth Democracy: Americans' Beliefs about How Government Should Work.* Cambridge Studies in Political Psychology and Public Opinion. Cambridge: Cambridge University Press.

Higham, John. 1993. "Multiculturalism and Universalism: A History and Critique." Special Issue on Multiculturalism. *American Quarterly* 45(2): 195–219.

———. 1963. *Strangers in the Land: Patterns of American Nativism 1860–1925.* New York: Atheneum.

Hoefer, Michael, Nancy Rytina, and Bryan Baker. 2008. *Estimates of the Unauthorized Immigrant Population Residing in the United States: January 2007.* Washington, DC: Office of Immigration Statistics, Department of Homeland Security.

Hollinger, David A. 1995. *Postethnic America: Beyond Multiculturalism.* New York: Basic Books.

Holmes, Steven. 2001. "The Nation: True Colors; The Confusion Over Who We Are." *New York Times*, June 3, sec. A.

Holthouse, David, and Mark Potok. 2008. *The Year in Hate: Active U.S. Hate Groups Rise to 888 in 2007*, Southern Poverty Law Center, no. 129, http://www.splcenter .org/intel/intelreport/article.jsp?aid=886 (accessed June 25, 2008).

Hood, M. V. III, and Irwin L. Morris. 1997. "¿Amigo o Enemigo? Context, Attitudes, and Anglo Public Opinion toward Immigration." *Social Science Quarterly* 78(2): 309–23.

Hood, M. V. III, Irwin L. Morris, and Kurt A. Shirkey. 1997. "'¡Quedate o Vente!': Uncovering the Determinants of Hispanic Public Opinion toward Immigration." *Political Research Quarterly* 50(3): 627–47.

Hopkins, Daniel J. 2009. "The Diversity Discount: When Increasing Ethnic and Racial Diversity Prevents Tax Increases." *Journal of Politics* 71(1): 160–77.

———. 2007. "Threatening Changes: Explaining Where and When Immigrants Provoke Local Opposition." Paper prepared for the annual meeting of the Midwest Political Science Association, Chicago.

Hopkins, Daniel J., Van C. Tran, and Abigail Fisher Williamson. 2009. "See No Spanish: Implicit Cues, Personal Experience, and Attitudes toward Immigration." Paper presented at the annual meeting of the Midwest Political Science Association, Chicago.

Hornstein, Harvey A. 1976. *Cruelty and Kindness: A New Look at Aggression and Altruism.* Patterns of Social Behavior Series. Englewood Cliffs, NJ: Prentice-Hall.

Howell, Susan E., and Deborah Fagan. 1988. "Race and Trust in Government: Testing the Political Reality Model." *Public Opinion Quarterly* 52(3): 343–50.

Huddy, Leonie, and Nadia Khatib. 2007. "American Patriotism, National Identity, and Political Involvement." *American Journal of Political Science* 51(1): 63–77.

Huddy, Leonie, and David Sears. 1995. "Opposition to Bilingual Education: Prejudice or the Defense of Realistic Interests?" *Social Psychology Quarterly* 58(2): 133–43.

Huddy, Leonie, Stanley Feldman, Charles Taber, and Gallya Lahav. 2005. "Threat, Anxiety, and Support of Antiterrorism Policies." *American Journal of Political Science* 49(3): 593–608.

Huntington, Samuel P. 2004. *Who Are We? The Challenges to America's Identity.* New York: Simon and Schuster.

Hurwitz, Jon, and Jeffery J. Mondak. 2002. "Democratic Principles, Discrimination and Political Intolerance." *British Journal of Political Science* 32(1): 93–118.

Izumi, Lance. 2001. "December 7th, September 11th, and Immigrant Assimilation," http://www.vdare.com/misc/izumi_assimilation.htm (accessed April 22, 2008).

Jacobson, Cardell K. 1985. "Resistance to Affirmative Action: Self-Interest or Racism?" *The Journal of Conflict Resolution* 29(2): 306–29.

Jacoby, William G. 2006. "Value Choices and American Public Opinion." *American Journal of Political Science* 50(3): 706–23.

Jaschik, Scott. 2009. "Special Sauce for ESL." *Inside Higher Ed.*, May 27, http://www.insidehighered.com/news/2009/05/27/esl (accessed September 10, 2009).

Jelen, Ted G. 1999. "Dimensions of Religious Free Exercise: Abstract Beliefs and Concrete Applications." *Review of Religious Research* 40(4): 349–58.

Jetten, Jolanda, Nyla R. Branscombe, Michael T. Schmitt, and Russell Spears. 2001. "Rebels with a Cause: Group Identification as a Response to Perceived Discrimination from the Mainstream." *Personality and Social Psychology Bulletin* 27(9): 1204–13.

Johnson, Kevin. 1997. "The New Nativism: Something Old, Something New, Something Borrowed, Something Blue." In *Immigrants Out! The New Nativism and the Anti-Immigrant Impulse in the United States*, ed. Juan Perea, 165–89. New York: New York University Press.

Jones-Correa, Michael, and David L. Leal. 1996. "Becoming 'Hispanic': Secondary Panethnic Identification among Latin American-Origin Populations in the United States." *Hispanic Journal of Behavioral Sciences* 18(2): 214–54.

Junn, Jane, and Natalie Masuoka. 2008. "Asian American Identity: Shared Racial Status and Political Context." *Perspectives on Politics* 6(4): 729–40.

Kallen, Horace. 1924. *Culture and Democracy in the United States*. New Brunswick, NJ: Transaction Publishers.

Keele, Luke. 2005. "The Authorities Really Do Matter: Party Control and Trust in Government." *Journal of Politics* 67(3): 873–86.

Keeter, Scott, Carolyn Miller, Andrew Kohut, Robert Groves, and Stanley Presser. 2000. "Consequences of Reducing Nonresponse in a National Telephone Survey." *Public Opinion Quarterly* 64(2): 125–48.

Kessler, Thomas, Amelie Mummendey, and Utta Kristin Leisse. 2000. "The Personal-Group Discrepancy: Is There a Common Information Basis for Personal and Group Judgment?" *Journal of Personality and Social Psychology* 79(1): 95–109.

Kim, Phillip H. 2004. "Conditional Morality? Attitudes of Religious Individuals toward Racial Profiling." *American Behavioral Scientist* 47(7): 879–95.

Kinder, Donald R., and Don Herzog. 1993. "Democratic Discussion." In *Reconsidering the Democratic Public*, ed. George E. Marcus and Russell Hanson, 347–77. University Park: Pennsylvania State University Press.

Kinder, Donald R., and Lynn M. Sanders. 1996. *Divided by Color: Racial Politics and Democratic Ideals*. Chicago: University of Chicago Press.

King, D. A. 2009. "Is Obama-Care to Include Illegal Immigrants?" *Marietta Daily Journal*, July 22, http://www.mdjonline.com/content/index/showcontentitem/area/1/section/17/item/136907.html (accessed August 18, 2009).

King, Desmond. 2005. *The Liberty of Strangers: Making the American Nation*. Oxford: Oxford University Press.

———. 2000. *Making Americans: Immigration, Race, and the Origins of the Diverse Democracy*. Cambridge, MA: Harvard University Press.

King, Gary, Michael Tomz, and Jason Wittenberg. 2000. "Making the Most of Statistical Analyses: Improving Interpretation and Presentation." *American Journal of Political Science* 44(2): 347–61.

Kobrynowicz, Diane, and Nyla R. Branscombe. 1997. "Who Considers Themselves Victims of Discrimination? Individual Difference Predictors of Perceived Gender Discrimination in Women and Men." *Psychology of Women Quarterly* 21(3): 347–63.

Kroenig, Matthew, and Jay Stowsky. 2006. "War Makes the State, but Not As It Pleases: Homeland Security and American Anti-Statism." *Security Studies* 15(2): 225–70.

Kuklinski, James H., Paul J. Quirk, Jennifer Jerit, David Schwieder, and Robert F. Rich. 2000. "Misinformation and the Currency of Democratic Citizenship." *Journal of Politics* 62(3): 790–816.

Kymlicka, Will. 1995. *Multicultural Citizenship: A Liberal Theory of Minority Rights.* New York: Oxford University Press.

Lee, Lichang, Jane Allyn Piliavin, and Vaughn R. A. Call. 1999. "Giving Time, Money, and Blood: Similarities and Differences." *Social Psychology Quarterly* 62(3): 276–90.

Lezin, Sophia. 1999a. "Fines Anger Latino Merchants; Municipal Ordinances Requiring English in Commercial Signs Galvanize Hispanics." *Atlanta Journal-Constitution*, March 7, sec. E.

———. 1999b. "Latino Merchant Files Suit in Norcross Sign Dispute." *Atlanta Journal-Constitution*, March 10, sec. C.

Lichtblau, Eric. 2003. "Bush Issues Racial Profiling Ban but Exempts Security Inquiries." *New York Times*, June 18, sec. A.

Lien, Pei-te. 1994. "Ethnicity and Political Participation: A Comparison between Asian and Mexican Americans." *Political Behavior* 16(2): 237–64.

Lien, Pei-te, M. Margaret Conway, and Janelle Wong. 2004. *The Politics of Asian Americans: Diversity and Community.* New York: Routledge.

Lipset, Seymour Martin. 1963. *The First New Nation: The United States in Historical and Comparative Perspective.* New York: Basic Books.

Lopez, Mark Hugo, and Gretchen Livingston. 2009. *Hispanics and the Criminal Justice System: Low Confidence, High Exposure.* Washington, DC: Pew Hispanic Center.

Lopez, Mark Hugo, and Susan Minushkin. 2008. *2008 National Survey of Latinos: Hispanics See Their Situation in U.S. Deteriorating; Oppose Key Immigration Enforcement Measures*, no. 93. Washington, DC: Pew Hispanic Center.

Louie, Josephine. 2005. *We Don't Feel Welcome Here: African Americans and Hispanics in Boston.* Cambridge, MA: The Civil Rights Project, Harvard University.

Lowe, Lisa. 1996. *Immigrant Acts.* Durham, NC: Duke University Press.

Major, Brenda, Wendy J. Quinton, and Toni Schmader. 2003. "Attributions to Discrimination and Self-Esteem: Impact of Group Identification and Situational Ambiguity." *Journal of Experimental Social Psychology* 39(3): 220–31.

Malkin, Michelle. 2009. "Ensuring Insurance for Illegal Aliens." *New York Post*, July 22, sec. Opinion, http://www.nypost.com/seven/07222009/postopinion/oped columnists/ensuring_insurance_for_illegal_aliens_180602.htm (accessed August 18, 2009).

———. 2004a. *In Defense of Internment: The Case for "Racial Profiling" in World War II and the War on Terror.* Washington, DC, and Lanham, MD: Regnery Publishing.

———. 2004b. "Racial Profiling: A Matter of Survival." *USA Today*, August 17, sec. A.

Martin, Philip. 1995. "Proposition 187 in California." Special Issue: Diversity and Comparability: International Migrants in Host Countries on Four Continents. *International Migration Review* 29(1): 255–63.

Mason, Andrew. 1999. "Political Community, Liberal-Nationalism, and the Ethics of Assimilation." *Ethics* 109(2): 261–86.

Masuoka, Natalie. 2006. "Together They Become One: Examining the Predictors of Panethnic Group Consciousness among Asian Americans and Latinos." *Social Science Quarterly* 87(5): 993–1011.

Maucker, Earl. 2003. "We Expected Language Stories to Hit Nerve; Animosity over Differences Still Proves Unsettling." *Sun-Sentinel*, May 18, sec. F.

Maykuth, Andrew. 2008. "Ruling: 'Speak English' Sign at Cheesesteak Shop Not Discriminatory." *Philadelphia Inquirer*, March 20, http://www.philly.com/inquirer/special/immigration_debate/20080320_Ruling_quot_Speak_English_quot_sign_at_cheesesteak_shop_not_discriminatory.html (accessed June 11, 2008).

McClain, Paula, Jessica Johnson Carew, Eugene Walton, and Candis Watts. 2009. "Group Membership, Group Identity, and Group Consciousness: Measures of Racial Identity in American Politics." *Annual Review of Political Science* 12: 471–85.

McClosky, Herbert. 1964. "Consensus and Ideology in American Politics." *American Political Science Review* 58(2): 361–82.

McClosky, Herbert, and John Zaller. 1984. *The American Ethos: Public Attitudes toward Capitalism and Democracy*. Cambridge, MA: Harvard University Press.

McConahay, John B. 1982. "Self-Interest versus Racial Attitudes as Correlates of Anti-Busing Attitudes in Louisville: Is It the Buses or the Blacks?" *Journal of Politics* 44(3): 692–720.

McDaniel, Eric, and Irfan Nooruddin. 2008. "Proud to Be an American: How National Pride Affects Visions of National Identity" (unpublished manuscript).

McHugh, Margie, Julia Gelatt, and Michael Fix. 2007. *Adult English Language Instruction in the United States: Determining Need and Investing Wisely*. Washington, DC: Migration Policy Institute.

Mendelberg, Tali. 2001. *The Race Card: Campaign Strategy, Implicit Messages, and the Norm of Equality*. Princeton, NJ: Princeton University Press.

Meyerson, Harold. 2006. "New Immigrants Teach an Old Lesson." *Washington Post*, March 29, sec. A.

Michelson, Melissa R. 2003. "The Corrosive Effect of Acculturation: How Mexican Americans Lose Political Trust." *Social Science Quarterly* 84(4): 918–33.

———. 2001. "The Effect of National Mood on Mexican American Political Opinion." *Hispanic Journal of Behavioral Sciences* 23(1): 57–70.

Migration Policy Institute. 2006. *New Estimates of Unauthorized Youth Eligible for Legal Status under the DREAM Act*, no. 1.

Miller, Arthur H., Patricia Gurin, Gerald Gurin, and Oksana Malanchuk. 1981. "Group Consciousness and Political Participation." *American Journal of Political Science* 25(3): 494–511.

Miller, David. 2008. "Immigrants, Nations, and Citizenship." *Journal of Political Philosophy* 16(4): 371–90.

———. 1995. *On Nationality*. Oxford: Clarendon Press.

Miller, John J. 1998. *The Unmaking of Americans: How Multiculturalism Has Undermined the Assimilation Ethic*. New York: Free Press.

Mills, Charles W. 1997. *The Racial Contract*. Ithaca, NY: Cornell University Press.

Miroff, Nick. 2007. "Prince William Passes Resolution Targeting Illegal Immigration." *Washington Post*, July 11, sec. A.

Montgomery, David. 2007. "Spanish Lesson: Two Constituencies, Two Campaigns? What You Need Is Another Tongue." *Washington Post*, June 3, sec. D.

————. 2006. "An Anthem's Discordant Notes." *Washington Post*, April 28, sec. A.

Mueller, John. 1988. "Trends in Political Tolerance." *Public Opinion Quarterly* 52(1): 1–25.

Müller, Jan-Werner. 2007. *Constitutional Patriotism*. Princeton, NJ: Princeton University Press.

Muller, Thomas. 1997. "Nativism in the Mid-1990s: Why Now?" In *Immigrants Out! The New Nativism and the Anti-Immigrant Impulse in the United States*, ed. Juan Perea, 105–18. New York: New York University Press.

Murray, Alice Yang. 2000. "The Internment of Japanese Americans." In *What Did the Internment of Japanese Americans Mean?* ed. Alice Yang Murray, 3–26. Boston: St. Martin's Press.

Mutz, Diana C., and Jeffery J. Mondak. 1997. "Dimensions of Sociotropic Behavior: Group-Based Judgments of Fairness and Well-being." *American Journal of Political Science* 41(1): 284–308.

National Conference of State Legislatures. 2008. "Q & A on Immigrant Legislation," http://ncsl.org/programs/immig/QandAIB.htm (accessed June 2, 2008).

Nelson, Sophia. 2008. "Black. Female. Accomplished. Attacked." *Washington Post*, July 20, sec. B.

Ngai, Mae. 2004. *Impossible Subjects: Illegal Aliens and the Making of Modern America*. Princeton, NJ: Princeton University Press.

Noel, Josh. 2007. "Hope Is Spoken at Literacy Center: Reading and Writing English Taught by Volunteers in Aurora." *Chicago Tribune*, December 23.

Oakes, Penelope. 2001. "The Root of All Evil in Intergroup Relations? Unearthing the Categorization Process." In *Blackwell Handbook of Social Psychology: Intergroup Processes*, ed. Rupert Brown and Samuel Gaertner, 3–21. Malden, MA: Blackwell.

Orey, Byron D'Andra. 2004. "White Racial Attitudes and Support for the Mississippi State Flag." *American Politics Research* 32(1): 102–16.

Orfield, Gary, and Chungmei Lee. 2007. *Historic Reversals, Accelerating Resegregation, and the Need for New Integration Strategies*, Los Angeles: The Civil Rights Project.

Owen, Diana, and Jack Dennis. 2001. "Trust in Federal Government: The Phenomenon and Its Antecedents." In *What Is It About Government that Americans Dislike?* ed. John Hibbing and Elizabeth Theiss-Morse, 209–26. Cambridge: Cambridge University Press.

Palmer, J. Jioni. 2006. "King Eyes Ethnic Profiling." *Newsday*, August 17.

Passel, Jeffrey, Randolph Capps, and Michael Fix. 2004. "Undocumented Immigrants: Facts and Figures." In The Urban Institute, http://www.urban.org/Publications/1000587.html (accessed June 2, 2008).

Paxton, Pamela, and Anthony Mughan. 2006. "What's to Fear from Immigrants? Creating an Assimilationist Threat Scale." *Political Psychology* 27(4): 549–68.

Pearson, Kathryn, and Jack Citrin. 2006. "The Political Assimilation of the Fourth Wave." In *Transforming Politics, Transforming America*, ed. Taeku Lee, S. Karthick Ramakrishnan, and Ricardo Ramirez, 217–42. Charlottesville: University of Virginia Press.

Perea, Juan, ed. 1997. *Immigrants Out! The New Nativism and the Anti-Immigrant Impulse in the United States*. New York: New York University Press.

Petit, Philip. 1997. *Republicanism: A Theory of Freedom and Government*. New York: Oxford University Press.

Pfeiffer, Eric. 2007. "Support Grows to make English Official." *Washington Times*, January 22, http://www.washtimes.com/national/20070122-010039-8297r.htm (accessed February 8, 2007).

Pickus, Noah M. 2005. *True Faith and Allegiance: Immigration and American Civic Nationalism*. Princeton, NJ: Princeton University Press.

———. 1998. "To Make Natural: Creating Citizens for the Twenty-First Century." In *Immigration and Citizenship in the Twenty-First Century*, ed. Noah M. Pickus, 107–40. New York: Rowman and Littlefield.

Portes, Alejandro, and Rubén G. Rumbaut. 2001. *Legacies: The Story of the Immigrant Second Generation*. Berkeley: University of California Press.

Prothro, James W., and Charles M. Grigg. 1960. "Fundamental Principles of Democracy: Bases of Agreement and Disagreement." *Journal of Politics* 22(2): 276–94.

Putnam, Robert D. 2007. "*E Pluribus Unum*: Diversity and Community in the Twenty-First Century: The 2006 Johan Skytte Prize Lecture." *Scandinavian Political Studies* 30(2): 137–74.

———. 2003. "Bowling Together." In *United We Serve: National Service and the Future of Citizenship*, eds. E. J. Dionne, K. Meltzer Drogosz, and R. Litan, 13–19. Washington, DC: Brookings Institution.

———. 2000. *Bowling Alone: The Collapse and Revival of American Community*. New York: Simon and Schuster.

Rahn, Wendy M., and Thomas J. Rudolph. 2005. "A Tale of Political Trust in American Cities." *Public Opinion Quarterly* 69(4): 530–60.

Ramakrishnan, S. Karthick. 2006. "But Do They Bowl? Race, Immigrant Incorporation, and Civic Voluntarism in the United States." In *Transforming Politics, Transforming America: The Political and Civic Incorporation of Immigrants in the United States*, eds. Taeku Lee, S. Karthick Ramakrishnan, and Ricardo Ramirez, 243–59. Charlottesville: University of Virginia Press.

Richardson, Lilliard, David Houston, and Chris Sissie Hadjiharalambous. 2001. "Public Confidence in Leaders of American Governmental Institutions." In *What Is It about Government that Americans Dislike?* ed. John Hibbing and Elizabeth Theiss-Morse, 83–97. Cambridge: Cambridge University Press.

Roberts, Dorothy. 1997. "Who May Give Birth to Citizens? Reproduction, Eugenics, and Immigration." In *Immigrants Out! The New Nativism and the Anti-Immigrant Impulse in the United States*, ed. Juan Perea, 205–19. New York: New York University Press.

Robinson, Greg. 2001. *By Order of the President: FDR and the Internment of Japanese Americans*. Cambridge, MA: Harvard University Press.

Rodriguez, America. 1996. "Objectivity and Ethnicity in the Production of the Noticiero Univisión." *Critical Studies in Mass Communication* 13: 59–81.

Rutenberg, Jim. 2008. "Deconstructing the Bump." *New York Times*, June 11, sec. A.

Rutten, Tim. 2009. "Immigration Debacle." *Los Angeles Times*, July 15, sec. Opinion, http://www.latimes.com/news/opinion/commentary/la-oe-rutten15-2009jul15%2C0%2C4385349.column(accessed August 18, 2009).

Sabato, Larry, Bruce A. Larson, and Howard R. Ernst. 2001. *Dangerous Democracy? The Battle over Ballot Initiatives in America*. Lanham, MD: Rowman and Littlefield.

Sacchetti, Maria. 2007. "A Working Vocabulary: Employers Host English Classes." *Boston Globe*, October 12, sec. Metro.

Sam, David. 2006. "Acculturation: Conceptual Background." In *The Cambridge Handbook of Acculturation Psychology*, ed. David Sam and John Berry, 11–26. Cambridge: Cambridge University Press.

Sandel, Michael J. 1996. *Democracy's Discontent: America in Search of a Public Philosophy*. Cambridge, MA: Belknap Press.

Schatz, Robert, Ervin Staub, and Howard Lavine. 1999. "On the Varieties of National Attachment: Blind versus Constructive Patriotism." *Political Psychology* 20(1): 151–74.

Schevitz, Tanya. 2000. "Multiracial Census Form Poses Dilemma; Organizations Fear Dilution of Numbers." *San Francisco Chronicle*, March 11, sec. A.

Schildkraut, Deborah J. 2009. "Amnesty, Guest Workers, Fences! Oh My! Public Opinion about 'Comprehensive Immigration Reform.'" Paper presented at the Dynamics of Public Opinion on Immigration in the U.S. and the West conference, University of Texas at Austin.

———. 2005a. *Press One for English: Language Policy, Public Opinion, and American Identity*. Princeton, NJ: Princeton University Press.

———. 2005b. "The Rise and Fall of Political Engagement among Latinos: The Role of Identity and Perceptions of Discrimination." *Political Behavior* 27(3): 285–312.

———. 2003. "American Identity and Attitudes toward Official-English Policies." *Political Psychology* 24(3): 469–99.

———. 2002. "The More Things Change ... American Identity and Mass and Elite Responses to 9/11." *Political Psychology* 23(3): 511–35.

———. 2001. "Official-English and the States: Influences on Declaring English the Official Language in the United States." *Political Research Quarterly* 54(2): 445–57.

Schildkraut, Deborah J., and Pete Furia. 2003. "Patriotism." In *Encyclopedia of Community*, ed. Karen Christensen and David Levinson. Vol. 3, 1059–66. Thousand Oaks, CA: Sage Publications.

Schlafly, Phyllis. 2008. "Immigration Breaks Backs of Taxpaying U.S. Citizens." In *WorldNetDaily*, http://www.wnd.com/index.php?fa=PAGE.view&pageId=61861 (accessed April 22, 2008).

———. 2006. "Patrick Buchanan Sounds Alarm in 'State of Emergency,'" http://www.townhall.com/columnists/PhyllisSchlafly/2006/08/28/patrick_buchanan_sounds_alarm_in_state_of_emergency(accessed September 13, 2006).

Schlesinger, Arthur M. 1998. *The Disuniting of America: Reflections on a Multicultural Society*. Rev. ed. New York: W.W. Norton.

Schmitt, Michael T., and Nyla R. Branscombe. 2002. "The Meaning and Consequences of Perceived Discrimination in Disadvantaged and Privileged Social Groups." In *European Review of Social Psychology*, ed. Wolfgang Stroebe and Miles Hewstone. Vol. 12, 167–99. Essex, UK: Psychology Press.

Schmitt, Michael T., Russell Spears, and Nyla R. Branscombe. 2003. "Constructing a Minority Group Identity Out of Shared Rejection: The Case of International Students." *European Journal of Social Psychology* 33(1): 1–12.

Sears, David. 1993. "Symbolic Politics: A Socio-Psychological Theory." In *Explorations in Political Psychology*, ed. Shanto Iyengar and William McGuire, 113–49. Durham, NC: Duke University Press.

Sears, David, and Carolyn Funk. 1990. "Self-Interest in Americans' Political Opinions." In *Beyond Self-Interest*, ed. Jane Mansbridge, 147–70. Chicago: University of Chicago Press.

Sears, David O., P. J. Henry, and Rick Kosterman. 2000. "Egalitarian Values and Contemporary Racial Politics." In *Racialized Politics: The Debate about Racism in America*, ed. David O. Sears, Jim Sidanius, and Lawrence Bobo, 75–117. Chicago: University of Chicago Press.

Sears, David, Colette Van Laar, Mary Carrillo, and Rick Kosterman. 1997. "Is It Really Racism? The Origins of White Americans' Opposition to Race-Targeted Policies." *Public Opinion Quarterly* 61(1): 16–63.

Sechrist, Gretchen B., Janet K. Swim, and Charles Stangor. 2004. "When Do the Stigmatized Make Attributions to Discrimination Occurring to the Self and Others? The Roles of Self-Presentation and Need for Control." *Journal of Personality and Social Psychology* 87(1): 111–22.

Shayo, Moses. 2009. "A Model of Social Identity with an Application to Political Economy: Nation, Class, and Redistribution." *American Political Science Review* 103(2): 147–74.

Shuck, Peter. 1998. *Citizens, Strangers, and In-Betweens: Essays on Immigration and Citizenship*. Boulder, CO: Westview Press.

Sidanius, Jim, and Felicia Pratto. 1999. *Social Dominance: An Intergroup Theory of Social Hierarchy and Oppression*. Cambridge: Cambridge University Press.

Sidanius, Jim, Seymour Feshback, Shana Levin, and Felicia Pratto. 1997. "The Interface between Ethnic and National Attachment: Ethnic Pluralism or Ethnic Dominance?" *Public Opinion Quarterly* 61(1): 102–33.

Sides, John, and Jack Citrin. 2007. "How Large the Huddled Masses? The Causes and Consequences of Public Misperceptions about Immigrant Populations." Paper presented at the annual meeting of the Midwest Political Science Association, Chicago.

Smith, Rogers M. 2004. "Identities, Interests, and the Future of Political Science." *Perspectives on Politics* 2(2): 301–12.

———. 2003. *Stories of Peoplehood: The Politics and Morals of Political Membership*. Cambridge: Cambridge University Press.

———. 1997. *Civic Ideals: Conflicting Visions of Citizenship in U.S. History*. Yale ISPS Series. New Haven, CT: Yale University Press.

———. 1993. "Beyond Tocqueville, Myrdal, and Hartz: The Multiple Traditions in America." *American Political Science Review* 87(3): 549–66.

———. 1988. "The 'American Creed' and American Identity: The Limits of Liberal Citizenship in the United States." *Western Political Quarterly* 41(2): 225–51.

Sniderman, Paul, and Edward Carmines. 1997. *Reaching Beyond Race*. Cambridge, MA: Harvard University Press.

Sniderman, Paul, and Thomas Piazza. 1993. *The Scar of Race*. Cambridge: Belknap Press.

Sniderman, Paul M., Louk Hagendoorn, and Markus Prior. 2004. "Predisposing Factors and Situational Triggers: Exclusionary Reactions to Immigrant Minorities." *American Political Science Review* 98(1): 35–49.

Sommers, Laurie Kay. 1991. "Inventing Latinismo: The Creation of 'Hispanic' Panethnicity in the United States." *Journal of American Folklore* 104(411): 32–53.

Song, Sarah. 2009. "What Does It Mean to Be an American?" *Daedalus* 138(2): 31–40.

Soto, Hiram. 2006. "Mexican Flag Kindles Passions Pro and Con." *San Diego Union-Tribune*, April 8, sec. B.

Spears, Russell. Forthcoming. "Group Identities." In *Handbook of Identity Theory and Research*, ed. Seth Schwartz, Koen Luyckx, and Vivian Vignoles. New York: Springer Publishing.

Stanton, John. 2009. "Kyl Says Concerns over Illegal Immigration Are Valid." In *Roll Call*, http://www.rollcall.com/news/37825-1.html (accessed August 25, 2009).

Stein, Robert M., Stephanie Shirley Post, and Allison L. Rinden. 2000. "Reconciling Context and Contact Effects on Racial Attitudes." *Political Research Quarterly* 53(2): 285–303.

Sullivan, John L., Amy Fried, and Mary G. Dietz. 1992. "Patriotism, Politics, and the Presidential Election of 1988." *American Journal of Political Science* 36(1): 200.

Tajfel, Henri, ed. 1982a. *Social Identity and Intergroup Relations*. New York: Cambridge University Press.

———. 1982b. "Social Psychology of Intergroup Relations." *Annual Review of Psychology* 33: 1–39.

Tajfel, Henri, and John Turner. 1986. "The Social Identity Theory of Intergroup Behavior." In *Psychology of Intergroup Relations*, ed. William Austin and Stephen Worchel, 7–24. Chicago: Nelson-Hall.

Takaki, Ronald. 1999. "Race at the End of History." In *The Good Citizen*, ed. David Batstone and Eduardo Mendieta, 81–92. New York: Routledge.

Tatalovich, Raymond. 1995. *Nativism Reborn? The Official English Language Movement and the American States*. Lexington: University Press of Kentucky.

Taylor, Charles. 1999. "Democratic Exclusion (and Its Remedies?)." In *Multiculturalism, Liberalism, and Democracy*, ed. Rajeev Bhargava, Amiya Kumar Bagchi, and R. Sudarshan, 138–63. Oxford: Oxford University Press.

———. 1998. "The Dynamics of Democratic Exclusion." *Journal of Democracy* 9(4): 143–56.

Theiss-Morse, Elizabeth. 2009. *Who Counts as an American? The Boundaries of National Identity*. New York: Cambridge University Press.

———. 2006. "The Obligations of National Identity: Charity, Welfare, and the Boundaries of the National Group." Paper presented at the annual meeting of the Midwest Political Science Association, Chicago.

———. 2005. "Benefitting the National Group – at Least Some of it: The Consequences of Limiting Who Counts as an American." Paper presented at the annual meeting of the Midwest Political Science Association, Chicago.

———. 2004. "Who's In and Who's Out: American National Identity and the Setting of Boundaries." Paper presented at the annual meeting of the Midwest Political Science Association, Chicago.

———. 2003. "Identification and Disidentification: Americans' Commitment to the National Collective and its Consequences." Paper presented at the annual meeting of the American Political Science Association, Philadelphia.

Tichenor, Daniel J. 2002. *Dividing Lines: The Politics of Immigration Control in America*. Princeton Studies in American Politics. Princeton, NJ: Princeton University Press.

Tocqueville, Alexis de. 1835/1990. *Democracy in America*. New York: Vintage Books.

Transue, John. 2007. "Identity Salience, Identity Acceptance, and Racial Policy Attitudes: American National Identity as a Uniting Force." *American Journal of Political Science* 51(1): 78–91.

Tuan, Mia. 1998. *Forever Foreigners or Honorary Whites? The Asian Ethnic Experience Today*. New Brunswick, NJ: Rutgers University Press.

Tucker, James. 2006. *The ESL Logjam: Waiting Times for Adult ESL Classes and the Impact on English Learners*. Los Angeles: NALEO Educational Fund.

Turner, John. 1999. "Some Current Issues in Research on Social Identity and Self-Categorization Theories." In *Social Identity: Context, Commitment, Content*, ed. Naomi Ellemers, Russell Spears, and Bertjan Doosje, 6–34. Malden, MA: Blackwell.

———. 1982. "Towards a Cognitive Redefinition of the Social Group." In *Social Identity and Intergroup Relations*, ed. Henri Tajfel, 15–40. Cambridge: Cambridge University Press.

Turner, John, and Katherine Reynolds. 2001. "The Social Identity Perspective in Intergroup Relations: Theories, Themes, and Controversies." In *Blackwell Handbook of Social Psychology: Intergroup Processes*, ed. Rupert Brown and Samuel Gaertner, 133–52. Malden, MA: Blackwell.

Tyack, David. 1999. "Preserving the Republic by Educating Republicans." In *Diversity and Its Discontents: Cultural Conflict and Common Ground in Contemporary American Society*, ed. Neil Smelsner and Jeffrey Alexander, 63–83. Princeton, NJ: Princeton University Press.

Tyler, Tom. 2006. *Why People Obey the Law*. Princeton, NJ: Princeton University Press.

Tyler, Tom, and Yuen Huo. 2002. *Trust in the Law: Encouraging Public Cooperation with the Police and Courts*. New York: Russell Sage Foundation.

Uriarte, Miren, and Roseann Tung. 2009. *English Learners in Boston Public Schools in the Aftermath of Policy Change*. Boston: Gaston Institute, University of Massachusetts.

Vidanage, Sharmaine, and David Sears. 1995. "The Foundations of Public Opinion toward Immigration Policy: Group Conflict or Symbolic Politics?" Paper presented at the annual meeting of the Midwest Political Science Association, Chicago.

Virtanen, Simo V., and Leonie Huddy. 1998. "Old-Fashioned Racism and New Forms of Racial Prejudice." *Journal of Politics* 60(2): 311–32.

Walzer, Michael. 1996. *What It Means to Be an American: Essays on the American Experience*. New York: Marsilio.

———. 1983. *Spheres of Justice: A Defense of Pluralism and Equality*. New York: Basic Books.

Waters, Mary C. 1990. *Ethnic Options: Choosing Identities in America*. Berkeley: University of California Press.

Weaver, Charles. 2003. "Confidence of Mexican Americans in Major Institutions in the United States." *Hispanic Journal of Behavioral Sciences* 25(4): 501–12.

Weisman, Jonathan, and Michael D. Shear. 2008. "Obama Fiercely Defends His Patriotism; Democrat Also Decries Criticism of Rival McCain on Service to Country." *Washington Post*, July 1, sec. A.

Weitzer, Ronald, and Steven Tuch. 2005. "Racially Biased Policing: Determinants of Citizen Perceptions." *Social Forces* 83(3): 1009–30.

———. 2004. "Race and Perceptions of Police Misconduct." *Social Problems* 51(3): 305–25.

———. 2002. "Perceptions of Racial Profiling: Race, Class, and Personal Experience." *Criminology* 40(2): 435–56.

Wellman, Christopher Heath. 2001. "Friends, Compatriots, and Special Political Obligations." *Political Theory* 29(2): 217–36.

Wenzel, James P. 2006. "Acculturation Effects on Trust in National and Local Government among Mexican Americans." *Social Science Quarterly* 87(5): 1073–87.

Wides-Munoz, Laura. 2009. "Mel Martinez's Senate Exit Signals Crossroads for GOP Efforts to Woo Hispanics." *Los Angeles Times*, August 23, http://www.latimes.com/

news/nationworld/nation/wire/sns-ap-us-mel-martinez-losing-hispanics,0,4585457
.story (accessed August 25, 2009).

Widmer, Ted. 2007. "Fighting Words – the Administration's Rhetorical Quagmire."
Boston Globe, April 29.

Will, George. 2006. "A Vote for English." *Washington Post*, May 25, sec. A.

Wilson, Doug. 2006. "Does It Unify Us?" http://www.townhall.com/opinion/columns/
DougWilson/2006/04/10/193116.html (accessed May 24, 2006).

Wong, Cara, and Grace E. Cho. 2005. "Two-Headed Coins or Kandinskys: White
Racial Identification." *Political Psychology* 26(5): 699–720.

Wong, Janelle. 2006. *Democracy's Promise: Immigrants and American Civic Institutions*. Ann Arbor: University of Michigan Press.

Wright, Stephen. 2001. "Strategic Collective Action: Social Psychology and Social
Change." In *Blackwell Handbook of Social Psychology: Intergroup Processes*, ed.
Rupert Brown and Samuel Gaertner, 409–30. Malden, MA: Blackwell.

Zaller, John. 1992. *The Nature and Origins of Mass Opinion*. New York: Cambridge
University Press.

Zaller, John, and Stanley Feldman. 1992. "A Simple Theory of the Survey Response:
Answering Questions versus Revealing Preferences." *American Journal of Political
Science* 36(3): 579–616.

Zolberg, Aristide R., and Long Litt Woon. 1999. "Why Islam Is Like Spanish: Cultural
Incorporation in Europe and the United States." *Politics and Society* 27(1): 5–38.

Zucchino, David. 2006. "Cheesesteak Joint Places Its Own Order: English Only." *Los
Angeles Times*, June 14, sec. A.

Index